Little VISITS

VOLUME FOUR

365 FAMILY DEVOTIONS

CONCORDIA PUBLISHING HOUSE • SAINT LOUIS

Copyright © 2005 Concordia Publishing House
3558 S. Jefferson Avenue, St. Louis, MO 63118-3968
1-800-325-3040 • www.cph.org

Scripture quotations, unless otherwise indicated, are from The Holy Bible, English Standard Version, copyright © 2001 by Crossway Bibles, a division of Good News Publishers. Used by permission. All rights reserved.

Scripture quotations marked NIV are from the HOLY BIBLE, NEW INTERNATIONAL VERSION®. NIV®. Copyright © 1973, 1978, 1984 by International Bible Society. Used by permission of Zondervan Publishing House. All rights reserved.

This publication may be available in braille, in large print, or on cassette tape for the visually impaired. Please allow 8 to 12 weeks for delivery. Write to the Library for the Blind, 7550 Watson Rd., St. Louis, MO 63119-4409; call toll-free 1-888-215-2455; or visit the Web site: www.blindmission.org.

Manufactured in the United States of America

Library of Congress Cataloging-in-Publication Data
365 family devotions.
     p. cm. -- (Little visits ; v. 3)
     ISBN 0-7586-0798-9
     1. Family--Prayer-books and devotions--English. 2. Devotional calendars.
I. Series.
     BV255 .A14 2002
     249--dc21   2002006608

1 2 3 4 5 6 7 8 9 10   14 13 12 11 10 09 08 07 06 05

Versions of these devotions originally appeared in various volumes of the magazine, *My Devotions*. This book is dedicated to the authors of these devotions, who have contributed their God-given time and talents to nurturing the faith of God's children. ✑

Preface

For a number of years, the title *Little Visits* has been associated with devotions that share the saving Gospel of Jesus Christ with children. From the very first edition of *Little Visits with God* to this current volume, these devotions reinforce scriptural truths and faith concepts centered on God's love for us through Christ.

Setting aside time for devotions is an excellent way to lead children to the Savior and to bring them face-to-face with God's Word. In Romans 10:7, we read that "faith comes from hearing the message, and the message is heard through the word of Christ." Find a time that best suits your family and be consistent. Set a format that is most harmonious with the ages and stages of your children. Using the order of worship provided on the facing page will build a sense of tradition and ritual into your family devotions. Developing such rituals or traditions helps to lay important building blocks for faith formation and creates a link between worship in the family of faith and worship within your own family.

These devotions have been written by pastors and educators who have drawn upon their experiences to provide illustrations from daily life and link them to God's Word. May you and your children be blessed as the Holy Spirit works through these words to teach your minds and touch your hearts.

The Editors

Daily Devotion for Family Use

Parents may feel free to adapt according to the children's ages and ability to participate.

_____ The Invocation

The parent may open the devotion with a call to worship.
Leader: In the name of the Father and of the Son and of the Holy Spirit.
Family: Amen.

_____ The Hymn

The family may sing together a related hymn or song of praise.

_____ The Scripture Reading

The designated Scripture may be read by parent or child.

_____ The Devotional Reading

The designated devotion may be read by parent or child.
The parent may lead the family in discussion using the questions provided.

_____ The Closing Prayer

The parent may lead the family in the closing prayer.

january

Contributors for this month:

Cheryl Andrix

Wendy Eckart

Cheryl Ehlers

Heidi Mueller

Valerie Schultz

Kathy Schulz

Susan Waterman Voss

Certain Future

Read from God's Word

Jesus said to her, "I am the resurrection and the life. Whoever believes in Me, though he die, yet shall he live, and everyone who lives and believes in Me shall never die. Do you believe this?" John 11:25–26*

Some people like to guess what will happen in the future. These guesses are called *predictions*. Some predictions are wild guesses; others are based on information. Some predictions come true, but many do not.

In 1948, the magazine *Science Digest* predicted that "landing and moving around on the moon offers so many serious problems for human beings that it may take science another 200 years to lick them." Just 21 years after this prediction, in July 1969, man walked on the moon for the first time.

The next time you get in the car, think of this prediction from the 1889 *Literary Digest*: "The ... horseless carriage [car] is a luxury for the wealthy ... and will never come into as common use as the bicycle."

The Bible has many predictions we call prophecies. Over 300 prophecies were made about Jesus. Each one was fulfilled—just as God said it would be. For example, the prophet Micah predicted not only Jesus' birth but also Jesus' birthplace: Bethlehem.

The Bible has predictions that still speak to us today. For example, it says that all who believe in Jesus will not die but will live forever. That is a prediction we can count on and rejoice in!

_____Let's do: Look in your Bible for prophecies that have been fulfilled: Psalm 22:18 and John 19:23–24; Job 19:25–27 and John 11:23, 25–26; Psalm 47:5 and Mark 16:19. Write them down and compare them.

_____Let's pray: Heavenly Father, thank You for the many promise predictions You have given us. Help us always to trust in Your promise of salvation, which comes through Your Son. In His name we pray. Amen.

K. S.

Dead ... and Alive

Read from God's Word

And you were dead in the tres-passes and sins .... But God, being rich in mercy, because of the great love with which He loved us, even when we were dead in our trespasses, made us alive together with Christ—by grace you have been saved. Ephesians 2:1, 4–5

Which animal is born blind, deaf, and hairless? Here's a hint: this amazing animal lives in Australia. It is a kangaroo. The newborn kangaroo, called a joey, finds its way into its mother's pouch. The joey lives in that pouch, safe and secure, until it is old enough to survive out in the world on its own.

The baby kangaroo is born in a unique way, just like you. You may not have been born physically blind or deaf, but you were born spiritually blind and dead. As the Bible says, "You were dead in the trespasses and sins" (Ephesians 2:1).

But in Baptism something wonderful happens. You are made spiritually alive in Jesus. Your physical birth makes you a member of your earthly family. Your spiritual birth, Baptism, makes you a member of God's family.

A joey crawls into its mother's pouch and receives food there. In Baptism we are put into a kind of "Jesus" pouch. In Jesus we live and grow, safe and secure, feeding on God's life-giving Word.

God provides for the baby kangaroo to be taken care of in a wonderful way. He provides for your care too. In Jesus you are saved by God's grace.

———Let's talk: Where do you feel the most secure? When were you made alive in Christ?

———Let's pray: You are alive, Lord Jesus! And so am I! Thank You for Your life-giving Word. Help me to live each day, secure in Your love. Amen.

K. S.

Old Is New Again

amal was not the most popular boy in school. He rarely got the answer right when Ms. Canes called on him in class. Sometimes he even wore the same shirt several days in a row. Some students made fun of him.

One Sunday Sara noticed Jamal and his mom sitting in the back row at church. Pastor Smith told Sara that Jamal's father had died and his mom was trying to find work. Now Sara understood why Jamal didn't wear the latest styles. She also wondered if missing his dad made it hard for him to study.

God worked in Sara's heart. She decided to try to be Jamal's friend. Other kids laughed at her at first, but then they also discovered how much fun Jamal could be. Jamal and Sara, and sometimes other students, studied together. As other kids accepted Jamal, his confidence grew.

If Jamal changed even a little because someone cared about him, imagine the change that takes place in us when we become children of God! In Baptism God makes each of us new because of Jesus' death and resurrection. We are new, not on the outside, but where it really counts—on the inside! Sara and Jamal learned that "if anyone is in Christ, he is a new creation."

Read from God's Word

Therefore, if anyone is in Christ, he is a new creation. The old has passed away; behold, the new has come.
2 Corinthians 5:17

_____Let's talk: How might the fact that God is changing you on the inside make you change on the outside?

_____Let's pray: Heavenly Father, thank You for making me a new creation through my Baptism. In Jesus' name I pray. Amen.

K. S.

Angels All Around

Read from God's Word

For He will command His angels concerning you to guard you in all your ways. On their hands they will bear you up, lest you strike your foot against a stone. Psalm 91:11–12 ✍

Abraham's sacrifice of Isaac, Daniel in the lions' den, Lot's rescue from Sodom, the shepherds in the field, and Jesus' temptation by Satan. All of these events in the Bible have one thing in common: each involved an angel.

Many people are interested in angels. In fact, 69 percent of all Americans say they believe in angels. The Angel Collectors Club of America has members from across the country. One collector has over 11,000 angels! Another woman claims she can introduce you to your guardian angel. Many people tell stories of times they believe angels saved their lives or prevented serious accidents.

Angels are amazing. They are mentioned more than 280 times in the Bible. They closed the mouths of the lions while Daniel was in the den. One told Abraham that he and Sarah would have a son; an angel kept Abraham from sacrificing that son. The angel Gabriel told Mary she would give birth to the Savior sent from God to rescue all His people (including you and me) from sin and death.

Angels are amazing heavenly creatures that serve our loving God. That same loving God provided His own Son to be our servant. Jesus is that servant who died so we might live forever with Him. No angel can do that!

_____Let's talk: Can you think of a time when an angel protected you? How do you feel about angels watching over you?

_____Let's pray: Thank You, Jesus, for Your tender, loving care. Keep us close to You here on earth and forever. Amen.

K. S.

God's Word, Forever

Read from God's Word

"As for what was sown on good soil, this is the one who hears the word and understands it. He indeed bears fruit and yields, in one case a hundredfold, in another sixty, and in another thirty." Matthew 13:23

Ancient lotus seeds, found in a dry lakebed in China, sprouted. What a remarkable event! In a matter of days, seeds that were asleep for years had grown little green shoots.

In today's Bible reading we learn of another kind of seed, older than the Chinese lotus seeds. This seed is God's Word, which sprouted in the hearts of people long ago and still sprouts today.

Jesus explained how God's Word grows through the story of the farmer who went out to sow his seed. Some seeds fell along a path and were eaten by birds. Some seeds fell on a rocky place and quickly died. Other seeds fell among weeds and died. There were some seeds that fell on good soil. These seeds produced more seeds for future crops.

The seed of God's Word was planted in you at Baptism or as you heard of God's love in Jesus. Faith in Jesus as your Savior from sin has taken root and continues to grow as you are led to hear and understand God's Word.

As faith grows in your heart, it yields seeds. As you tell others about Jesus, using His Word and reflecting on His love, the Spirit is working. With God's help, you can plant the seeds of the Gospel. God does the growing. How remarkable!

_____Let's talk: Read Matthew 13:1–9 and 18–23. How is the seed of God's Word planted? How does that seed continue to grow?

_____Let's pray: Father, thank You for planting Your seed of faith in my heart. Help the seed grow. Give me courage to spread this seed to others. In Jesus' name I pray. Amen.

K. S.

Read from God's Word

Now after Jesus was born in Bethlehem of Judea in the days of Herod the king, behold, Wise Men from the east came to Jerusalem, saying, "Where is He who has been born King of the Jews? For we saw His star when it rose and have come to worship Him." ... And going into the house they saw the child with Mary His mother, and they fell down and worshiped Him. Then, opening their treasures, they offered Him gifts, gold and frankincense and myrrh. Matthew 2:1–11

Gifts from the Heart

M om," called Andy, "I've been invited to Roberto's birthday party! I'll have to get him a *really* great gift."

"Do you want to give Roberto a great gift because you are his friend or because he invited you to his party?" asked Mom.

"I guess I want to get him something nice because he is doing something nice for me."

Andy's desire came from the heart. The Wise Men also had a desire to bring gifts from the heart. Today is Epiphany, a special day in the church year to celebrate the coming of the Wise Men to see Jesus.

These important men wanted to show Jesus their love. They brought wonderful gifts for Jesus—gold, myrrh, and frankincense. These gifts were normally given to the kind of kings who wore crowns.

Jesus didn't wear a crown, but He is greater than any other king who has ever lived. He showed His love for us by coming to live on earth as a man. He lived a perfect life and then, in the greatest act of love, He gave His life on the cross for the forgiveness of our sins.

Our King, Jesus, has given us the best gift from His heart! Because we love Him, our heart overflows and we give Him gifts in return.

_____Let's talk: What gifts of the heart can you bring to Jesus? What gift from Jesus can you share with others?

_____Let's pray: Dear God, You lead the Wise Men to Jesus by showing them a star. Show us the way to Jesus by leading us to Your Word, the Bible. In His name. Amen.

K. S.

Warnings Ignored

On May 30, 1889, the rain began to fall. By the next morning, the Conemaugh River raced down the valley toward Johnstown, Pennsylvania, and flooded the town of 30,000 people. This flood was bad enough, but then the South Fork Dam broke and a wall of water swept through. More than 2,200 people lost their lives to the worst flood in American history.

Although engineers had warned the people about the dam's weakness, their warnings were ignored.

There are many examples in the Bible of people who were warned about the danger of not believing in God. Jesus wept over the city of Jerusalem because the people there did not believe He was the Son of God. Later, Jerusalem was destroyed.

The tears of Jesus show us God's great love. He wants us to be with Him in heaven but does not want to scare us into loving Him, so He guides us through our lives. He doesn't want us washed away in a flood of sin.

Read from God's Word

Therefore we must pay much closer attention to what we have heard, lest we drift away from it. For since the message declared by angels proved to be reliable and every transgression or disobedience received a just retribution, how shall we escape if we neglect such a great salvation? It was declared at first by the Lord, and it was attested to us by those who heard, while God also bore witness by signs and wonders and various miracles and by gifts of the Holy Spirit distributed according to His will. Hebrews 2:1–4 ✑

We can live each day with the promise of forgiveness instead of living in fear that our sins will destroy us. "If we confess our sins, He is faithful and just to forgive us our sins and to cleanse us from all unrighteousness" (1 John 1:9). God's great love continues to flood our lives today.

_____Let's talk: What promise does God give us? How does this promise make you feel?

_____Let's pray: Jesus, forgive us. Keep our sins from leading us away from You. Grant us Your peace. Amen.

K. S.

The King Has Come

Then Herod ... sent them to Bethlehem, saying, "Go and search diligently for the child, and when you have found Him, bring me word, that I too may come and worship Him." After listening to the king, they went on their way. And behold, the star that they had seen when it rose went before them until it came to rest over the place where the child was. When they saw the star, they rejoiced exceedingly with great joy. And going into the house they saw the child with Mary His mother, and they fell down and worshiped Him. Then, opening their treasures, they offered Him gifts, gold and frankincense and myrrh. Matthew 2:7–11

Andy found 10 Lone Ranger comic books in his grandpa's attic and discovered that each comic book was worth $15! What a good thing to see! What a manifestation!

The word *epiphany* comes from the Greek word for manifestation (to bring to light or cause to appear). During the Epiphany season, we celebrate the coming of Jesus for all people. We see this tiny baby as our Savior.

Matthew 2:6 tells us a prophet confessed long ago that there "shall come a ruler." The we read about the Wise Men visiting the baby Jesus. Matthew puts these two things together to say that Jesus is the Messiah who was proclaimed by the prophets and now He has come.

Throughout Epiphany we will hear how Jesus went to the temple as a young boy, was baptized, called His disciples, and performed miracles. These events remind us that Jesus was both human and God. The Father sent us the best gift of all when He gave us Jesus, a king who would bring hope and love to His children. He paid the price for all sin and gave His children eternal life when He suffered and died on the cross.

Remember this manifestation: Jesus is the best gift of all.

_____Let's do: Review the Apostles' Creed in your Small Catechism. What does it tell us about Jesus?

_____Let's pray: Dear God, thank You for Your Son, Jesus Christ. Help me remember that He is my Savior and King. In Jesus' name. Amen.

H. M.

The Mystery

Read from God's Word

To me, though I am the very least of all the saints, this grace was given, to preach to the Gentiles the unsearchable riches of Christ, and to bring to light for everyone what is the plan of the mystery hidden for ages in God who created all things, ... in whom we have boldness and access with confidence through our faith in Him.
Ephesians 3:8–9, 12 ✎

t was a mystery. When his mom reminded Jake to make his lunch, he said yes but he got distracted in a computer game. He didn't remember putting anything except an apple in his brown bag. But there in front of him was also a sandwich, corn chips, and a brownie. How did that happen?

God inspired Paul to write about another mystery—the mystery of salvation by God's grace. How did that happen? We didn't plan it or deserve it. We often do things we shouldn't do or we don't do things we should do, but God loves us anyway. We live with a sinful condition called original sin, which makes us enemies of God. All this grace is a mystery. Why does God love sinners?

Jake's mom had gotten up early, peeked in the bag, and saw the lonely apple. She fixed his favorites and kept her actions a secret.

Like Jake, we receive more than we deserve. We receive all of God's riches because of what Christ did when He died on the cross to take away our sins.

God's grace in Christ is no secret. God gives us this grace because of Christ's work through the riches of His Word, Baptism, and Holy Communion.

The mystery is solved. God did it in love for Jesus' sake.

_____Let's do:　Write your own prayer. Remember to thank God for the grace He gives us through Christ.

_____Let's pray: Dear God, thank You for Your grace, which sent Your Son to save us. In Jesus' name. Amen.

H. M.

Read from God's Word

For He delivers the needy when he calls, the poor and him who has no helper. He has pity on the weak and the needy, and saves the lives of the needy. From oppression and violence He redeems their life, and precious is their blood in His sight. Psalm 72:12–14 ✍

What Do We Deserve?

"I feel terrible," Jasmine said to her mother. "I told everyone that Abby got a C in science. It isn't true; I was just jealous. Abby always does better than I do in science. I don't deserve her friendship."

Jasmine knew it was wrong to lie and felt guilty. She was afraid she had ruined a friendship with Abby and the other girls. Jasmine wanted everything to be right again. As she talked to her mom, God led her to repent.

"When we are repentant," her mother said, "we want to confess our sins to God. We admit that we've done wrong and ask for His forgiveness. Repentance includes trying to change our behavior and apologize with God's help. Although we deserve punishment because of our wrong, God gives us forgiveness because Jesus has already taken the punishment we deserve. All the sin that causes people to feel terrible is removed. We are free!"

"I'm so thankful for all Jesus has done for me," Jasmine said with tears in her eyes. "I know Jesus forgives me, but I had to hear it again. I really am sorry for what I did, and I do want God to help me tell Abby that I'm sorry."

It wasn't long before Jasmine picked up the phone and called Abby.

_____Let's do: Is there someone to whom you want to apologize? Write about the situation. Ask God to help you apologize.

_____Let's pray: Dear God, thank You for forgiving my sin. Help me to seek Your forgiveness and the forgiveness of others. In Jesus' name. Amen.

H. M.

The Special Day

B rad was nervous but certain that he wanted the special event to happen. He had begged his mom to let him. Today was the day he had been waiting for. He put on his new clothes.

The special time had come. Brad stood in front of the church at the baptismal font. Brad knew two of the people who stood near him. They were his sponsors. There were others there, too, including a family with a new baby.

Pastor made a mark in the shape of a cross on the forehead and upon the heart of baby Jacob and then on 10-year-old Brad. The pastor said some important words to the sponsors. Then he poured the water and said to each child, "I baptize you in the name of the Father and of the Son and of the Holy Spirit." Next came the blessings, the burning candles, and the prayers.

Through Baptism God added Brad and Jacob to His own people. Through Baptism God gave forgiveness of sins, faith, new life, and salvation to both boys.

The waiting was over. Jacob and Brad were part of the body of Christ, children of the heavenly Father. Although they were different ages and from different families, they are brothers in Jesus Christ. Each went home blessed in their new faith.

Read from God's Word

As the people were in expectation, and all were questioning in their hearts concerning John, whether he might be the Christ, John answered them all, saying, "I baptize you with water, but He who is mightier than I is coming, the strap of whose sandals I am not worthy to untie. He will baptize you with the Holy Spirit and with fire. Luke 3:15–16

_____Let's do: Find out about your Baptism. Write about it.

_____Let's pray: Dear God, thank You for making me Your child
through Baptism. Help me to remember my Baptism
every day. In Jesus' name. Amen.

H. M.

Set Aside

Read from God's Word

Now when all the people were baptized, and when Jesus also had been baptized and was praying, the heavens were opened, and the Holy Spirit descended on Him in bodily form, like a dove; and a voice came from heaven, "You are My beloved Son; with You I am well pleased."
Luke 3:21–22

Heidi's family keeps three extra-special things in the cabinet: Grandma's bracelet, Mom's stuffed piranha, and Heidi's baptismal outfit. These are set aside to remember special occasions. Grandma got the bracelet from her siblings, who visited the World's Fair in 1933. Mom received her stuffed piranha when her sister returned from Brazil. Heidi's baptismal outfit was made from her grandmother's wedding dress.

Today the church remembers Jesus' baptism, which marks the beginning of His public ministry. Although the event happened many years ago, it is very significant. Luke records that the window of heaven opened and the Holy Spirit appeared in the form of a dove. The heavenly Father's voice announced to everyone who Jesus was—His very own Son.

Jesus' baptism sets Him aside as the Chosen One. God the Father tells us Jesus is His Son, the long-expected Messiah. We do not need to look for someone else to save us.

Jesus takes on all of our sin in His baptism. He saves us from our sin by taking the blame and punishment for it all, and we then take His place as children of God. This doesn't seem fair, does it? Jesus gets the punishment and we get the reward. This shows how much God loves us—that's truly extra special!

_____Let's do: Do a Bible search. What other time were people saved in the Jordan? Write about it.

_____Let's pray: Dear God, thank You for loving me enough to make me one of Your children. In Jesus' name. Amen.

H. M.

Buried

Paradise Inn on Mount Rainier, Washington, recorded 789.5 inches of snow during the winter of 1916–17. This much snow completely covers everything and takes a long time to melt. Just think of all the things buried under that snow!

In today's reading Paul tells us that in our Baptism, we were "buried" with Christ. Does that mean we were physically buried in the ground? No! When we are baptized, our sin is covered over. Why is that? Paul says we are buried into Jesus' "death." Jesus died on the cross for us. He received the punishment for our sins and, therefore, put them away. Our sins are now forgiven and we can enjoy the reward Jesus won for us, which is eternal life.

We remember that we are new people in Christ. When we remember that the old self is buried, it is like writing down all the things we've ever done wrong or ever will do wrong and burying that paper beneath 789.5 inches of snow. We don't even have to worry that our sins will show up later after a thaw. God has taken them completely away.

God the Father looks at us and sees that our sin was buried by Jesus' death and resurrection. Isn't that wonderful?

Read from God's Word

We were buried therefore with Him by baptism into death, in order that, just as Christ was raised from the dead by the glory of the Father, we too might walk in newness of life. For if we have been united with Him in a death like His, we shall certainly be united with Him in a resurrection like His. Romans 6:4–5 ◌

_____Let's do: Write down something you have done wrong and feel badly about. Pray about those things. Bury the words under a sticker. God has forgiven you; they're gone forever!

_____Let's pray: Dear God, please forgive my sins for Jesus' sake. Thank You for making me new. In Jesus' name. Amen.

H. M.

Walk in the Light

Read from God's Word

Again Jesus spoke to them, saying, "I am the Light of the world. Whoever follows Me will not walk in darkness, but will have the light of life." John 8:12
〜

In the Blind Man game one person is blindfolded and another person guides him around. The person who cannot see is in complete darkness. He must depend on a guide so he can find his way. For the activity to be successful the player trusts the guide and the guide does not break that trust.

The kind of trust in this activity reminds us of our relationship with Jesus. We were born like the blindfolded person. We wandered around in life's sinful darkness without hope until Jesus came at our Baptism and through His Word. He claims us as His own and guides us. He is the light that breaks our darkness and shows us the way. We can completely trust Him. He will lead us in the way of truth. In the Bible reading for today Jesus says, "I am the Light of the world. Whoever follows Me will not walk in darkness, but will have the light of life." We follow Jesus by reading His Word and letting Him guide us.

In the Bible we read about God's love. He sent Jesus, His Son, to die on the cross so our sins can be forgiven. Jesus is the only light we need in this world. He's the best guide ever!

_____Let's do: Find a friend and play the Blind Man game. Write about what it feels like to be in total darkness. How important is it to have a guide?

_____Let's pray: Dear God, thank You for being our light, guiding us in the way of truth, and giving us hope. Help us to read Your Word so we can learn more about You. In Jesus' name. Amen.

H. M.

The Perfect Gift

C an you match the person or animal below with the perfect gift from the second column?

_____ 1. Cinderella

_____ 2. Frosty the Snowman

_____ 3. The Tin Man from Oz

_____ 4. The Three Little Pigs

_____ 5. Old Mother Hubbard

_____ 6. Noah

_____ 7. Popeye

a. Umbrella

b. Dog bone

c. Spinach

d. Glass slipper

e. A freezer

f. Heart

g. Bricks

How did you do? Not in this little quiz—how did you do for Christmas? Was there a gift under the tree that was a perfect match for you? Is it still the perfect gift? Three weeks after Christmas, you might say no. You might have mastered your new computer game or scuffed your new skates. Your "perfect" gift is not so perfect anymore.

In Ephesians Paul wrote about the perfect gift God has given to all who believe in Him. It never wears out. It never goes out of fashion. It has a beyond-this-lifetime warranty. This gift is perfect for everyone!

> ### Read from God's Word
>
> _For by grace you have been saved through faith. And this is not your own doing: it is the gift of God, not a result of works, so that no one may boast. Ephesians 2:8–9_

Jesus purchased it for us. It cost Him His life, and He gave it willingly. He wants us to have the best present ever—forgiveness of sins and life everlasting. He wants us to be with Him forever.

Let's say, "Thanks for the perfect gift, Jesus. It's just what I've always wanted and needed!"

_____ Let's do: How can you show your thanks to God for this wonderful Christmas gift? Write your ideas on an index card and put it where you will see it every day.

_____ Let's pray: Dear Jesus, thank You for giving me the perfect Christmas gift! You're just what I needed! Amen.

C. E.

The Price Is Right

And He who was seated on the throne said, "Behold, I am making all things new." Also He said, "Write this down, for these words are trustworthy and true." And He said to me, "It is done! I am the Alpha and the Omega, the Beginning and the End. To the thirsty I will give from the spring of the water of life without payment. The one who conquers will have this heritage, and I will be his God and he will be My son."
Revelation 21:5–7

"The Price Is Right" is a game show that has been on television for many years. The contestants guess the price of items. If you watch the reruns, you know that prices have changed over the years.

Compare the 1960 prices of these items with their prices today.

	1960	Today
Postage stamp	$ .04	_____
Loaf of bread	$ .20	_____
Gallon of gas	$ .31	_____
New car	$2,000	_____

Can you think of anything that has not changed in price over the years? The Bible reading for today has an answer! In Revelation Jesus says, "I am ... the Beginning and the End. To the thirsty I will give from the spring of the water of life without payment."

A drink from the spring of the water of life has no cost to us. The price was paid by the death and resurrection of Jesus. And Jesus promises to give the thirsty person this no-cost drink.

God gave us—the thirsty ones—the drink of new life in the waters of Baptism. There our sins were washed away, giving us a new start as forgiven children. God gave us His Word, which satisfies as no other words can.

The price is right! The prize is ours—life with Jesus, forever!

_____Let's do: Reread Revelation 21:5–7. Write down "trustworthy and true" words about Jesus. Share your list with someone.

_____Let's pray: Dear Jesus, thank You for giving us promises that we can count on! Thank You for the gift of eternal life. Amen.

C. E.

On Top

Place your right hand on the table. Have your friend place his right hand on top of yours. Now place your left hand on top of your friend's right hand. Your friend lays his left hand on the top. Pull your right hand from the bottom and place it on the top. Keep it going—taking turns, faster and faster.

Now say "winner" every time you place your hand on top. You go from being a winner to a loser in seconds. You go from feeling good to feeling bad.

We often feel good for a moment, when we receive a high test score or help someone, for example. But it doesn't take long to feel squashed by sin. We forget an assignment, we break a rule.

In our Bible reading today Paul explained that he tried his best to be good and do good, but he didn't succeed. He was at the bottom of the pile.

But "thanks be to God—through Jesus Christ our Lord!" Paul wrote that our "goodness" does not depend on *what* we do, but on *whose* we are. We are God's. He seeks us out from the bottom of the pile. He forgives us because of Jesus' goodness and makes us belong to Him. God put us on top as winners!

Read from God's Word

For we know that the law is spiritual, but I am of the flesh, sold under sin. I do not understand my own actions. ... For I do not do the good I want, but the evil I do not want is what I keep on doing. Now if I do what I do not want, it is no longer I who do it, but sin that dwells within me. So I find it to be a law that when I want to do right, evil lies close at hand. For I delight in the law of God, in my inner being, but I see in my members another law waging war against the law of my mind and making me captive to the law of sin that dwells in my members. Wretched man that I am! Who will deliver me from this body of death? Thanks be to God through Jesus Christ our Lord! Romans 7:14–25 ✍

_____Let's do: Reread Romans 7:14–25 carefully. Write about a time when you felt this struggle.

_____Let's pray: Thank You, God, for giving us victory through faith in Jesus. In His name we pray. Amen.

C. E.

Read from God's Word

And those twelve stones, which they took out of the Jordan, Joshua set up at Gilgal. And he said to the people of Israel, "When your children ask their fathers in times to come, 'What do these stones mean?' then you shall let your children know, 'Israel passed over the Jordan on dry ground.' For the LORD your God dried up the waters of the Jordan for you until you passed over as the LORD your God did to the Red Sea, which He dried up for us until we passed over, so that all the peoples of the earth may know that the hand of the LORD is mighty, that you may fear the LORD your God forever."
Joshua 4:20–24

Monumental Event

Match the following monuments or towers with their locations:

1. ____ Pyramids   a. Pisa
2. ____ Gateway Arch   b. China
3. ____ Leaning Tower   c. Paris
4. ____ Big Ben   d. St. Louis
5. ____ Great Wall   e. London
6. ____ Statue of Liberty f. Egypt
7. ____ Eiffel Tower   g. New York City

The people of Israel were instructed to build a monument to remember their special crossing of the Jordan River. Can you imagine how excited they were when they walked through that riverbed? They would never forget how God had led them and helped them. They wanted their children and grandchildren to know God's great actions.

Their monument was a collection of 12 rocks. Each of the 12 tribes took one large stone from the riverbed to add to the monument. In the years to come, people would see the monument and ask about it. The Israelites would use those questions as opportunities to tell about the wonderful way God saved them.

The cross is a reminder to all people of what God did to save us from sin and its consequences. We never want to forget what Jesus did for us! We want to tell about this "monumental" event.

____Let's do: Read Joshua 4:1–24. Draw a "monument" to remind you of Jesus. Then make the monument using paper, clay, blocks, or your favorite building material.

____Let's pray: Dear Jesus, Your death and resurrection are so important to me! Because of You, I can live forever with You! Help me share this Good News. Amen.

C. E.

Hide-and-Seek

Walk around right now and spot some places that would be good for hiding. Find a good hiding spot; finish your devotion there. If you are with other people, you'll have to find a place large enough for your group.

Now you're ready to remember the Genesis account. Adam hid because he and his wife, Eve, had sinned. They felt ashamed and wanted to hide from God. They knew they had done something wrong and needed help.

Think of things you have done that make you want to hide. Sin causes us to feel like hiding. We might try to hide our mistakes for a while, but we realize that we can't hide them from God. We need help.

Now come out from your hiding place. Find a comfortable place to read Luke 19:10. This is good news. Jesus came "to seek and to save the lost." Jesus was sent by God to forgive our mistakes. He died so we don't have to

Read from God's Word

But the serpent said to the woman, "You will not surely die. For God knows that when you eat of it your eyes will be opened, and you will be like God, knowing good and evil." ... She took of its fruit and ate, and she also gave some to her husband. ... Then the eyes of both were opened, and they knew that they were naked. ... The man and his wife hid themselves from the presence of the LORD God among the trees of the garden. But the LORD God called to the man and said to him, "Where are you?" And he said, "I heard the sound of You in the garden, and I was afraid, because I was naked, and I hid myself." Genesis 3:4–10

hide from God. We don't have to fear Him. Jesus gathered all our sins and hid them away forever. They will never be found again!

Now we can live forever with Jesus! Don't hide this great news any longer! Instead, share it with everyone you meet!

———Let's talk: Read Genesis 3:1–10 aloud. List other stories from the Bible in which something or someone was hidden. What do these stories teach you about God?

———Let's pray: Dear Father in heaven, thank You for finding me. Thank You for saving me from my sins. In Jesus' name. Amen.

C. E.

See You at the Pole

Have you ever heard of an activity at some schools called "See you at the pole"? The school's flagpole is a meeting place. No one requires students to go; students who love Jesus choose to come together to pray.

In today's Bible reading we have another "pole" story. The Israelites were wandering in the wilderness. A scary and weird thing happened. God sent poisonous snakes all around them. Many people were bitten and died. Moses and the people asked God to remove the snakes. God told him to make a bronze snake and put it on a pole. Anyone who was bitten could look at the snake on the pole and be healed.

Both of these stories include people who trust God for help. Both stories teach that God is powerful and saves those who believe in Him.

Jesus was lifted up on another type of pole—a cross. Everyone who looks at the cross and trusts in Jesus will be saved from death. It is as though we have all been bitten by a snake and will die. Our only hope is that God helps us to look to Jesus on the cross and to trust in Him as our Savior.

St. John wrote, "And as Moses lifted up the serpent in the wilderness, so must the Son of Man [Jesus] be lifted up, that whoever believes in Him may have eternal life" (John 3:14–15).

_____Let's do: Read Numbers 21:4–9. Draw a picture of Jesus on the cross. Draw yourself in the picture looking at the cross. Add anything else to the picture to help you remember that Jesus died for you!

_____Let's pray: Dear Jesus, help me to stand firm in faith and love for You. Grant grace and mercy to all. Amen!

C. E.

The Way in the Desert

C an anything survive in the desert? The saguaro cactus does. The cactus arms stretch out with pleated spines. These pleats expand like an accordion when it rains so the cactus can store water. God created the saguaro cactus so it could thrive and survive in the desert.

The Bible talks a lot about survival in the desert. In the Book of Isaiah God said He would provide for His people. God kept His promise. He provided springs of water. He helped His people out of the sand and heat of the desert.

Our sinful condition is like the struggles of a thirsty person wandering in the desert. Can anyone survive? Yes, just the way the Israelites did—with God's help. God promised to make "a way" for us to survive. He did that by sending His own dear Son to live on earth and to die on the cross. God refreshes us with the living water of His Word and Sacraments. When we hear the pastor forgive our sins or read God's Word, it's like getting a drink of cool water in the hot desert.

Imagine Jesus with His arms stretched out, dying for your sins. He's making the way for you. He loves you so much and He's giving you a drink. Refreshed, now you can proclaim His praise.

Read from God's Word

"Remember not the former things, nor consider the things of old. Behold, I am doing a new thing; now it springs forth, do you not perceive it? I will make a way in the wilderness and rivers in the desert. The wild beasts will honor Me, the jackals and the ostriches, for I give water in the wilderness, rivers in the desert, to give drink to My chosen people, the people whom I formed for Myself that they might declare My praise." Isaiah 43:18–21

_____ Let's do: Draw a cactus. Around the picture write words from the Bible reading that give you hope.

_____ Let's pray: Dear Jesus, thank You for giving me a way to be with You forever. Thank You for the refreshing waters of Your Word and Sacraments. Amen.

C. E.

Read from God's Word

Let love be genuine. Abhor what is evil; hold fast to what is good. Love one another with brotherly affection. Outdo one another in showing honor. Do not be slothful in zeal, be fervent in spirit, serve the Lord. Rejoice in hope, be patient in tribulation, be constant in prayer. Contribute to the needs of the saints and seek to show hospitality. Romans 12:9–13

Active Love

"Good night, Mom," said Eric. "I love you."

"Good night, Eric," said Mom. "I believe you."

"Aren't you supposed to say, 'I love you too'?"

"Usually I do," she said. "But today you showed me you love me in lots of ways. Love is more than words, Eric," said Mom. "Today I didn't have to ask you to set the table for dinner. You saw that it needed to be done and you did it. Thank you."

"No problem, I guess."

"You helped your brother with his bike and you helped Sis study her spelling words. That's active love. Jesus lived a life of active love. He was always caring for others. He showed His disciples active love when He washed their feet. He showed active love when He died on the cross."

"Wait a minute, Mom. I don't want to die for anyone."

"Oh, Eric," Mom said, giving him a hug. "Nobody's asking you to do that. Jesus paid fully for our sins. He suffered, died, rose again, and lives in the hearts of all who believe in Him. I could see His love at work through you today."

"Really? It was kind of fun," Eric said. "Well, good night."

"Good night," Mom said. "Oh, Eric?"

"Yeah, Mom?"

"I love you too."

_____Let's talk: What are some things you can do for family members or friends to let Jesus' love reach out from you?

_____Let's pray: Dear Jesus, thank You for showing me how much You love me. Help me to show Your love. Amen.

V. S.

Be Imitators

Read from God's Word

For it is God who works in you, both to will and to work for His good pleasure. Philippians 2:13 ↝

"Come on, Adam, you have three Shaq cards. Just trade me one," begged Michael.

"No, I don't think so," Adam stalled.

"You know he's my favorite player," Michael said. "I'll never forgive you if you don't trade." He was getting frustrated.

It was true that Shaq was Michael's favorite. He wore a T-shirt that told everyone so. He had a hat with the team name on it. He even tried to talk his mom into letting him get his hair cut in the same style as his favorite player.

Whom do you try to be like? Some people we want to copy make better role models than others.

Ephesians 5:1–2 tells us to be imitators of God. It also tells us to live a life of love, just as Christ loved us. Imitating someone means acting just like him or her. How can we act just like God? We can't. In fact, we often do just the opposite of what God wants us to do.

We can be thankful that Jesus lived a perfect life in our place. He's more than our role model. He's our Savior. He died to take the punishment for the times we fail to imitate Him. And He works in our lives the power "to will and to work for His good pleasure."

_____Let's talk: Do you sometimes become confused about who you are supposed to be or how you are supposed to act? How will God help you imitate Him? Where can you look to find God's answers to those questions?

_____Let's pray: Dear God, thank You for showing me, in Your Word, Jesus' life of love and forgiveness. Help me to be an imitator of Christ. In His holy name I pray. Amen.

V. S.

Read from God's Word

So then, as we have opportunity, let us do good to everyone, and especially to those who are of the household of faith.
Galatians 6:10 ✍

We Are Family

The rain had been coming down all day. Matt and Emily were stuck in the house playing a game.

"You took two turns," Matt accused. "You're cheating."

"I am not," Emily snapped back.

Aaron, who had been painting a picture in the kitchen, proudly brought his artwork in to show the others.

"Do you like the forest I painted?" he asked.

"*Forest?* It looks like green spaghetti," Emily laughed.

Ouch! Unkind words can sting and hurt others. Does talking back or putting other people down ever happen at your house? Galatians 6:10 tells us to be good or kind to all people. Goodness and kindness are God's way of treating others. Those words are difficult to obey, and sometimes they are even more difficult with the people in our own family.

Thank God for His Son, Jesus Christ. Christ is the head of each Christian family. As we look to Him and His life of love, we can share more of His love with our family. Jesus took our sin to the cross, and there He won a victory over all our mean words. We have His victory and the help of His Spirit to treat others with goodness and kindness. Jesus can help us replace angry words with kindness and understanding, even on a rainy day.

_____Let's do: Write a prayer for each member of your family. Say these prayers every night before you go to sleep.

_____Let's pray: Dear Jesus, please help me be kind to others—especially my own family. Thank You for putting me into my family and showing me how to love. Amen.

V. S.

You're in the Army Now!

I t was the end of the Civil War, the night before the Northern armies were released from their military duty. The men were waiting for morning. They were glad the war was over but they were uncertain about what was coming next.

A few soldiers stuck candles in the muzzles of their muskets. They lighted the candles and began to march down the street. Other soldiers joined them. Soon the whole company—officers, privates, and bands playing music—marched with thousands of candle flames. They began to cheer! They had marched together on battlefields. Now they simply marched for joy. Their fighting had not been for nothing. The Union had been preserved; the slaves had been freed.

As soldiers in the Christian army we live in the middle of a battleground. God's Holy Spirit in us is at war with the devil, the temptations of the world, and our own sinful flesh. But Jesus has already won our victory. He died on the cross to free us from the slavery of sin. As soldiers, we bring the Good News that frees other slaves of Satan. Even now, all the company of heaven—angels and saints—rejoices and cheers us on as we "put on the whole armor of God."

Read from God's Word

Finally, be strong in the Lord and in the strength of His might. Put on the whole armor of God, that you may be able to stand against the schemes of the devil. For we do not wrestle against flesh and blood, but against the rulers, against the authorities, against the cosmic powers over this present darkness, against the spiritual forces of evil in the heavenly places. Therefore take up the whole armor of God, that you may be able to withstand in the evil day, and having done all, to stand firm. Ephesians 6:10–13 ✍

_____Let's talk: Do you know anybody in the armed forces? What kind of training do they have? Read Ephesians 6:10–20. What kind of training prepares us for spiritual "warfare"?

_____Let's pray: Dear Jesus, being in an army sounds a little scary. Sometimes I'm not very brave about being a Christian. Please teach me and give me courage. Amen.

W. E.

The Lord's Day

Read from God's Word

For a day in Your courts is better than a thousand elsewhere. I would rather be a doorkeeper in the house of my God than dwell in the tents of wickedness. For the LORD God is a sun and shield; the LORD bestows favor and honor. No good thing does He withhold from those who walk uprightly. Psalm 84:10–11

In the 1924 Olympics, Scotland's fastest runner, Eric Liddell, was expected to run the 100-meter race and win the gold medal. But Olympic officials announced that the qualifying heats for the 100-meter race would be run on Sunday.

Eric knew that God said, "Remember the Sabbath day, to keep it holy" (Exodus 20:8). He felt he would not be keeping the commandment if he ran the race.

Eric told the Olympic officials he would not run the race on Sunday. The officials asked him to run the 400-meter race on another day instead. He did and won the gold medal for Scotland and set a world record of 47.6 seconds.

After the Olympics, Eric became a missionary in China. He was still there during World War II when the Japanese captured him. Eric shared the love of God with his captors. Throughout his life God showed His love for Eric, and Eric reflected God's love.

God loves us so much that He sent His only Son to die for us. Setting aside one day of the week to worship God is one way we reflect God's love. It helps us to remember the great things God has done for us. We are blessed through the treasures of the divine service as we worship with other believers in Christ.

_____Let's talk: What things interfere with your worship and Bible study time? How can you avoid such conflicts?

_____Let's pray: Dear Jesus, thank You for Your sacrifice on the cross and Your victory over sin, death, and the devil. Help me to reflect the love You have for me. Amen.

K. S.

The Right Uniform

osh felt very proud. He'd worked hard to learn the zone defense, dribble with his left hand, and keep his back to the basket. It had paid off. Josh made the basketball team!

All the guys wore their green and white jerseys to school so everyone would know they were on the school's team. Now Josh stood in the middle of the gym floor with his teammates, listening to the opening prayer.

Wearing a uniform lets others know you are part of a team. Christians may not wear shirts with numbers, but the Bible tells us we have a special uniform. John 13:35 says that our *love* will show others who we are and whose we are. With the Holy Spirit's help we have clothed ourselves with Christ. A Christian's uniform is seen in loving acts. It can be worn each day all day. It never wears out.

Jesus makes us part of the team and equips us to play. Through faith in Him, given by the Holy Spirit in our Baptism, we can reflect His love to the people around us. On our own we have nothing to be proud of. But we can wear our Christian uniform proudly because it shows others Jesus Christ and His great love.

_____Let's talk: How does it make you feel to be part of a group or team? Can you think of someone who might like to be included on the team of believers in Jesus Christ?

_____Let's pray: Dear Jesus, thank You for including me on Your team of believers. Thank You for dying on the cross for me. Help me to share Your love with others. Amen.

V. S.

Children of God

See what kind of love the Father has given to us, that we should be called children of God; and so we are. The reason why the world does not know us is that it did not know Him. Beloved, we are God's children now, and what we will be has not yet appeared; but we know that when He appears we will be like Him, because we shall see Him as He is. And everyone who thus hopes in Him purifies himself as He is pure. 1 John 3:1–3

Tracy took a break from cleaning to watch TV and munch a cookie. Just then her dad got home, and she could tell by looking at his face that he was upset. "You'll never amount to anything!" Her dad exploded and ordered her to get back to work. "Get down on your hands and knees and dust under the piano!"

Tracy was hurt by her father's words, which seemed so unfair. She began to cry.

Sometimes people we love and trust hurt us deeply. The hurt is especially painful when we don't deserve it. Even Jesus—the only perfect person who ever lived—felt the pain of being betrayed by His disciples. Jesus was even abandoned on the cross by His Father.

When God abandoned His Son, He allowed Jesus to suffer the pain of hell in our place so the gates of heaven would be open for us. But God did not leave Jesus in the grave. Jesus' resurrection and ascension completed God's plan for our victory. We, too, will rise from the dead and ascend to live with God forever!

You'll never amount to anything? Not true! God has chosen you to be His own dearly beloved child and live in His kingdom!

_____Let's talk: What types of feelings did Tracy's dad bring home from work? What are some helpful and not-so-helpful ways to deal with feelings like those?

_____Let's pray: Heavenly Father, thank You for letting me know I'm special because of Jesus. Help me to remember that I am loved by You always. In Jesus' name. Amen.

C. A.

The Real Thing

Two-year-old Allen discovered a bowl of artificial fruit on the end table in Aunt Susan's basement. She knew it was okay for him to play with it. What she didn't count on was that Allen might think the fruit was real.

He picked up a fuzzy peach. Before Aunt Susan could say a word, he bit into it. Allen was shocked. What he thought was real turned out to be unreal. Our world is often like that. Imitations exist everywhere; even in places we least expect them to be.

There are a lot of people who believe in a god or "divine being" but who don't believe in the one, true, living God. Their services may seem like ours and their buildings may appear like our churches. The difference is that they are not worshiping the God who created them, who provides their way of salvation, and who has the power to bring them to faith. There is no substitute for the triune God— Father, Son, and Holy Spirit.

Read from God's Word

And we know that the Son of God has come and has given us understanding, so that we may know Him who is true; and we are in Him who is true, in His Son Jesus Christ. He is the true God and eternal life. Little children, keep yourselves from idols. 1 John 5:20–21

Pray for knowledge to see through the imitations. Be thankful that the Holy Spirit has brought you to faith in Jesus, the Savior, who laid down His life on Calvary to make you His forever. "He is the true God and eternal life."

_____ Let's talk: How can Bible study help us see the difference between our God and a false god?

_____ Let's pray: Dear God, thank You for bringing us to faith in You. Help us see through the imitations in our world and remember that You are the only, true, living Lord. In Jesus' name. Amen.

S. W. V.

Planning

It's fun to build a house with playing cards. You start with two cards, bent slightly and resting on their edges. You place another card flat on top of those two. From there you keep building higher and higher.

However, one sudden movement or slip of the hand can destroy hours of work. The entire structure can suddenly crash into a big mess.

The tower of Babel became a mess, too, but for a different reason. God wasn't happy with the plans the people had made. He saw that they were proud and tried to make themselves important. The tower may have seemed like a good idea to them, but it didn't fit into God's plans for their welfare.

God wants us to ask for His help as we make our decisions. Sometimes we decide for ourselves and then ask for God's help. That's backward! God has the wisdom to steer us in the right direction from the start. He invites us to pray for His guidance in making all our plans and decisions.

That doesn't mean that everything will work out perfectly. We are still sinful people living in a sinful world. But God wants what is best for us. He proved that by giving us salvation through the sacrifice of His Son, Jesus Christ.

_____Let's talk: Can you think of a time when your plan failed and later you were very glad? How might that have shown God's hand in the matter? How can we remember to ask for God's help in making decisions?

_____Let's pray: Dear Lord God, help us remember that You want what is best for us. We pray that our decisions fit into Your will for our lives. In Jesus' name. Amen.

S. W. V.

Cold-and-Flu Season

Winter is cold-and-flu season. Commercials on television remind us of the awful condition of aches, pains, fever, and stuffy heads.

You know all the remedies—painkillers, decongestants, cough medicine, chicken soup, orange juice, and heating pads. Often a doctor is consulted and, if necessary, stronger medication is given.

The cold or flu eventually goes away. Gradually we start to feel normal again, and life goes on. So when others ask what happened that made the illness go away, what will we say? We can tell others about the medicine Dad bought at the drugstore or how much the doctor's bill was. We can brag about Aunt Marie's chicken soup or give a long explanation of the human immune system. But those answers do not tell the whole story.

It is God who heals us. He alone is responsible for the creation of our wonderful bodies, which can renew and replace injured cells. He provides doctors and medicines for us. The Lord makes us well.

Out of His great love for us, God heals our souls as well as our bodies. When we are sick with sin, He forgives us and heals our injured hearts and spirits. Through Jesus' victory over every evil, He gives us a joyful hope and a glorious future with Him forever.

Read from God's Word

Bless the LORD, O my soul, and all that is within me, bless His holy name! Bless the LORD, O my soul, and forget not all His benefits, who forgives all your iniquity, who heals all your diseases, who redeems your life from the pit, who crowns you with steadfast love and mercy. Psalm 103:1–4

_____Let's talk: How can an illness help us to share God's love with others? In what ways does God give us responsibility for our own health?

_____Let's pray: Dear Lord God, thank You for Your great work of healing. Help us remember that You are our source of health—physical and spiritual. In Jesus' name I pray. Amen.

S. W. V.

february

Contributors for this month:

Joel Brondos

Dawn Napier

Christine Ross

Carolyn Sims

Cathy Spieler

Angie Bierlein Watt

Cherie Werner

Not Good Enough

Read from God's Word

For by works of the law no human being will be justified in His sight, since through the law comes knowledge of sin. But now the righteousness of God has been manifested apart from the law, although the Law and the Prophets bear witness to it— the righteousness of God through faith in Jesus Christ for all who believe. For there is no distinction: for all have sinned and fall short of the glory of God, and are justified by His grace as a gift, through the redemption that is in Christ Jesus. Romans 3:20–24 ✍

Inspector Mom could spot a stray sock behind the dresser, a toy in the corner, or a dust bunny under the bed. Anyone else would think a room was clean enough, but Mom always showed that it wasn't.

God's Law inspects our lives even more closely than a mom. When God's Law finds something dirty or disorderly (and it always does), it accuses us. We may think our lives are good enough, but God's Law always shows that our lives are not perfectly clean.

How do we get the Law to be quiet and stop accusing us? We can't—but Jesus did. He allowed Himself to be inspected by the Law in our place. His life is the only one perfectly clean from all sin and selfishness. His life is the only one that satisfies the Law. We are justified and redeemed because Jesus stopped the Law from accusing us.

When the Law comes to inspect our lives and accuse us, we can recall that we have been baptized into Christ. He has passed inspection for us and because of Him, we cannot be accused by the Law any longer. Redeemed and justified in Christ, we will come to enjoy an eternity of wonderful days in the clean rooms He has prepared for us in heaven.

_____Let's talk: The name *Satan* means "the accuser." How might Satan use the Law to accuse us? How does Jesus silence Satan's accusations?

_____Let's pray: Dear heavenly Father, help us to face all our accusers, to confess the truth, and to stand on the Last Day with Your Son, who has redeemed us from the accusations and curses of the Law. In Jesus' name we pray. Amen.

J. B.

Shadows

Read from God's Word

Therefore let no one pass judgment on you in questions of food and drink, or with regard to a festival or a new moon or a Sabbath. These are a shadow of the things to come, but the substance belongs to Christ.
Colossians 2:16–17

In some regions of North America people observe February 2 as Groundhog Day. According to the tradition, if the groundhog comes out of his hole and sees his shadow, he gets scared and jumps back into his hole. This is supposed to mean another six weeks of winter. But if the day is cloudy, the groundhog isn't scared of his shadow, and spring weather is supposed to come sooner.

Throughout the history of the Christian church February 2 has been celebrated as the Presentation of Our Lord. On this day, 40 days after His birth, the baby Jesus was taken by His parents to the temple. There, an old prophet named Simeon held Jesus in his arms and gave thanks to God for sending the Savior. Simeon spoke the words (Luke 2:22–40) many of us now sing in church after Holy Communion, "Lord, now let Your servant depart in peace."

Simeon's words remind us that Jesus was not afraid to be our Savior. He was not scared away when He saw the dark shadows of death. He took on human flesh and was sacrificed for our sins. Instead of looking to groundhogs or shadows, we look to our Lord Jesus Christ. In Him we have the guarantee of "eternal spring" with Him in heaven.

_____Let's talk: How many special days in the year can you list? In what ways can those days be used to remember Jesus?

_____Let's pray: Father, on this day we remember Jesus' presentation in the temple. Grant that through our Baptism we may be presented to You with pure and clean hearts. In the name of Your Son, our Savior. Amen.

J. B.

Big and Strong

Can you name five superheroes? Sometimes we like to pretend we are superstrong and powerful, able to overcome all the dangers and enemies that threaten us.

Jesus did not have a cape, a ray gun, or a mask to conquer all His enemies. He used nails and a cross. He did something that didn't seem very heroic at all. He died.

Jesus knew that a strong enemy might be able to accept being beaten by a powerful hero. But how much more earth-shattering the victory would be if someone utterly weak overcame the enemy! So Jesus smashed the evil powers and rulers by being weak. God did not use superpower to save us. He used superweakness!

Sometimes we feel weak and foolish. The apostle Paul did too. But Jesus told him, "My grace is sufficient for you, for My power is made perfect in weakness." See 2 Corinthians 12:9–10 for Paul's response.

Read from God's Word

For Jews demand signs and Greeks seek wisdom, but we preach Christ crucified, a stumbling block to Jews and folly to Gentiles, but to those who are called, both Jews and Greeks, Christ the power of God and the wisdom of God. For the foolishness of God is wiser than men, and the weakness of God is stronger than men. For consider your calling, brothers: not many of you were wise according to worldly standards, not many were powerful, not many were of noble birth. But God chose what is foolish in the world to shame the wise; God chose what is weak in the world to shame the strong. 1 Corinthians 1:22–27

God's gifts of Baptism, Holy Communion, and the Bible don't seem very powerful to the world. That may be why we call them *means of grace* instead of *means of power.* They keep us close to Christ, who, unlike any superhero, has truly won the victory for us. When we are in Christ, we are strong even in weakness.

_____Let's talk: What circumstances make you feel weak? How does faith in Christ affect your weakness?

_____Let's pray: Lord God, You were not afraid to become weak to overcome my enemies: sin, death, and the devil. Thank You for being my very present help and strength. In Jesus' name. Amen.

J. B.

Born That Way

John slammed the door so hard an antique plate from his mother's collection fell and broke. He was angry. As his mom handed him the broom, she asked John not to get so angry. John replied, "I can't help it. I was born that way."

Clair left her clarinet at home. She couldn't help it that she was so forgetful. When she took her clarinet home to practice, she left it there. And when she brought it to school for band, she left it there. She was born that way—forgetful.

People try to use the excuse "I was born that way" to avoid judgment and punishment. Our sinful nature tells us we "can't help it." Instead of looking for an explanation for our sins, we can look to the One who paid for our sins, Jesus Christ. Then we will realize that Christians don't need excuses. We have forgiveness and life in the name of the Father, Son, and Holy Spirit.

Instead of looking for excuses for our sins, we look for "excuses" to do something good. We don't have to give reasons for being faithful in hearing the Word, courageous in the face of hardship, or steadfast in times of trial. We simply say, "I can't help it. I was *reborn* that way."

_____Let's talk: What excuses have you made for your sins and shortcomings? What is the difference between excusing sin and forgiving sin?

_____Let's pray: Dear Lord God, You created all things good, but we have used Your good creation in selfish and unloving ways. Move us to confess our sins. For Jesus' sake. Amen.

J. B.

Free to Serve

om was grinning from ear to ear as Joel walked out the door with a loaded trash bag.

Usually Mom has to bug him while he's watching TV, playing video games, or getting ready to play with his friends. But this time, she hadn't asked. This time, Joel asked her, "Mom, what can I do to help?"

Previously, Mom had to use reminders and a firm tone of voice to get Joel to do his chores. His stubbornness led her to use commands. But now something had come over him that led her to respond with an award-winning smile.

No number of commands or threats could ever have forced Jesus to serve stubborn, selfish people like us. But He offered to save us; He was obedient even when He didn't have to be. His freedom from sin left Him perfectly free to serve sinners in love. Jesus willingly took out the garbage of our sinful lives and disposed of it by His death on the cross.

When we are forgiven in the name of Jesus, we are freed from our sins. Through that forgiveness Jesus also frees us from serving ourselves. His Word and Spirit bring about such a cheerful heart that God helps us to be happy—even when we're doing our chores.

Read from God's Word

For you were called to freedom, brothers. Only do not use your freedom as an opportunity for the flesh, but through love serve one another. Galatians 5:13

_____Let's talk: What would lead you to offer help instead of waiting to be told what to do? What does Jesus give that makes it possible for us to help at home, in school, in church, or in our neighborhood?

_____Let's pray: Dear Lord God, free me from my stubborn and selfish ways that I may serve You in everlasting righteousness, innocence, and blessedness, for Jesus' sake. Amen.

J. B.

Read from God's Word

Bring the full tithes into the storehouse, that there may be food in My house. And thereby put Me to the test, says the LORD of hosts, if I will not open the windows of heaven for you and pour down for you a blessing until there is no more need.
Malachi 3:10

The Dilemma

Collin had been working hard shoveling snow and had finally been paid. Now he could buy the computer game he wanted.

Oh, no, he thought as he counted his money. It was just exactly enough. That was a problem.

Collin's parents had taught him that the first 10 percent of his earnings went right to God. But this time, giving up that 10 percent meant waiting another month for his game. He wasn't sure he could wait much longer. Besides, if it didn't snow anymore, he couldn't earn any more money.

During church Collin heard again about Jesus' love for him. Collin remembered how much God had already blessed him and he was thankful for many things in his life. When the offering plate passed by him, he put his money in. Collin prayed that God would use the money so others would hear the news about Jesus, their Savior. Collin knew he would have to wait longer for the computer game, but it didn't seem to matter too much.

Collin saved up the extra money he needed and tithed even more. When he went to the store to buy his game, he was surprised to find it on sale.

God blesses us in many ways with forgiveness, salvation, families, strength to shovel, and even money. We are truly rich.

——Let's do: Write down different ways you spend your money. Think about the words from today's Bible reading.

——Let's pray: Lord God, heavenly Father, thank You for the many blessings You give to me. Help me give to You with a generous heart. In Your Son's name I pray. Amen.

C. W.

Jesus Knows

Justin shuffled slowly through the snow on his way home. His parents had been fighting almost nonstop lately. He was afraid of what might happen next. Justin was sure they didn't love him anymore.

When he looked up, he realized that he had taken a wrong turn and was standing in front of his church instead of his house. He sat down on the steps, too tired to turn around.

Pastor James came outside just as it was getting dark. "Hi, Justin! How are you doing?"

"Hi, Pastor," Justin mumbled.

Pastor knew the situation with Justin's family and had counseled them a few times.

"Are things getting any better at home, Justin?" he asked.

Justin tried to hide his tears, but he couldn't. Pastor James put his arm around Justin and let him cry. "I know it's hard, Justin. I bet you think no one cares how you feel, but there is Someone who knows and cares very much.

"Jesus knows all our feelings. In fact, while He was on earth, Jesus experienced those same feelings. When He was on the cross, He felt abandoned and unloved by His Father, just like you might sometimes feel abandoned and unloved by your parents. Jesus knows how you feel. He loves you. And He will help you through this difficult time."

Read from God's Word

Since then we have a great high priest who has passed through the heavens, Jesus, the Son of God, let us hold fast our confession. For we do not have a high priest who is unable to sympathize with our weaknesses, but one who in every respect has been tempted as we are, yet without sin. Let us then with confidence draw near to the throne of grace, that we may receive mercy and find grace to help in time of need. Hebrews 4:14–16

———Let's talk: Have you ever thought that no one knew how you were feeling? Have you ever felt alone and unloved? Read Hebrews 4:14–16 again. What do you think now?

———Let's pray: Jesus, You know exactly how I feel each day. Help me trust You for what is best for me in every situation. Amen.

C. W.

Read from God's Word

Beloved, let us love one another, for love is from God, and whoever loves has been born of God and knows God. Anyone who does not love does not know God, because God is love. In this the love of God was made manifest among us, that God sent His only Son into the world, so that we might live through Him. In this is love, not that we have loved God but that He loved us and sent His Son to be the propitiation for our sins. Beloved, if God so loved us, we also ought to love one another. No one has ever seen God; if we love one another, God abides in us and His love is perfected in us. 1 John 4:7–12 ❧

Signs of Love

You can't miss the signs. The stores are full of items to help us celebrate. Perhaps you have shiny red hearts decorating your classroom.

Long ago a man named "Valentine" lived in Rome. Although there are many legends about Valentine, we know for sure that he loved Jesus and shared Jesus' love with others. Because Valentine refused to deny his faith in Jesus Christ in front of the government, he was put in prison. On February 14 in the year 270, he was killed because of his faith.

Some children who will be exchanging cards or candy don't know that legend. But, worse, some of those children don't know about Jesus. In fact, they may never have heard of Him. If someone does not know Jesus, there is no salvation.

But we know that God's heart of love allowed His own Son to be sacrificed on the cross for His sinful people. Because of His love, we have love to share with those who *do* know and those who *don't* know Christ. When God's children buy valentine cards or heart-shaped boxes of chocolate, they can think of sharing God's love with others, the love they first received from God.

_____Let's talk: What are the signs of Valentine's Day that surround you? How can each one remind you of Jesus?

_____Let's pray: Heavenly Father, help me to focus on Jesus every day. Teach me how much You and others love me too. In Jesus' name. Amen.

C. R.

Hot Cross Buns

We smelled the wonderful aroma as we walked through the door. Grandma had hot cross buns, fresh and warm from the oven, cooling on the counter. As far back as we could remember our family has had hot cross buns on Ash Wednesday.

How did the custom of eating hot cross buns get started? We don't know, and maybe it doesn't matter. Lent would still be Lent whether we ate that spicy raisin bun or not. But the special buns remind our family of Jesus' suffering on the cross for our sins. The frosting cross reminds us of Him.

On Ash Wednesday, we remember our sin and eventual death. But God's family also celebrates the Sacrament of Holy Communion. At the Lord's Supper believers receive the body and blood of Christ in, with, and under the visible bread and wine. The main blessing of this meal is the forgiveness of sins, and Christ also offers life and salvation.

Read from God's Word

"This is My blood of the covenant, which is poured out for many for the forgiveness of sins." Matthew 26:28

Even if you are not old enough to attend the Lord's Supper, you can be sure you have the forgiveness of sins and life everlasting because Christ has won it for you and all believers on the cross.

Look to the cross this season. See there the great sacrifice of the Savior for all people—and especially for you.

_____Let's do: Name special foods that remind you of special times in the church year. Write about how each one is special.

_____Let's pray: Dear Father, thank You for the gift of Your Son. Help me to see the blessings of Jesus' sacrifice for me. For Jesus' sake. Amen.

C. S.

Partly Right

Read from God's Word

Jesus said to him, "I am the Way, and the Truth, and the Life. No one comes to the Father except through Me." John 14:6

Mackenzie was frustrated. She missed the whole math problem just because she forgot a decimal point, a tiny dot. But her teacher said, "Partly right is not good enough."

James made his free throw, but the referee blew the whistle. James had stepped over the line; the free throw didn't count.

A celebrity on TV said he believes God is love but couldn't believe a loving God would send people to hell. The celebrity was partly right, but he was also partly wrong. God's love sent His Son, Jesus, to the manger, to a world of misunderstanding, and even to the cross for all people. Jesus' victory over sin, death, and the devil became *the way*—the only way to the Father in heaven.

God's Holy Spirit works constantly to bring all people to *the truth*—the only truth of saving faith in Jesus. He works through the Bible and through the Sacraments of Baptism and Holy Communion. Other Christians share the word about their new relationship with God through Jesus.

Being partly right about God's love isn't enough. So the Spirit works to bring people to know the full truth of God's love for us through Jesus. That's how God's children receive *the life*—the only life that will be with Him in heaven.

___Let's do: Draw a picture of what the words of John 14:6 say or write them using calligraphy in a meaningful way.

___Let's pray: Heavenly Father, I thank You for loving the world and for sending Your Son to be the way to a relationship with You. May Your Holy Spirit increase my faith. In the name of Your Son, Jesus Christ, I pray. Amen.

C. R.

Heads and Hearts

"You are missing some valentines, J. T." his mom said. "Where are the others?"

"There are a couple kids in class who don't like me. I can't imagine that they will want a card from me."

J. T.'s mom spoke quietly, "Sounds like we need to add a couple of names to the bedtime prayer list."

"Mom, you can't be serious! Pray for the kids who make fun of me?" J. T. exclaimed.

"We discussed this very topic in devotions yesterday. I have to ask God to help my heart do what I know I should do. Now it's your turn. God is leading you to put your faith into action. He will even help you do it."

J. T. knew that Jesus set the example for us by praying for the very people who wanted to kill Him and by asking God to forgive them even while He was on the cross. J. T.'s heart was struggling with forgiveness.

Read from God's Word

We love because He first loved us. If anyone says, "I love God," and hates his brother, he is a liar; for he who does not love his brother whom he has seen cannot love God whom he has not seen. And this commandment we have from Him: whoever loves God must also love his brother. 1 John 4:19–21

"Why is it so much harder to do what I know is right than to talk about it?" confessed J. T. "I guess if Jesus could die for me and others who mistreated Him, with His help I can give everyone in my class a valentine."

J. T.'s mom smiled, handed him the cards, and shared her favorite pen.

_____Let's do: Write a prayer for someone who is not one of your good friends.

_____Let's pray: Dear Jesus, it is only through You that I can care for people I may not like. Help me. Amen.

C. R.

Love Others

Nicholas says, "I can't love David. He's a ball hog and he never makes layups. Every time he gets the ball, he heads straight for the basket!"

Alyssa says, "I can't love Anna. She won't switch times with me, no matter how I explain to her why I can't acolyte on Sunday."

Derek says, "I can't love Ryan. No matter how many times I try to explain what happened at recess, he refuses to listen."

Nicholas, David, Alyssa, Anna, Derek, and Ryan are all in the same classroom. They are all Christians. In their classroom there are problems. In their classroom there are opportunities. In their classroom God is helping them grow in friendship and understanding. They are growing with the help of God's Spirit to make problems into opportunities to love one another as Jesus loves.

It isn't easy to love those who hurt us. That's why Jesus showed us how to do it. He was selfless, understanding, and forgiving. He even became the perfect sacrifice for sinners.

We can't be perfect like Jesus, but with God's help we, the imperfect people, can love other imperfect people. And by this kind of love others will know we are part of God's family.

_____Let's do: Look at hymn 373 in *Lutheran Worship*. Write down the ways God uses to help you learn to love like Jesus. Take special note of the verbs.

_____Let's pray: Dear Jesus, You showed all people what love looks like. Help me to share Your kind of love. Amen.

C. R.

Perfect Love

Read from God's Word

Love is patient and kind; love does not envy or boast; it is not arrogant or rude. It does not insist on its own way; it is not irritable or resentful; it does not rejoice at wrongdoing, but rejoices with the truth. Love bears all things, believes all things, hopes all things, endures all things.
1 Corinthians 13:4–7

Mrs. Jones read 1 Corinthians 13 aloud during Sunday school. Then she handed each class member a paper with the following activity:

____ is patient and kind; ____ does not envy or boast; ____ is not arrogant or rude. ____ does not insist on its own way; ____ is not irritable or resentful; ____ does not rejoice at wrongdoing, but rejoices with the truth. ____ bears all things, believes all things, hopes all things, endures all things.

"Each of you will take your turn reading the paragraph aloud and placing your own name in each blank. Jill, will you begin please?"

After a few giggles, Jill began. "Jill is patient, Jill is kind . . ."

This exercise helped the class members understand ways they hadn't loved but could grow in love for one another.

Next they read the passage again. This time they substituted the name of Jesus in the blanks. The class began, "Jesus is patient, Jesus is kind…"

When they finished, Mrs. Jones said, "Jesus is our example of perfect love. He was our substitute, taking God's punishment against us for our sin. Through Jesus we are forgiven for not loving perfectly. We are given many opportunities to love others."

____Let's do: Consider the list of ways to show love. Write five of your favorites on a piece of paper.

____Let's pray: Dear God, forgive me through Jesus when I am not loving. Send Your Spirit to teach me how to love. In Jesus' name I pray. Amen.

C. R.

Read from God's Word

But God shows His own love for us in that while we were still sinners, Christ died for us. Romans 5:8 ✍

Jesus Loves You

U se the code to discover a Bible verse that tells what Jesus does for us.

A=1 B=2 C=3 D=4 E=5 F=6 G=7
H=8 I=9 J=10 K=11 L=12 M=13
N=14 O=15 P=16 Q=17 R=18 S=19
T=20 U=21 V=22 W=23 X=24 Y=25
Z=26 1=27 2=28 3=29 4=30 5=31
6=32 7=33 8=34 9=35

"T _ _ _   _ _   _ _ _   _ _   _ _ _ _
20, 8, 9, 19   9, 19   8, 15, 23   23, 5   11, 14, 15, 23

_ _ _ _   _ _ _ _ _   _ _: _ _ _ _ _
23, 8, 1, 20   12, 15, 22, 5   9, 19:   10, 5, 19, 21, 19

_ _ _ _ _ _   _ _ _ _   _ _ _ _   _ _ _
3, 8, 18, 9, 19, 20   12, 1, 9, 4   4, 15, 23, 14   8, 9, 19

_ _ _ _   _ _ _   _ _."
12, 9, 6, 5   6, 15, 18   21, 19.

_   _ _ _ _   _:_ _
27   10, 15, 8, 14   29: 27, 32

Today is a day to celebrate love. Remember all you have learned about love through the past week. Most of all, remember Jesus. Christ's love for His Father led Him to be obedient, even unto death. His love for us caused Him to die for our sins so we may one day live with God perfectly. What amazing love this is!

_____Let's talk: Discuss all the ways Jesus' love touches your life.

_____Let's pray: Dear Father, thank You for sending Jesus to save me from my sins. Thank You for Your great love for me through Him, in whose name I pray. Amen.

C. R.

Finders Keepers?

E rin couldn't believe her eyes. She glanced into the wastebasket and noticed the crumpled green bill. Someone had accidentally thrown away a hundred-dollar bill!

Erin thought about everything she could do with that much money. She could buy toys and gifts. She could put some of it in the offering at church. She also thought about God's commandment "Do not steal." This wasn't really *stealing*, was it? She didn't take it from anybody; she just *found* it.

Then Erin thought about the person who had lost the money. That person must be feeling sad and worried. He might have needed to buy food or pay the electric bill.

Erin didn't have to think any longer. She quickly turned the money in to the school office.

Erin knew God loved her and cared for her. He showed that when Jesus died to take away her sins. That love was so strong in Erin's heart that she loved and cared about other people too.

The Bible tells us that we keep God's laws best when we obey them out of love. Erin didn't return the money because she was afraid God would punish her if she didn't. She returned the money because she loved God and all His people. That kind of love is worth more money than anyone has.

Read from God's Word

Owe no one anything, except to love each other, for the one who loves another has fulfilled the law. The commandments, "You shall not commit adultery. You shall not murder. You shall not steal. You shall not covet," and any other commandment, are summed up in this word: "You shall love your neighbor as yourself." Love does no wrong to a neighbor; therefore love is the fulfilling of the law. Romans 13:8–10

_____Let's talk: What would you do if you found something that someone else lost? Why?

_____Let's pray: Dear Jesus, thank You for all Your gifts to me. Please help me show my love for You by the way I care about others. Amen.

C. S.

Read from God's Word

"Let not your hearts be troubled. Believe in God; believe also in Me. In My Father's house are many rooms. If it were not so, would I have told you that I go to prepare a place for you? And if I go and prepare a place for you, I will come again and will take you to Myself, that where I am you may be also."
John 14:1–3

The Best House, Ever!

Last summer when Carolyn attended a family reunion, the thing she looked forward to the most was a visit to the house in which her mother had grown up.

When she finally reached the farm, Carolyn saw a sagging shack surrounded by a broken fence. The yard was full of weeds, and the house was full of clutter. No one had lived there for many years, and no one had taken care of it. It was nothing like the mansion she had imagined.

The Bible tells us about another house we are eager to see. It is the house Jesus is preparing for us in heaven. That house, He says, has many rooms—one of them picked out especially for Carolyn and one of them picked out especially for you!

That house will not disappoint us. God is busy right now getting everything ready. Jesus died to pay the price so we can go to heaven to be with Him forever. He doesn't want us to worry about dying, so He gives us a picture we can understand. "Trust Me," He says. "I will bring you to the most wonderful home you could ever imagine. I'll be waiting for you there."

That will be the best family reunion ever!

_____Let's do: Draw a picture of what you think the next life will be like. Be sure to put yourself and Jesus in the picture.

_____Let's pray: Dear heavenly Father, I know I will see You someday because Jesus is my Savior. Help me look forward to all the wonderful things You have prepared for me. In Jesus' name I pray. Amen.

C. S.

Who's in Charge?

On Presidents' Day we remember all the presidents who have led the United States. Some of them accomplished important work. Others have names we hardly remember.

Leaders of other nations have titles such as Prime Minister or King. Like United States presidents, they all are the representatives God allows to govern people on earth. They are a blessing from God to us, so they deserve our respect and prayers of gratitude.

Although leaders may do great things, they are not perfect. That is why God tells us to pray for our leaders and ask for His continued blessings on them.

Perhaps God has given you the gifts needed to be a leader. Perhaps He is preparing you right now to be a president some day. Perhaps He is preparing you to be a leader in your city or church or family. We need leaders who honor God and follow His ways—just like you do. Be ready to serve faithfully in whatever position God calls you. You can be certain that the God who loves you and forgives your sins for Jesus' sake can use you to be a blessing to others. He is in charge of the whole world, and He is in charge of you!

Read from God's Word

Paul, an apostle of Christ Jesus by command of God our Savior and of Christ Jesus our hope. To Timothy, my true child in the faith: Grace, mercy, and peace from God the Father and Christ Jesus our Lord. 1 Timothy 1:1–2

_____Let's talk: What makes a leader great? How could you be a leader in your family or school?

_____Let's pray: Dear heavenly Father, thank You for the leaders of our nation. For Jesus' sake, please forgive our leaders when they sin and give them wisdom to honor You in all they do. In Jesus' name. Amen.

C. S.

Read from God's Word

For to this you have been called, because Christ also suffered for you, leaving you an example, so that you might follow in His steps. He committed no sin, neither was deceit found in His mouth. When He was reviled, He did not revile in return; when He suffered, He did not threaten, but continued entrusting Himself to Him who judges justly. He himself bore our sins in His body on the tree, that we might die to sin and live to righteousness. By His wounds you have been healed. 1 Peter 2:21–24

A Guard

Four-year-old Ivan found just the right hill for sledding, but it was dangerous. Within a few feet of the bottom was a busy street. His father knew what could happen if Ivan failed to stop, so he intended to catch him at the end of the hill.

"Watch out, Dad," he shouted. "Here I come!" Ivan's sled knocked his father's feet out from under him. His father had just enough time to grab Ivan and keep him from the traffic only a few feet away. Ivan's father hurt his back when he fell and had to stay in bed for three days; but he saved his son and that was all that mattered.

Jesus is like Ivan's father. He saves us when our lives are out of control because of sin. We cannot stop ourselves from doing wrong. But Jesus protects us from the evil the devil would like us to suffer.

Jesus paid a price to be our Savior. He had to die on the cross to rescue us. He loves us so much that He died willingly so we could be safe from all dangers. Then He rose from the dead so we could live with Him forever.

Sin, death, and the devil have been defeated. We are safe.

_____Let's do: Is there someone you would like to help? Write that person's name and the way you could help him or her. Then do it.

_____Let's pray: Dear Jesus, thank You for giving Your life to save me. I will love You forever! Amen.

C. S.

Who Knows It All

When the principal asked Miguel why he had disturbed the class, Miguel muttered, "I don't like school. Kids shouldn't have to go to school after third grade."

"Do you think you have learned everything?" asked the principal.

"I know how to read. And I know how to multiply and divide. What more is there?"

Can you think of some things Miguel hasn't learned yet? Perhaps he will learn different kinds of math that will help him with his career. Perhaps he could learn more in social studies so he can help others.

Some people think that just because they go to Sunday school and church or because they attend a Christian school or read devotions every night, they can stop studying the Bible or going to Bible class. But God's Word is like a deep mine full of treasures. No one can ever learn or know or understand them all. Even pastors and teachers never stop reading and studying the Bible.

Timothy first learned about the Scriptures when he was a child. He kept on learning, just as St. Paul told him to. God wants you to keep on learning His Word. It reminds you about Jesus' love. His Word makes your faith stronger and gives you power to live as His child.

What are some things you still want to learn?

Read from God's Word
But as for you, continue in what you have learned and have firmly believed, knowing from whom you learned it and how from childhood you have been acquainted with the sacred writings, which are able to make you wise for salvation through faith in Christ Jesus. All Scripture is breathed out by God and profitable for teaching, for reproof, for correction, and for training in righteousness, that the man of God may be competent, equipped for every good work. 2 Timothy 3:14–17

_____ Let's do: Write down three things you still don't know about God and His Word. Where can you find the answers?

_____ Let's pray: Dear God, thank You for teaching me about Jesus in the Bible. Help me to learn about You. I ask this in Jesus' name. Amen.

C. S.

When I am afraid, I put my trust in You. In God, whose word I praise, in God I trust; I shall not be afraid. What can flesh do to me? Psalm 56:3–4 ✍

When Mom Is Late

Day care was closing. Maya was worried. Mom had never been this late. While she waited she could hear sirens coming closer.

"Please, God," prayed Maya, "don't let my mom be hurt. Please let her get here soon." Hot tears formed behind Maya's eyes. *Where could her mother be?*

Have you ever felt that frightened? When people we depend on are late, we often panic. Sometimes terrible things do happen. There are some things we have no control over. But there are things we can do when we are worried or upset.

In the Bible reading for today David was frightened. His enemies wanted to kill him. He was helpless, but God invited David to throw his worries onto God's shoulders and trust Him to provide everything. God protected David and blessed him in many ways.

Our minds can rest on how strong God is and on how much He loves us. God will never let anything happen to us that will not work out for our good. Even when sadness and pain come, He is there to bring us joy and healing. Even when we worry, God loves us.

Maya's mother rushed in and apologized for being late. She had been stuck in traffic. Maya sighed a prayer of thanks and smiled all the way home.

——Let's do: Write down things you worry about, making a cross shape around the words. Then pray about them.

——Let's pray: Dear Jesus, whenever I am afraid, help me trust in You. Amen.

C. S.

Report Card Day

Max stuffed his report card deep into his backpack and headed home, avoiding his friends. They would make the honor roll—but he wouldn't.

Max could fix a broken toaster and make his baby sister stop crying. He could cook dinner and get downtown on the bus. But there is no place on a report card for those things.

Do you have to make the honor roll, be a cheerleader, or get elected to the student council to be successful at school? Do you have to be successful at school to be successful at life?

God grades us on what He has done for us. He sees every person as someone He created and loves. Because His Son, Jesus, died for us, God looks at us "cross-eyed"—that is, through the cross. When He sees us, He sees Jesus, who was perfect. Now we're perfect too.

You are on God's honor roll because He gives you honor. You can bring cheer into the lives of others because God blesses you with life and joy. You are a leader in God's army because He has work for you to do and He gives you the strength to do it. God has erased your failures and given you straight As.

Read from God's Word

I appeal to you therefore, brothers, by the mercies of God, to present your bodies as a living sacrifice, holy and acceptable to God, which is your spiritual worship. Do not be conformed to this world, but be transformed by the renewal of your mind, that by testing you may discern what is the will of God, what is good and acceptable and perfect. Romans 12:1–2 ✍

_____Let's talk: How are you using the talents God has given you to encourage others?

_____Let's pray: Thank You, God, for making me special. Let me always remember that You provide the strength for me to do whatever You want me to do. For Jesus' sake. Amen.

C. S.

Getting Fired

Five-year-old Antonio didn't want to do what the principal told him to do. "You're fired!" he shouted, thinking his words would make the principal go away.

Some people think they can fire God and do things their way. They don't want anybody else to be in charge of their lives. Do you think a person's words can make God go away? Of course not!

God is ruler of all things and of all people. He loves all people—even those who do not love Him in return or do not yet know about Him. He will do what is best for us.

When we sin, we feel uncomfortable and afraid because we know we aren't living up to what our perfect God wants us to do. But Jesus died for our sins so we don't have to be afraid. We can enjoy having God with us every day. He is our friend and comforter. He forgives us and loves us, even when we are in trouble.

When you feel uncomfortable with your sin, ask God to forgive you and help you learn what He wants to teach you. He wants to spend years with you on earth and an eternity with you in heaven.

_____Let's talk: Do you know someone who is difficult to love? How can you show love to that person like God shows love to you?

_____Let's pray: Dear God, I'm glad You are in charge of me and of the world. Please help me to love others, even when it is hard. In Jesus' name. Amen.

C. S.

Sunday—Church Day

"Time to wake up. It's church day!"
"Mom, I'm tired!" Tanner grumbled.

"I'm a little tired too. But Jesus took good care of us all week. We get to go to His house to thank Him."

I remember my mother happily preparing breakfast while we dressed for church. She would find time to sing and play some hymns on the piano. Her mother did that too. Their joy reminds me of Psalm 122:1—"I was glad when they said to me, 'Let us go to the house of the LORD!'"

The prophet Elijah was tired and afraid, and he needed physical and spiritual nourishment. He felt like giving up, but an angel of the Lord came to feed him. Elijah then had strength to go on. Elijah traveled to the mountain of God, where the Lord revealed Himself to Elijah.

Often we feel tired and afraid. Sometimes we even feel like giving up. At these times we need to be fed and refreshed by the Word of God. God helps us leave our sins at the foot of the cross, where Jesus paid for them with His own life. God helps us worship Him with our Christian friends at church, where He reveals Himself to us and gives us strength to accomplish the tasks that lie ahead.

Read from God's Word

Ahab told Jezebel all that Elijah had done, and how he had killed all the prophets with the sword. ... Then he was afraid, and he arose and ran for his life. ... And behold, an angel touched him and said to him, "Arise and eat." And he looked, and behold, there was at his head a cake baked on hot stones and a jar of water. And he ate and drank and lay down again. And the angel of the LORD came again a second time and touched him and said, "Arise and eat, for the journey is too great for you." And he arose and ate and drank, and went in the strength of that food forty days and forty nights. ...
1 Kings 19:1–8

_____Let's talk: How do you enjoy worshiping the Lord? What are some of your favorite hymns? How does the service strengthen your faith?

_____Let's pray: Thank You, dear Lord, for each opportunity to go to church. Help us remember that it is Your house on earth, where we can visit You. In Jesus' name. Amen.

A. B. W.

The Power of Prayer

Read from God's Word

So Peter was kept in prison, but earnest prayer for him was made to God by the church. Now when Herod was about to bring him out, on that very night, Peter was sleeping between two soldiers, bound with two chains, and sentries before the door were guarding the prison. And behold, an angel of the Lord stood next to him, and a light shone in the cell. He struck Peter on the side and woke him, saying, "Get up quickly." And the chains fell off his hands. . . . When he realized this, he went to the house . . . where many were gathered together and were praying.
Acts 12:5–12

Angie and her family watched television and saw the destruction caused by an earthquake in California. A section of double-deck freeway had collapsed.

They prayed for survivors trapped in the freeway structure. On the fourth day, when hope was growing slim, a man was found alive. The first thing he said was, "Thank God, I'm alive!" Angie also thanked God he was alive—she had been praying for him.

Today's Bible reading finds Peter in prison, facing execution. Awaiting trial, Peter slept between two soldiers, bound with chains. Suddenly an angel appeared in a bright light. While the soldiers slept, Peter's chains fell off.

"Follow me," the angel said as they walked safely past all the guards. The iron gate to the city opened for them by itself. It's no wonder Peter thought he was dreaming!

Now free, Peter went to the house where many people had gathered to pray for him. They had been praying earnestly for him, but the people in the house were surprised to see Peter just the same.

The same God who rescued Peter has rescued us from sin and the devil through the suffering and death of His own Son. He also gives us the privilege of prayer. Because He loves us, we know He will hear our prayers and respond in the best way, His way.

_____Let's talk: Read Acts 12:1–17. Are you sometimes surprised when your prayers are answered? Should you be? Why or why not?

_____Let's pray: Thank You, dear Lord God, for the privilege of prayer. In Jesus' name. Amen.

A. B. W.

Be a Friend—
Bring a Friend

P astor's words from Sunday's ser-
mon rang in Angie's ears all week
long. "Do you really care that people
around you are going to hell?" Our
church sign read, "Be a friend—bring
a friend."

Angie finally got her nerve up
Saturday night to invite a neighbor to
go to church with her. She couldn't
come tomorrow, the neighbor said, but
wanted to come another time. Angie
thought, *that wasn't so hard.*

When she went to sleep, Angie
had a dream about the Last Day, the
day when Jesus came again to separate
the believers from the nonbelievers. He
took the believers home to heaven.

In her dream she was standing on
the shore of a large body of water,
watching stars fall from the sky.
Planets whizzed past her, disappearing
beyond the horizon.

Angie grabbed the arm of the
stranger next to her. She tried several times to ask him if he knew Jesus. But
she couldn't get the word *Jesus* out of her mouth. The dream ended there,
and she woke up with troubled thoughts.

We won't always have time to share with others the faith, peace, and
joy we have in Jesus. He promises to help us say, "Jesus came from heaven
to save us from suffering forever because of our sins. He offers you forgiveness and eternal life."

Read from God's Word

*"For as the lightning comes
from the east and shines as far
as the west, so will be the coming
of the Son of Man. ...
Immediately after the tribulation
of those days the sun will be
darkened, and the moon will not
give its light, and the stars will
fall from heaven, and the powers
of the heavens will be shaken.
Then will appear in heaven the
sign of the Son of Man, and then
all the tribes of the earth will
mourn, and they will see the Son
of Man coming on the clouds of
heaven with power and great
glory. And He will send out His
angels with a loud trumpet call,
and they will gather His elect
from the four winds, from one
end of heaven to the other."
Matthew 24:27, 29–31* ✐

_____Let's do: Write about a connection between the words of
Matthew 24:31 and the words of "My Hope Is Built
on Nothing Less" (*LW* 368).

_____Let's pray: Jesus, give me the words to share my love for You.
Amen.

A. B. W.

No Kindness Is Wasted

Read from God's Word

"For I was hungry and you gave me food. I was thirsty and you gave me drink. I was a stranger and you welcomed me. I was naked and you clothed me. I was sick and you visited me. I was in prison and you came to me.' Then the righteous will answer Him, saying, 'Lord, when did we see You hungry and feed You, or thirsty and give You drink? And when did we see You a stranger and welcome You, or naked and clothe You? And when did we see You sick or in prison and visit You?' And the King will answer them, 'Truly, I say to you, as you did it to one of the least of these My brothers, you did it to Me.'" Matthew 25:35–40

Far north in Michigan's Upper Peninsula is an old, large white pine tree. It grows near the shore of Lake Superior on an Indian reservation. Solemnly it stands in the middle of a burial ground that dates back to about 1841.

Eliza Waishkey, then 15, planted the twig near her grandfather's grave in 1848. He was John Waishkey, chief of the Waishkey band of Chippewa Indians. This little thing Eliza did honored her grandfather's memory. Today, more than 150 years later, the tree lives on.

The Bible teaches us that nothing we do for the Lord is ever wasted. Any act of kindness or love, no matter how small, is seen by the Lord. Today's Scripture reading tells us that it's as though we have done the loving or kind act for Jesus.

These acts of kindness, or good works, do nothing to earn us salvation. Jesus has already given His perfect life to pay our debt of sin. Faith in the Savior is our way to heaven. Only in thanks to Him, and motivated by His love, can we respond with acts of love done to God's glory.

The possibilities of "thanks-living" are endless:
Taking out an elderly neighbor's garbage
Picking flowers for someone
Helping around the house without being told

_____Let's talk: Read Matthew 25:31–46. When are our kind deeds pleasing to God? What loving things can you do for others?

_____Let's pray: Lord Jesus, let each day of my life be one of "thanks-living." Please give me chances to love and serve You by loving and serving others. Amen.

A. B. W.

The War We Fight

The Civil War battle was acted out for the spectators like a huge play. The soldiers wore uniforms and carried guns. Some soldiers rode horses and carried swords. Muskets (muzzle-loading rifles) and cannons fired everywhere. (The bullets fired were blanks so no one would be hurt.) After each skirmish, soldiers lay "dead and wounded." This all seemed so real!

Do you know that Christians are involved in a war too? We are the battleground on which the war between good and evil is fought. The devil wants to win us to his side.

God sent Moses and Aaron to the ruler of Egypt to ask him to free the people of Israel from slavery. God instructed Moses about what should be done when Pharaoh asked for a miracle. Aaron was to throw down his staff and it would become a snake.

When Aaron did this, Pharaoh's magicians did the same thing with their staffs. But Aaron's snake swallowed up all the magicians' snakes. God is more powerful than any of those who oppose Him!

Jesus is all-powerful; He won the battle with Satan. God's Holy Spirit lives within each of us Christians. With His help, we are winners. We are winners because Jesus has overcome all the forces of the devil for our sake.

_____Let's talk: What are some evil things that cross your path? With the Holy Spirit's help, how can you say no to them?

_____Let's pray: Dear Father in heaven, help us in the struggle between good and evil every day of our lives. I pray this in Jesus' name. Amen.

A. B. W.

Read from God's Word

Then the Lord said to Moses and Aaron, "When Pharaoh says to you, 'Prove yourselves by working a miracle,' then you shall say to Aaron, 'Take your staff and cast it down before Pharaoh, that it may become a serpent.'" So Moses and Aaron went to Pharaoh and did just as the Lord commanded. Aaron cast down his staff before Pharaoh and his servants, and it became a serpent. Then Pharaoh summoned the wise men and the sorcerers, and they, the magicians of Egypt, also did the same by their secret arts. For each man cast down his staff, and they became serpents. But Aaron's staff swallowed up their staffs. Still Pharaoh's heart was hardened, and he would not listen to them, as the Lord had said. Exodus 7:8–13

Read from God's Word

Jacob ... dreamed, and behold, there was a ladder set up on the earth, and the top of it reached to heaven. And behold, the angels of God were ascending and descending on it! And behold, the LORD stood above it and said, "I am the LORD, the God of Abraham your father and the God of Isaac. The land on which you lie I will give to you and to your offspring. ... Behold, I am with you and will keep you wherever you go, and will bring you back to this land. For I will not leave you until I have done what I have promised you." Then Jacob awoke from his sleep and said, "... How awesome is this place! This is none other than the house of God, and this is the gate of heaven." Genesis 28: 10–17 ✍

Look Up to God

As Jesse came into the house, Mom asked, "What's wrong?"

Jesse replied, "How do you know something's wrong?"

"Your body language tells me how you feel," Mom explained. "Your face is long, your shoulders sag, and your head hangs down."

Read about Jacob's ladder when you feel down. Jacob had been sent away from home. One night Jacob lay down to sleep, with a rock for a pillow. He dreamed about a ladder that went from earth to heaven. Angels of God were ascending and descending on it, and the Lord stood at the top. God blessed Jacob and promised to be with him.

There are times when we feel alone and really down. That is when God wants us to look up. We can think about how the Lord blesses us and promises to be with us at all times.

God gives us reminders in His creation to look up—trees and plants grow toward heaven, rainbows draw our eyes upward after a rain. They remind us that God keeps His promises. "Set your minds on things that are above, not on things that are on earth. For you have died, and your life is hidden with Christ in God. When Christ who is your life appears, then you also will appear with Him in glory" (Colossians 3:2–4).

_____Let's talk: Read Genesis 28:1–5 and 10–17. What other reminders of God can you think of in nature? Where can we find God's promise of a Savior?

_____Let's pray: Thank You, Lord God, for giving us people and things to cheer us. Keep our eyes on Jesus, who rose from the dead to make us right with You. In His name. Amen.

A. B. W.

God is Enough

D o you have fun learning words? Dawn's dad likes to say "I've had sufficient" when their family is finished with dinner. It means he has had enough to eat. The word sufficient means "enough."

In today's Bible verse God tells us His grace is sufficient (enough) for us. Grace is a very good word to learn.

Grace is undeserved love. We sin many times each day. Yet God forgives us, though we don't deserve it. He forgives us for Jesus' sake. Jesus earned forgiveness for us when He hung on the cross. We can't do anything but receive God's grace and be thankful.

Below are some more passages that tell about this wonderful grace God has for us. Read them. Then fill in the blanks with words that show how God is sufficient for us in all things.

"God shows His love for us in that while we were still sinners, Christ died for us" (Romans 5:8). His _____ is sufficient for me!

Read from God's Word

So to keep me from being too elated by the surpassing greatness of the revelations, a thorn was given me in the flesh, a messenger of Satan to harass me, to keep me from being too elated. Three times I pleaded with the Lord about this, that it should leave me. But He said to me, 'My grace is sufficient for you, for my power is made perfect in weakness.' Therefore I will boast all the more gladly of my weaknesses, so that the power of Christ may rest upon me. For the sake of Christ, then, I am content with weaknesses, insults, hardships, persecutions, and calamities. For when I am weak, then I am strong. 2 Corinthians 12:7–10

"For God so loved the world, that He gave His only Son, that whoever believes in Him should not perish but have eternal life" (John 3:16). His _____ is sufficient for me!

"Cast all your anxieties on Him, because He cares for you" (1 Peter 5:7). His _____ is sufficient for me!

____Let's talk: How is God's love enough for you? How is His Son enough for you? How is His care enough for you? Think of some other words to complete this sentence: His _____ is sufficient for me!

____Let's pray: I praise You for Your grace, dear heavenly Father. Help me celebrate Your great love and care in Jesus. Amen

D.N.

march

Contributors for this month:

Diana Lesire Brandmeyer

Carol Delph

Nicole Dreyer

Rodney Rathmann

Christine Ross

Cathy Spieler

Tim Wesemann

Judy Williams

Do You Know?

The group of friends usually spent their recess laughing. Today, Diana had nothing to say. So silently she prayed. *Dear Father, help me. I don't know what to say to Julie. Why did her sister have to die?*

Then the words came. "What can I do to help you?"

Julie's eyes filled with tears. "Talk to me. Nobody will talk to me about Carrie. People look away when I walk by. I'm embarrassed." Her voice trailed off.

"Why are you embarrassed? You didn't do anything."

"Maybe they think I should have helped her," said Julie. "The worst part is that I feel lonely inside. I just wish there was more than just dying. I mean, you die and that's it."

"Julie, there *is* more. Do you know about Jesus?" Diana asked.

"He was just a teacher or something," said Julie.

Read from God's Word

"But you will receive power when the Holy Spirit has come upon you, and you will be My witnesses in Jerusalem and in all Judea and Samaria, and to the end of the earth." Acts 1:8

Diana thought for a moment, and then prayed some more. *Dear God, please send me the right words!* "Jesus loves you, Julie. He loves you so much that He died and rose again so your sister and you could live forever with Him. Would you like to talk to my pastor? He can help you understand about Jesus. I'll come with you."

Jesus promised to give His followers power to witness. He did that for Diana. He will do it for you.

_____Let's talk: What truths can you tell someone about Jesus?

_____Let's pray: Dear Father, put words in my mouth that help me tell everyone about Your Son, my Savior. In Jesus' name. Amen.

D. L. B.

Read from God's Word

"For thus says the LORD: When seventy years are completed for Babylon, I will visit you, and I will fulfill to you My promise and bring you back to this place. For I know the plans I have for you, declares the LORD, plans for wholeness and not for evil, to give you a future and a hope. Then you will call upon Me and come and pray to Me, and I will hear you." Jeremiah 29:10–12 ∽

In Tune

D o I *have* to practice my saxophone again?"

"Your concert is coming up soon," answered Emily's mother.

"But I won't ever be good at it," Emily said. "When I try to play a C, it sounds like a truck tire deflating." She warmed up her reed, put the mouthpiece to her lips, and struggled to make the note sounds clearly.

She hit an A and then a B. She tried for the C. The sound that came out was awful. "See! I just can't get it right. I'll sound awful in the school concert."

"I have an idea," her mother said. "Why don't we get a high school student to help you? Would you like to try that?"

"Do you think that would really help, Mom? Do you think I can learn this music before the concert?" Emily asked.

"I'm not sure about that, but I do know that God will enable you to do your best, Emily. And that will be good enough for me."

God did His best for us by sending Jesus to forgive our sins. He provides us a future with Him in heaven. This hope encourages us to use our talents and gifts to God's glory—at home, at school, and even in the band.

_____Let's do: What do you think the phrase "plans for wholeness" means in Jeremiah 29:11?

_____Let's pray: Dear Jesus, give me strength to adjust my attitude to Your will. Amen.

D. L. B.

What's in the Future?

Read from God's Word

"Therefore do not be anxious about tomorrow, for tomorrow will be anxious for itself. Sufficient for the day is its own trouble." Matthew 6:34 ⌒

The paper said that in the future we won't have to be in our car to roll up the window," said Rory. "The article said we could just use a cell phone to dial the car, punch in a code, and the window would go up."

"With all these new ideas, you probably won't ever have to learn to drive, Rory," said his dad. "You'll just sit in the driver's seat and tell the car where to go by talking on your phone."

"I wouldn't like that," said Rory. "I want to be able to drive the car myself."

"I'm sure there will always be changes in a lot of things we use, Rory. You can already see your grandmother as you call her on the cell phone."

"That would be okay. But, Dad, what if someone called and you didn't want to see them—like some girls? It's kind of scary with all these new things," said Rory.

God's Word tells us not to worry about what is going to happen tomorrow or in the future. We know that Jesus will always be with us because He died for us and won the victory for us over sin. We won't need to worry about our future. Our future is with God in heaven.

_____Let's do: Look up Matthew 28:20. How do these words help calm your fears?

_____Let's pray: Dear God, help me remember the loving sacrifice of Jesus and the future that He provided for me. In His name I pray. Amen.

D. L. B.

Read from God's Word

So I find it to be a law that when I want to do right, evil lies close at hand. For I delight in the law of God, in my inner being, but I see in my members another law waging war against the law of my mind and making me captive to the law of sin that dwells in my members. Wretched man that I am! Who will deliever me from this body of death? Thanks be to God through Jesus Christ our Lord! So then, I myself serve the law of God with my mind, but with my flesh I serve the law of sin. Romans 7:21–25

Going Under

The fishing ship off the coast of Vancouver was sinking. The two fishermen on board hurried into the lifeboat. One of the fishermen noticed a nylon rope trailing behind them. He pulled on it, trying to bring it into the lifeboat. It wouldn't come. The lifeboat was still tied to the fishing ship!

The fisherman looked for something to cut the rope. They found nothing. If they weren't rescued soon, the larger ship would pull the lifeboat under with it. How long would it be before a rescue ship arrived? Would their lifeboat be pulled out from under them, leaving them in the water?

Sin is like the rope to that fishing ship—pulling us to destruction. We hurt somebody's feelings. We tell a small lie. We cheat on a test. We may feel bad, but we are still doomed by our sinful acts and sinful nature unless Jesus rescues us.

The fishermen finally chewed through the rope until it broke. How can we cut the rope of sin? We can't, but God can and He did. Jesus cut off the ropes of sin, death, and the devil. We're no longer tied to the death-ship. We are free through Jesus' death and resurrection. We are free to be His resurrection children.

_____Let's do: Draw a picture of a lifeboat with you inside. Write the first part of Romans 7:25 around the boat.

_____Let's pray: Dear Father, I know that I sin, but sometimes I don't even realize I'm doing it. Thank You for Christ's victory over sin. In Jesus' name I pray. Amen.

D. L. B.

What a Relief

Aimee felt miserable as she lay on her bed. She'd been sent to her room for shouting mean words at her brother. Aimee was confused. She thought, *How can I sing songs about God's love one hour and call my brother names the next? I don't understand myself.*

Do you ever wonder why you do bad things? All Christians feel this way at times. Even the apostle Paul wrote, "I do not understand my own actions. For I do not do what I want, but I do the very thing I hate" (Romans 7:15). We do bad things because of sin.

God's Spirit helps us to be aware of our sinful actions. We may have broken a commandment against God or our neighbor. We tell (or confess to) God our sin and ask Him to forgive us. God, who is faithful and just, forgives us through His Son, Jesus Christ. We hear words of absolution (or forgiveness) in church each Sunday from the pastor, just as if God were saying them Himself.

We no longer feel miserable about our sin. Our hearts and minds are set free. We are friends again with God and with our neighbors. God helps us say we are sorry. What a relief to know that God forgives us through His Son, Jesus.

Read from God's Word

If we say we have no sin, we deceive ourselves, and the truth is not in us. If we confess our sins, He is faithful and just to forgive us our sins and to cleanse us from all unrighteousness.
1 John 1:8–9

_____Let's do: Write about a time when God's Spirit led you to ask for forgiveness and you felt a sense of relief afterwards.

_____Let's pray: Dear God, thank You for loving me so much that You sent Jesus to die that I might be forgiven. In His name I pray. Amen.

C. R.

Read from God's Word

But far be it from me to boast except in the cross of our Lord Jesus Christ, by which the world has been crucified to me, and I to the world. Galatians 6:14 ✍

The Donkey's Cross

The cross is a very important symbol for Christians. You see crosses in churches and on steeples. You see cross pins and necklaces. You see crosses in Sunday school classrooms and in the living rooms and bedrooms of Christians. But did you know you can see a cross on most donkeys?

The next time you see a donkey at a zoo or farm, take a good look. A line of dark hair begins at the base of the mane and goes partway down the center of the back. It forms the vertical piece of the cross. The arms of the cross are shaped from darker hair that goes across the shoulders of the donkey.

It is likely that a cross-marked donkey carried Jesus into Jerusalem. Five days later Jesus was the one who carried the sins of the whole world to the cross. He suffered the punishment for our sins and died in our place.

Jesus is stronger than death. His resurrection hands are imprinted with the marks of His love. Now all believers will rise again and live with Him forever in heaven. The cross—wherever we see it—is a reminder of what Jesus has done for us.

_____ Let's do: Look in an encyclopedia or on the Internet for different kinds of crosses. Sketch some of them. How is each one significant?

_____ Let's pray: Thank You, Jesus, for dying on the cross for my sins and for the sins of all people. Whenever I see a cross, let it remind me of Your gift to me. Amen.

J. W.

Stone Posts

Cathy noticed those squared-off, stone posts as they drove to her grandparents' house. Some posts stood at the corners of the fence line. Others lined the road.

The posts made Cathy wonder about the people who built them. They were pioneers, bold adventurers who had endured hardship and trials to claim the land from the wilderness.

Cathy liked modern conveniences—riding in a warm car and stopping for a breakfast sandwich at a drive-through restaurant when she got hungry. Sleeping in a covered wagon and fixing breakfast over a fire seemed much harder.

The early settlers must have worked long and hard to make and place those posts! The posts show that the land was important to them. Those people got through with strength and determination. Those posts stand as a kind of memorial to their labor.

Read from God's Word

Then Joshua called the twelve men from the people of Israel, … and Joshua said to them, "Pass on before the ark of the LORD your God into the midst of the Jordan, and take up each of you a stone upon his shoulder, according to the number of the tribes of the people of Israel, that this may be a sign among you. When your children ask in time to come, 'What do those stones mean to you?' then you shall tell them that the waters of the Jordan were cut off before the ark of the covenant of the LORD. When it passed over the Jordan, the waters of the Jordan were cut off. So these stones shall be to the people of Israel a memorial forever." Joshua 4:4–7

Our Bible reading tells of a memorial to the people of Israel, but it was not a tribute to the people's labor. It stood on the west bank of the Jordan River as a memorial to God's strength and power. God intervened in the lives of His people for their good, and He intervenes in our lives too. He sent His Son to rescue us from sin. That's worth remembering!

_____ Let's do: What reminds you of God's strength? In what way is the cross a memorial of God's power and love for us?

_____ Let's pray: Dear Father in heaven, thanks for Your love and forgiveness through Christ. Give me Your strength to do Your will in my life. In Jesus' name I pray. Amen.

C. S.

The Color Purple

Then Abram fell on his face. And God said to him, "Behold, My covenant is with you, and you shall be the father of a multitude of nations. No longer shall your name be called Abram, but your name shall be Abraham, for I have made you the father of a multitude of nations. I will make you exceedingly fruitful, and I will make you into nations, and kings shall come from you. And I will establish My covenant between Me and you and your offspring after you throughout their generations for an everlasting covenant, to be God to you and to your offspring after you. And I will give to you and to your offspring after you the land of your sojournings, all the land of Canaan, for an everlasting possession, and I will be their God." Genesis 17:3–8 ❧

In Acts 16:14 we meet Lydia, a woman who sold rare purple cloth. Kings and rich people wore costly purple clothing. Shellfish used in making the purple dye for the cloth swarmed in the nearby Mediterranean Sea. It took 10,000 shellfish to produce a single gram of purple dye.

God promised the Holy Land to Abraham. He also told Abraham that kings would come from him and he would be the father of many nations. Abraham believed God.

Later, Abraham purchased ground to bury his wife, Sarah. Abraham believed in God's promise. But Abraham himself could not save his wife or his people from eternal death. He looked forward to the promised Savior, the Messiah, who would deliver all people from their sin.

Jesus was not born in the land of purple, but in a lowly stable. While on earth this King of kings fulfilled all of God's promises in the Promised Land. Soldiers robed Jesus in purple on the day of His death. They crowned Him King of the Jews and nailed Him to the cross.

During this Lenten season your church may have purple cloths on the altar. This royal color reminds us of Jesus and His death. In God-given faith we look forward to our Lord's promise to take us to live with Him in His kingdom forever.

_____Let's do: Draw a robe fit for King Jesus. Color it purple.

_____Let's pray: Dearest Jesus, I praise You for the robe of righteousness You won for me on Calvary. Amen.

C. D.

Two Seas

The Dead Sea area is salty, hot, and dry, surrounded by barren hills with unproductive land. But the Sea of Galilee is full of beauty and life. The region is charming and plush—almost like a resort.

How could these seas be so different? One sea is giving and living. One sea is taking and lifeless.

Jesus proved Himself to be God by the Sea of Galilee. He surprised people and performed many great miracles. He taught there with authority and shared the Good News.

Our Lord gathered up all our sin—which is like the Dead Sea—all that was and is ugly and dying in our life. He took all our sin, death, and the torments of the devil to the cross. There He conquered them all and won for us new life with Him forever. Like the Sea of Galilee—our resurrected Lord keeps living and giving.

Sunday, is the Lord's Day. The Lord of the Sea of Galilee comes to us in divine worship. He invites us to gather in His name. He comes by the means of His powerful Word. He comes in Baptism and the Lord's Supper. He continues to live and give us new life.

Read from God's Word

Getting into one of the boats, which was Simon's. [Jesus] asked him to put out a little from the land. And He sat down and taught the people from the boat. And when He had finished speaking, He said to Simon, "Put out into the deep and let down your nets for a catch." ... And when they had done this, they enclosed a large number of fish, and their nets were breaking. They signaled to their partners in the other boat to come and help them. ... But when Simon Peter saw it, he fell down at Jesus' knees, saying, "Depart from me, for I am a sinful man, O Lord." ... And Jesus said to Simon, "Do not be afraid; from now on you will be catching men." And when they had brought their boats to land, they left everything and followed Him. Luke 5:3–11 ✍

_____Let's do: Read Luke 5:1–11. Write down ways that God continues to help You grow in faith.

_____Let's pray: Lord Jesus, thank You for taking the deadness of our life—all our sin—and giving us new life. Amen.

C. D.

Read from God's Word

When He was at table with them, He took the bread and blessed and broke it and gave it to them. And their eyes were opened, and they recognized Him. And He vanished from their sight. They said to each other, "Did not our hearts burn within us while He talked to us on the road, while He opened to us the Scriptures?" And they rose that same hour and returned to Jerusalem. And they found the eleven and those who were with them gathered together, saying, "The Lord has risen indeed, and has appeared to Simon!" Then they told what had happened on the road, and how He was known to them in the breaking of the bread. Luke 24:30–35

Crock-Pot of Love

Jack has Alzheimer's disease, an illness that affects the memory. His wife visits him every day in the nursing home, wondering if Jack will recognize her.

One day his wife brought him a big bowl of her famous chili. Jack grinned the whole time he was sipping the soup. He recognized his wife's love in that chili even though he didn't recognize her.

Cleopas and his partner were walking to Emmaus. Suddenly Jesus was with them, but the two travelers did not recognize Him. Jesus explained to the two what was said about Him in the Scriptures. After begging Jesus to stay with them, the three prepared to eat together. As Jesus broke the bread and gave thanks, the two saw that it was Jesus who was with them. When He was gone, they were so excited they ran back seven miles to tell others.

We don't always see Jesus around us, but He is there in His Word and Sacraments. That Word is God's love letter read over and over to us. That Word, used by the Holy Spirit, shapes our thoughts, words, and deeds. That Word burns in our hearts, too, and we are excited to tell God's love story to others.

_____Let's do: Write down a Bible verse that speaks about love.

_____Let's pray: O Lord Jesus, in all my actions and reactions make love my every motive. Amen.

C. D.

Hand-Me-Down Faith

In 1871 George White of Fisk University formed a choir made up of 15 former slaves and children of slaves. This group traveled around the country singing songs the slaves had sung before freedom. As the songs are sung over and over, year after year, generation after generation, the story of the slaves goes on.

We may not have been born slaves, owned by another person, but we were all born into the slavery of sin. Sin shows up in the way we talk to our parents or the way we treat our teachers and friends. Sin has a hold on us, but we can be thankful that God in Christ has released that grip. Jesus lived without sin to free us from our bondage. We are no longer slaves, but sons and daughters of God.

Now we can sing the songs and tell the story of Jesus over and over, year after year, generation after generation. We, as heirs, believe, teach, and confess that Christ released us from punishment for our sins through His perfect sacrifice on the cross and His resurrection. We worship and use the hymns and liturgies handed down to us. We read and study God's Word. We write new songs, telling of the Lord's salvation. We live each day as freed slaves, heirs of God.

Read from God's Word

I mean that the heir, as long as he is a child, is no different from a slave, though he is the owner of everything, but he is under guardians and managers until the date set by his father. In the same way we also, when we were children, were enslaved to the elementary principles of the world. But when the fullness of time had come, God sent forth His Son, born of woman, born under the law, to redeem those who were under the law, so that we might receive adoption as sons. And because you are sons, God has sent the Spirit of His Son into our hearts, crying, "Abba! Father!" So you are no longer a slave, but a son, and if a son, then an heir through God. Galatians 4:1–7 ✍

_____Let's do: Reread the Bible verses. What special words does the Spirit of God help you call out? Find out what the word *Abba* means.

_____Let's pray: Lord God, thank You for making me Your child, free from the slavery of sin. Use me to tell future generations about You and Your righteousness. In Jesus' name. Amen.

C. D.

Faced with Joy

Read from God's Word

Looking to Jesus, the founder and perfecter of our faith, who for the joy that was set before Him endured the cross, despising the shame, and is seated at the right hand of the throne of God. Hebrews 12:2

Mrs. Delph received a card from a five-year-old girl, thanking the teacher for telling her about Jesus. In the picture, the teacher's face was blank—no eyes, no nose, no mouth. She was expressionless.

However, we use our eyes and mouth to show all sorts of expressions—laughter, sadness, questions, tears, joy. Those looks show others our thoughts and feelings.

During Lent we feel sadness, have questions, and cry tears of sorrow. We look with sad eyes on the sufferings of our Savior, knowing our sin was its cause. We sing somber Lenten hymns. We read the Lenten texts and wonder at the kind of love God has for us. We hear of Christ's unfair trials, harsh treatment, and awful death on the cross. We are sorry when we realize why the dead body of our Savior was sealed in the tomb.

In Hebrews we read that Christ endured the cross for the joy of claiming you and me to be His forever. It doesn't mean He had a smile on His face when He was suffering and dying. It means He had an amazing love that could endure awful things for you and for me. His enduring love gives us victory over sin, death, and the devil. His love gives our face an expression of joy every week, month, or year!

_____Let's do: Use *Lutheran Worship* to find the Bible verses listed for the Sundays in Lent. Look under the heading "Propers of the Day." Read several verses and write about your favorite.

_____Let's pray: Dear Savior, thank You for expressing Your love for me on the cross. Amen.

C. D.

Who Is Hiding?

H ave you ever hidden from someone? Were you playing a game or were you in trouble?

After Adam and Eve sinned, they hid among the trees in the Garden of Eden. God found them and led them out of Eden. They were sinners. But God gave them the promise of a Savior from their sin.

Was this the end of the story? No! Outside of Paradise Adam and Eve no longer had to hide. God chose to hide Himself instead.

Throughout the Old Testament God's people must have been amazed at the creative ways He hid Himself. "Truly You are a God who hides Yourself" (Isaiah 45:15). The people started calling on God's name, knowing that in His name they could find their loving Creator and Sustainer.

In Jesus, God hid Himself in a glorious way. He used the flesh for His divine nature. On the cross, God in the

And they heard the sound of the LORD God walking in the garden in the cool of the day, and the man and his wife hid themselves from the presence of the LORD God among the trees of the garden. But the LORD God called to the man and said to him, "Where are you?" And he said, "I heard the sound of You in the garden, and I was afraid, because I was naked, and I hid myself." Genesis 3:8–10

flesh died. Victory, forgiveness, and life were hidden in death. On the third day He rose in a glorified body.

Until the Last Day, God in Christ is again hiding! We call on His name in prayer. God speaks to us through His servants, our pastors. He offers His saving presence in Word and Sacraments. The Lord continues to be near His beloved people and promises us that He is coming again.

_____Let's talk: Look at Isaiah 55:8–9. What about God is hidden from us?

_____Let's pray: Thank You, Lord Jesus, for revealing Your love to me. Amen.

C. D.

And he said, "Bring the garment you are wearing and hold it out." So she held it, and he measured out six measures of barley and put it on her. Then she went into the city. And when she came to her mother-in-law, she said, "How did you fare, my daughter?" Then she told her all that the man had done for her, saying, "These six measures of barley he gave to me, for he said to me, 'You must not go back empty-handed to your mother-in-law.'" Ruth 3:15–17 ✍

Grandma's Hand

C arol watched Grandma's hands making beds, washing windows, or planting seeds. She was surprised when they sat down for supper. Grandma did not fold her hands when they prayed. One hand clutched the wrist of the opposite hand. She held the other hand out with her palm up. Carol thought that was a strange way to pray, with your hand out.

In the reading from Ruth, Boaz pours out more grain into Ruth's shawl than the law required. She was poor; it was a gift. She did not walk away empty-handed. She walked away with more than she deserved—more than she could even imagine.

Actually, when we pray, we ask God for handouts too.

Because we are sinful, we don't deserve to ask or to receive anything of God. God, in Christ, solved that problem. On the cross, Jesus reached out His hands and gave us more than we could ask for or imagine, bearing the punishment we deserved. He rose victorious over the things that separated us from God. He made things right between God and man.

Now we are invited to pray in Jesus' name. Our heavenly Father hears our prayers for Jesus' sake. He answers them wisely. He pours out more blessings than we deserve—more than we can even imagine!

_____Let's do: Write a prayer of thanks for the many blessings God has poured into your hands this week. Don't forget the blessings of Jesus' outstretched arms.

_____Let's pray: Gracious Father, let the word *amen* sound again and again from me and all Your people for Your goodness and mercy. In Jesus' name. Amen.

C. D.

Spring Training

Read from God's Word

Every athlete exercises self-control in all things. They do it to receive a perishable wreath, but we an imperishable. 1 Corinthians 9:25

Nikki really looks forward to Major League Baseball spring training. The players practice hitting, fielding, and running—the *fundamentals*.

Nikki understood why she would have to practice baseball. She is young and is just learning to play. But why would Major Leaguers have to practice? It's because before they can succeed, they need to be good at the fundamentals.

Christians practice the fundamentals every day, too, but not to be perfect. Christians can never be perfect; no one can. But God in Christ frees us from the need to be perfect. He helps us practice our skills so others can see how much God loves us and that He sent Jesus to be perfect, to die on the cross for us, rise again, and take us to heaven one day.

Every time we listen to God's Word or talk to Him in prayer, whenever we say "I'm sorry" or "I forgive you," each time we praise God or thank Him, we are sharing the fundamentals God gives us.

For baseball players, spring training ends on opening day when the umpire yells, "Play ball!" For Christians, spring training doesn't end on earth. The opportunity to share God's love will end only when Jesus says, "Welcome home!" Then we will come into His Father's house. What a perfect season that will be!

_____Let's talk: Read Hebrews 12:11. What does the Bible say about practicing?

_____Let's pray: Dear Jesus, thank You for giving Your Spirit to help me share the fundamentals of my faith in You. Amen.

N. D.

Read from God's Word

Jesus Christ is the same yesterday and today and forever. Hebrews 13:8 ⮎

Yesterday, Today, Forever

When Nikki's daddy was little, there were no space flights or televisions. Computers, CD players, and digital cameras didn't exist.

But Daddy did listen to the radio, and he played football. He had a dog, and he was in the Boy Scouts. Daddy went to church and Sunday school. He went on vacations to the beach. He had lots of fun!

When Nikki was little, she watched the first rockets go into space on a black and white TV! She played softball with her friends. She was in the Girl Scouts. She went to church and Sunday school. She went on vacations to the beach. She had lots of fun!

Today, you can use a computer to do your assignments, and you can talk on a cell phone. Astronauts ride in the space shuttle and live on the space station. But many things haven't changed: pets, sports, Scouts, vacations, church, and Sunday school. And you can have lots of fun!

No matter how many changes there are, one thing will never change: *Jesus loves us!* He loves us so much that He died on the cross to save us. He changed our debt of sin into a certain victory. There is nothing in this world that can change that wonderful gift.

_____Let's talk: Why would Romans 8:38–39 be a good verse to put on a birthday card?

_____Let's pray: Dear Jesus, sometimes changes scare me. I'm so glad Your love never changes. I love You! Amen.

N. D.

St. Patrick's Day

More than 1,600 years ago a 16-year-old boy named Patrick was kidnapped and sold into slavery in Ireland. He didn't see his family for the next six years. Patrick did not go to church either because most of the Irish people did not know about Jesus.

Patrick escaped when he was 22. Then he went to school to become a priest, and he asked the church to send him back to Ireland!

Patrick believed that God wanted him to teach the Irish people about Jesus. People who did not want Patrick to preach in their country hurt him, but they couldn't stop him from spreading the Good News. Thanks to Patrick and other missionaries like him, Ireland heard the story of God's love in Jesus.

Today we celebrate St. Patrick's Day. Some people celebrate because they are Irish. Others celebrate just for fun.

Read from God's Word

For "everyone who calls on the name of the Lord will be saved." But how are they to call on Him in whom they have not believed? And how are they to believe in Him of whom they have never heard? And how are they to hear without someone preaching? And how are they to preach unless they are sent? As it is written, "How beautiful are the feet of those who preach the good news!" But they have not all obeyed the gospel. For Isaiah says, "Lord, who has believed what he has heard from us?" So faith comes from hearing, and hearing through the word of Christ. Romans 10:13–17

Today we can have fun and wear a green shirt and green socks. But we can also remember one of God's servants who was not afraid to tell others about Jesus, even when his life was in danger. We will have fun, but we will also pray for all the people in the world who don't believe in Jesus. We want to thank God for Patrick and all missionaries who are spreading the Gospel.

_____Let's do: St. Patrick used a shamrock to teach the Irish people about God—the Father, Son, and Holy Spirit. Draw a shamrock and describe how it connects to the devotion.

_____Let's pray: Thank You, dear God, for the people who told me about Your Son, my Savior. Help me tell others. In Jesus' name. Amen.

N. D.

Christ of the Deep

Read from God's Word

Out of the depths I cry to You, O LORD! O Lord, hear my voice! Let Your ears be attentive to the voice of my pleas for mercy! If You, O LORD, should mark iniquities, O Lord, who could stand? But with You there is forgiveness, that You may be feared. I wait for the LORD, my soul waits, and in His word I hope; my soul waits for the Lord more than watchmen for the morning, more than watchmen for the morning. O Israel, hope in the Lord! For with the LORD there is steadfast love, and with Him is plentiful redemption. And He will redeem Israel from all his iniquities. Psalm 130 ᔍ

Do you have a special picture of Jesus? It's not really a picture of Jesus—it's a picture of a statue. This bronze statue is 8 1/2 feet tall, weighs 30,000 pounds, and is underwater.

The Christ of the Deep statue stands 20 feet underwater in the Atlantic Ocean, off the coast of Key Largo, Florida. It is a copy of an Italian statue that is under the Mediterranean Sea. Guido Galletti created the statue to inspire everyone who explored and loved the sea. The copy was made for America as a symbol of peace.

The statue depicts Jesus standing with His arms open wide and His smiling face looking up. The ocean is so clear there you can just look down to see it. When I saw the statue, I swam down and held His hand!

The Christ of the Deep statue reminds me that Jesus loves me very much. In fact, He loves me so much He was willing to die for my sins and the sins of all people. When I remember swimming down to the statue and holding Jesus' hand, I also remember that Jesus is always with me, no matter how deep my troubles are. Jesus will never let go of me, and He will never let go of you.

———Let's talk: What can we learn about God from Psalm 130?

———Let's pray: Christ of the Deep, help me to remember that You are always with me, no matter how deep my troubles are. Amen.

N. D.

Joseph, the *Other* Dreamer

M iss Michaels told her fourth graders that they were celebrating Joseph the Dreamer today. "Does anyone remember who he was?" she asked.

"Joseph had dreams that he would be in charge of his brothers, so they sold him into slavery," said Nick. "He worked for Potiphar in Egypt."

"Prince Joseph saved the people when there wasn't enough to eat," said Raigan.

"Very good, but you're all wrong," laughed Miss Michaels. "I was thinking about another dreamer. In his dreams Joseph was told by God when to get married, when to run away, and when to come back home."

Baruti laughed and said, "I know. He's Jesus' dad!"

"You're right," said Miss Michaels. "He was Jesus' earthly father. This Joseph was in trouble too, but he trusted God. Joseph moved his family to Egypt to protect Jesus from King Herod's soldiers. When it was safe to come home, he took Jesus there. Joseph loved his adopted Son very much. Joseph was scared, but God helped him to trust in Him and overcome his fears.

"Sometimes we get scared too, and it's hard for us to trust God," said Miss Michaels. "But God gives us His Spirit to remind us that God loves us and is always with us.

Read from God's Word

Behold, an angel of the Lord appeared to him in a dream, saying, "Joseph, son of David, do not fear to take Mary as your wife, for that which is conceived in her is from the Holy Spirit. She will bear a son, and you shall call His name Jesus, for He will save His people from their sins." All this took place to fulfill what the Lord had spoken by the prophet: "Behold, the virgin shall conceive and bear a son, and they shall call His name Immanuel" (which means, God with us). Matthew 1:20–23 ✐

_____Let's talk: Read Matthew 1:18–24 and 2:13–23. Think about a time when you were afraid. How did God help you?

_____Let's pray: *Abba*, Father, forgive us when we are afraid to trust You. Thank You for giving Your Son. In His name we pray. Amen.

N. D.

Read from God's Word

Therefore, if anyone is in Christ, he is a new creation. The old has passed away; behold, the new has come.
2 Corinthians 5:17

The Poetry of Spring

"Today is the first day of spring," Miss Michaels told the fifth graders, "so we are going to write a funny poem about things in spring. This kind of poem is called a limerick. Let's see if we can make a list of spring things to write about."

They listed baby animals, flowers, rain, sunshine, eggs, bunnies, and birds. When they were finished, Sierra said, "We forgot the most important word: *Easter.*"

"That *is* an important spring word," agreed Miss Michaels, "because Easter is the time when we celebrate Jesus' resurrection. Right now, during Lent, we are remembering how Jesus suffered and died for us, but the new life in the spring can remind us of the new life we have in Jesus."

"But we can't write a funny poem about Jesus, can we?" asked Tim.

"Well, maybe not, but there are lots of people in the Bible we can write about."

"How about Zacchaeus?" suggested Chris. Arryn and Leza wrote this poem:

> There once was a man named Zacchaeus
> Who tried really hard to see Jesus.
> He climbed up a tree
> Where he finally could see
> When his Savior said, "Come down and meet us!"

"Jesus gave Zacchaeus new life, just like He gives us," said Miss Michaels. "Now that's something to write about!"

_____Let's do: Write a limerick about a Bible character.

_____Let's pray: Lord God, thank You for giving me new life
and salvation through Jesus, in whose name
I pray. Amen.

N. D.

March Madness

Read from God's Word

Now at the feast he used to release for them one prisoner for whom they asked. And among the rebels in prison, who had committed murder in the insurrection, there was a man called Barabbas. And the crowd came up and began to ask Pilate to do as he usually did for them. And he answered them, saying, "Do you want me to release for you the King of the Jews?" For he perceived that it was out of envy that the chief priests had delivered him up. But the chief priests stirred up the crowd to have him release for them Barabbas instead. And Pilate again said to them, "Then what shall I do with the man you call the King of the Jews?" And they cried out again, "Crucify Him." And Pilate said to them, "Why, what evil has He done?" But they shouted all the more, "Crucify Him." So Pilate, wishing to satisfy the crowd, released for them Barabbas, and having scourged Jesus, he delivered Him to be crucified.
Mark 15:6–15 ✎

Sports fans do some crazy things to support their teams. They paint their faces, wear funny hats, and wave banners. Fans jump up and down and yell and scream!

Sometimes people do crazy things because the rest of the crowd is doing them. When you're cheering for your team, that can be fun. But sometimes what the crowd is doing is not what Jesus wants us to do. Some crowds have burned cars and destroyed property just because their team lost!

Crowds in Jesus' time made wrong choices too. When Pilate wanted to release Jesus, who was innocent, the people wanted a murderer freed instead. They were upset because they wanted Jesus to be an earthly king, not a heavenly King. The crowd was so angry they told Pilate to crucify their Lord.

But Jesus knew the people were confused. He still loved them, although they crucified Him. Jesus loved them so much He asked God to forgive them (Luke 23:34).

Jesus knows that sometimes we follow the crowd instead of Him. But Jesus still loves us and He wants to forgive us. That's why Jesus died on the cross and rose again. Jesus' victory over sin, death, and the power of the devil is the greatest championship of all time! Three cheers for Jesus, our Champion!

_____Let's talk: Read 1 Corinthians 15:57–58. How can God help you make the right choices today?

_____Let's pray: Dear Jesus, forgive me when I follow the crowd instead of You. Thank You for loving me. Amen.

N. D.

Read from God's Word

Him we proclaim, warning everyone and teaching everyone with all wisdom, that we may present everyone mature in Christ. Colossians 1:28

But Joseph said to them, "Do not fear, for am I in the place of God? As for you, you meant evil against me, but God meant it for good, to bring it about that many people should be kept alive, as they are today. So do not fear; I will provide for you and your little ones." Thus he comforted them and spoke kindly to them. Genesis 50:19–21

Hate or Love?

"Why does Mrs. Green hate Joey?" asked Brad.

Brad's mom was surprised at the question. "What gave you that idea?"

"She gets on him in class. It's kind of like he is her enemy," Brad went on.

"Just because she gets on him in class about the way he acts doesn't mean she hates him," his mom tried to explain.

"I think he's cool, and I just think she's mean to him all the time."

"Do you really think that talking back to the teacher is cool?"

"Well, sure. It means you're tough," Brad said honestly.

"I don't think the way Joey acts is cool," his mom explained. "He doesn't follow the rules, and he doesn't show respect for his teacher. It has nothing to do with being tough. Mrs. Green wants Joey to do his best, and that also means respecting her. She cares about Joey. He just hasn't realized it yet."

God has put some people, including teachers, in authority over others. These people don't just teach math and reading or coach sports. They also teach us how to love and respect others. Christ showed us that kind of love. He gave His life for us on the cross so we may be presented before God as perfect and live with Him eternally.

——Let's talk: Who are the people in authority in your life? How do they show God's love?

——Let's pray: Dear Lord, help us to respect those in authority over us and to see Christ's love in their actions. In Jesus' name. Amen.

C. S.

Turned into Good

Two boys looked over the fence at an elderly woman who had just moved into their neighborhood. One boy whispered to the other, "Let's scare her."

On a large piece of paper they drew pictures of the most frightening things they could think of, including a snake and a ghost. They sneaked into the woman's yard, taped the picture to her window, and ran away.

The woman watched with amusement. As she studied the picture, she wasn't frightened at all.

Later that day the boys began to feel badly about what they did and came back to apologize. Instead of scolding them, she thanked them for their picture. As a sign of friendship she gave her new neighbors milk and cookies.

Joseph's brothers sold him into slavery. Like the boys in our story, they did a terrible thing and were sorry for it. In both stories all was forgiven. Not only that, but in each instance good developed out of the evil.

Joseph told his brothers. "You meant evil against me, but God meant it for good." Isn't it great to know that we have a God who forgives us and turns evil into good? By the sacrifice of His Son He has made our sinful lives into beautiful lives of service.

_____Let's do: Can you think of a bad happening in your life that later turned into good? Write about it.

_____Let's pray: Dear God, help me ask for forgiveness when I feel miserable over the wrong things I've done. Help me remember Your love. Hear me for Jesus' sake. Amen.

R. R.

Read from God's Word

But Joseph said to them. "Do not fear, for am I in the place of God? As for you, you meant evil against me, but God meant it for good, to bring it about that many people should be kept alive, as they are today. So do not fear: I will provide for you and your little ones." Thus he comforted them and spoke kindly to them. Genesis 50:19–21

Read from God's Word

Bearing with one another and, if one has a complaint against another, forgiving each other; as the Lord has forgiven you, so you also must forgive.
Colossians 3:13

Forgiveness

Joe and Jamal teased each other on their way to health class. They were not paying attention to their surroundings.

As the two friends turned the last corner, right by the school office, Jamal ran right into Mrs. Kingston. He knocked her against the wall. Her gasp brought both boys to a quick stop.

Jamal had not meant to hurt anyone. He was just goofing around and someone was hurt. Jamal took Mrs. Kingston's arm and helped her to a chair.

"I'm so sorry," he said quickly. "Are you okay?" He worried that she had broken something. It seemed like forever before she could speak. She patted Jamal's hand the whole time, as if she was reassuring him.

Finally she spoke. "Thank you for helping me to this chair. I think I just got the wind knocked out of me. I'll be just fine. Now run along so you are not late for class."

Jamal hesitated, but she waved her hand for him to go on. How could she forgive him so easily? It was amazing!

Mrs. Kingston gave Jamal and Joe a beautiful example of God's love. He forgives our sins because of Jesus. We don't deserve it. We didn't earn it. He just gives it. It's amazing!

_____Let's do: Write words to describe God's kind of forgiveness.

_____Let's pray: Thank You, God, for sending Jesus, who forgives me so easily. Help me to be that forgiving to others. In His name I pray. Amen.

C. S.

Standing Tall

Read from God's Word

I can do all things through Him who strengthens me.
Philippians 4:13

I t isn't fair," Jordan grumbled, dumping his backpack on the floor. "I miss Alex. I don't know anyone else who likes to share computer games and stuff."

"You'll just have to learn to be strong," said his dad.

"How am I supposed to learn to be strong?" Jordan complained.

"Remember the trees we saw in the documentary about Biosphere II?"

"Sort of," said Jordan.

"The trees break at the top because the Biosphere doesn't have strong winds, only breezes. Without those strong gusts the trees don't develop stress wood—the wood that gives them the strength to stand tall," said Jordan's dad.

Jordan wrinkled his nose. "I'm not a tree, Dad. Standing in the wind won't make me stronger."

"No, Jordan, for you to get stronger, you need Jesus. He died for you, and He lives in you. He is your stress wood. Philippians 4:13 says: 'I can do all things through Him who strengthens me.'"

"Then if Jesus is where I get my strength, my problems must be like the wind. Is that right, Dad?" asked Jordan.

"Sometimes problems come in gentle breezes like a lost math book."

"And sometimes they come in gusts like friends moving away," finished Jordan. "I think I will pray for a new friend."

"You're getting stronger, Jordan," said his dad.

_____Let's do: Write about a time when God gave you strength to make it through a problem.

_____Let's pray: Dear Jesus, thank You for living in us, making us strong for the problems that blow our way. Amen.

D. L. B.

Special Friends

Read from God's Word

So then, as we have opportunity, let us do good to everyone, and especially to those who are of the household of faith. Galatians 6:10

L ong ago there lived two boys. One was the son of the king; the other was a humble peasant.

Despite their different backgrounds, they became the best of friends. The friendship of the prince for the peasant boy was so strong that when he learned it was God's plan for the peasant boy to become king, he unselfishly helped his friend.

This is a true story of David and Jonathan as recorded in 1 Samuel 18–20. Jonathan, the prince, who might have been king, helped his friend David, the peasant, to become king instead because he knew it was God's will.

Like the friendship of Jonathan and David, the bond between Christian friends everywhere is a special one. Christian friends pray for one another, help one another, and share with one another how God has rescued them from sin through the death of His Son.

Having friends who love Jesus and His Word as we do will help to keep us close to Him. They will remind us of God's promises when we become discouraged.

Friends who love Jesus are precious gifts from God. Only with God's help can we develop the kind of deep and lasting friendship that David and Jonathan enjoyed.

_____Let's do: Write about how one of your Christian friends has helped you love Jesus more.

_____Let's pray: Dear Lord, thank You for my friends who love You. Thank You for Jesus, my best friend. I pray this in His name. Amen.

R. R.

Keep on Loving

Read from God's Word

Let brotherly love continue. Do not neglect to show hospitality to strangers, for thereby some have entertained angels unawares. Remember those who are in prison, as though in prison with them, and those who are mistreated, since you also are in the body. Let marriage be held in honor among all, and let the marriage bed be undefiled, for God will judge the sexually immoral and adulterous. Keep your life free from love of money, and be content with what you have, for He has said, "I will never leave you nor forsake you." So we can confidently say, "The Lord is my helper; I will not fear; what can man do to me?"
Hebrews 13:1–6 ⤸

Kim and Brian didn't say a word. They sat there looking at each other. Mom and Dad just left the room after telling Kim and Brian they were planning to get a divorce.

"Maybe if we wouldn't have argued so much, this wouldn't have happened," said Kim. Brian reminded her that Mom had just said the divorce wasn't because of anything they had done.

Tears came to Brian's eyes. The future seemed uncertain, and his heart seemed to hurt in his chest. What could they do?

You probably know people like Kim and Brian. How do you think they feel? How would you feel?

Our Bible reading reminds us that God will never leave us. He will always be with us, no matter what troubles enter our lives. It also says, "Let brotherly love continue." That means you and I need to continue sharing love in a special way with our friends who are hurting. We do this as a response to the love of Jesus, our Savior.

Jesus showed His love for us by suffering and dying for us. He kept on being our friend although sin separated us from God. With His help we, too, can keep on being friends to those who hurt us.

_____Let's do: Write down two things you want to remember from the Bible reading for today.

_____Let's pray: Dear God, help me show Your love to those around me whose lives are hurt by sin. In Your Son's name I pray. Amen.

J. W.

Read from God's Word

For we ourselves were once foolish, disobedient, led astray, slaves to various passions and pleasures, passing our days in malice and envy, hated by others and hating one another. But when the goodness and loving kindness of God our Savior appeared, He saved us, not because of works done by us in righteousness, but according to His own mercy, by the washing of regeneration and renewal of the Holy Spirit. Titus 3:3–5

Grandpa

Sonia's grandfather needs a lot of help now. She has to help Grandma get him from the wheelchair to his recliner. He can't get dressed by himself. At mealtimes Grandma has to feed him.

At other times Grandpa laughs when they talk about things Sonia did when she was little. Or he remembers where they were when something happened, something no one else can remember.

When Sonia was little, Grandpa liked to tease her and they played games. He can't do those things now. It's hard for him to do almost anything. But sometimes he will surprise her by telling her where to find something she's been looking for.

It has taken Sonia a while to realize that inside, Grandpa is still the same guy she has always loved and who has always loved her. He may look different on the outside. He may not be able to do all the things that he once did, but his love has never changed.

God has a remarkable unchanging love. Even when we were sinners He sent Jesus to rescue us from sin. He even claimed us to be His forever by the washing of Baptism.

Grandpa may forget who Sonia is or what day it is, but God will never forget Grandpa or any of His children. His love is completely unforgettable!

____Let's talk: In what ways does God work through older people?

____Let's pray: Thank You, Lord God, for loving us through all our years. Keep us always close to You. In Jesus' name. Amen.

C. S.

Focused!

Sarah stared out the window, concentrating deeply. Her friend Elizabeth came into the room. Sarah didn't even notice her. Finally she spoke. "What are you looking at, Sarah?"

Sarah was so focused that her friend's voice startled her. "You scared me, Elizabeth!"

"So, what is so interesting out there?" Elizabeth asked again.

"Outside? Nothing," replied Sarah. "I was thinking about my art project. When I get focused on a project, sometimes I don't even notice my friends sneaking up!"

The Bible verse for today tells us that Jesus was very focused on God's plan to save the world. That plan included Jesus' betrayal, suffering, death on a cross, resurrection, and return to heaven. That's a lot to happen in a short time!

Jesus knew His Father's plan. And so with great resolve (which means He was very focused), He headed to Jerusalem to suffer, die, and rise to life. Even when one of Jesus' friends was sneaking around behind His back, planning to betray Him, Jesus kept His focus on the cross and on saving us. Although His friends ran away, Jesus didn't run. He had us in His focus as He went to Jerusalem to suffer and die. It is a clear picture of His love for us. Focus on that fact!

Read from God's Word

When the days drew near for Him to be taken up, He set His face to go to Jerusalem.
Luke 9:51

_____Let's talk: What are some things God gives you to help you stay focused on Him?

_____Let's pray: Jesus, keep me focused on Your cross and Your empty tomb. Amen.

T. W.

Read from God's Word

And it is my prayer that your love may abound more and more, with knowledge and all discernment, so that you may approve what is excellent, and so be pure and blameless for the day of Christ, filled with the fruit of righteousness that comes through Jesus Christ, to the glory and praise of God. Philippians 1:9–11 ✐

Blameless

Daniel took the stairs two by two as he raced to his classroom. When he got to the door, he stopped and tried to catch his breath. Why did this always happen to him? It was always Mom who was late, or it was a traffic problem. Daniel hated coming in late.

He felt everyone's eyes focus on him when he opened the door. So far so good. Mrs. Brown didn't say anything until later.

"You certainly have a long drive to school each day," she said as she sat next to me in the library.

"Yes, I'm sorry I was late again," Daniel said quietly. "It really isn't my fault," he whispered.

"I know," she said. "Your mother told me it's her fault that you don't get started early enough." Mrs. Brown paused. "Your mother said she would take all the blame."

Daniel replayed his earlier thoughts. It really hadn't been *all* Mom's fault. He felt ashamed that he had blamed her. And he was amazed at her love.

Jesus took all the blame for all sin. He wasn't even partly at fault. He was totally innocent, but He became totally guilty so we could be "pure and blameless for the day of Christ." To God be glory and praise.

_____Let's talk: What are ways your love can grow according to Philippians 1:9–11? How will that growth help you?

_____Let's pray: Dear Jesus, thank You for living in us, making us strong for the problems that come. Amen.

D. L. B.

He Understands

Mrs. Alexander was sleeping after her emergency surgery. Her family was relieved. Mr. Alexander yawned as he sat next to his wife's hospital bed. David was hungry; he hadn't eaten since breakfast. Theresa paced the hospital floor or patted her mom's hand.

The Alexander family was going through a difficult time. Mom had experienced pain and surgery. Their day was filled with stress. Each person, in his or her own way, needed comfort.

Mark 11:12 reads, "On the following day, when they came from Bethany, He was hungry." What comfort could the Alexanders find in that simple verse? Jesus had just ridden into Jerusalem while the people shouted "Hosanna" and waved palms. Jesus would experience exhaustion, stress, concern, pain, and even death—and oh, yes, also hunger—that Holy Week. Whatever emotions or struggles we go through, Jesus can relate to it!

Read from God's Word

On the following day, when they came from Bethany, He was hungry. Mark 11:12 ⮎

It is a wonderful gift to have a friend who can relate to our experiences. But Jesus is more than a friend. He is our God. He can do all things and help in all situations. He died on the cross to pay for our sin, rose again to guarantee us eternal life with Him, and lives in our hearts through every joy and pain of ours. What a comfort to trust in Jesus through it all!

_____Let's talk: What did you experience today that Jesus also
          experienced?

_____Let's pray: Jesus, help me when I am going through difficult
          times. Give me Your comfort. Amen.

T. W.

april

Contributors for this month:

Jennifer L. AlLee

Jeanette A. Dall

Jeanne Dicke

Joan Gerber

Judy Williams

April Fools

April 1 used to be the first day of the new year. But about 400 years ago the people in Europe had to get used to the new Gregorian calendar. In the new calendar, January 1 became the first day of the year. Some people still celebrated April 1 as New Year's Day. They were called "April fools," and their friends enjoyed playing tricks on them. They would give them candy boxes filled with straw or bouquets of onions instead of flowers.

In the Bible God talks about another kind of fool—people who do not believe in Him. God shows Himself in the wonderful world He created. We can see His creative power and might in the uniqueness of His creation and the way it all works together. He shows His love through His Son, Jesus Christ. He comes to us in the words of the Bible. But some people still do not believe there is a God.

God sent His Son to show how much He cares for all people in the world—even those who do not believe. Jesus lived, suffered, died, and came alive again for each of us. So today, on April Fools' Day, perhaps you can tell someone who is a "fool" about our loving God, who sent His Son to live and die for them too.

Read from God's Word

The fool says in his heart, "There is no God." They are corrupt, they do abominable deeds, there is none who does good. The LORD looks down from heaven on the children of man, to see if there are any who understand, who seek after God. They have all turned aside; together they have become corrupt; there is none who does good, not even one. ... There they are in great terror, for God is with the generation of the righteous. You would shame the plans of the poor, but the LORD is his refuge. Oh, that salvation for Israel would come out of Zion! When the LORD restores the fortunes of His people, let Jacob rejoice, let Israel be glad. Psalm 14 ⬎

_____Let's talk: How does it feel when someone plays a trick on you? How does it feel to know how much God loves and cares for you? Do you know someone who doesn't love God? Don't trick them, but show them through your words and actions that God loves them.

_____Let's pray: Dear God, thank You for all whom You have given us to show Your love and care for us. Thank You especially for Your Son, Jesus. Please help us show Your love to others. In Your Son's name we pray. Amen.

J. W.

Read from God's Word

John to the seven churches that are in Asia: Grace to you and peace from Him who is and who was and who is to come, and from the seven spirits who are before His throne, and from Jesus Christ the faithful witness, the firstborn of the dead, and the ruler of kings on earth. To Him who loves us and has freed us from our sins by His blood and made us a kingdom, priests to His God and Father, to Him be glory and dominion forever and ever. Amen. Behold, He is coming with the clouds, and every eye will see Him, even those who pierced Him, and all tribes of the earth will wail on account of Him. Even so. Amen. Revelation 1:4–7

Symbol of Freedom

Lori was all smiles. She had just received an A on her social studies report. Lori told the class how she and her family took a boat to Ellis Island and saw the Statue of Liberty and what she had learned on the tour.

The tour guide said that millions of people have left their homelands for new lives of freedom in the United States. As they arrive in their new homeland, many pass the Statue of Liberty.

The Statue of Liberty was a gift from the country of France. The statue carries a tablet on which is written the date of the Declaration of Independence. It is a reminder that Americans have freedoms because people were willing to fight to gain them. The early Americans, or colonists, fought a war to gain independence from British rule.

We Christians have a different symbol of freedom—the empty cross. This cross stands for freedom from sin, death, and the devil. This freedom did not come easily. Jesus, God's Son, was willing to fight for it. He died on a cross for our freedom. But Jesus is stronger than death. He came alive again. As a result of the freedom Jesus earned for us, we are promised a new homeland—heaven. We will live there forever with our Savior.

_____Let's talk: Name other symbols of the freedoms we enjoy as citizens of a free country and as Christians. How do they make you feel?

_____Let's pray: Dear Lord God, help us lift high Your cross and proclaim Your love so that all the world may adore Your sacred name. In Jesus' name. Amen.

J. W.

God Understands

Read from God's Word

This, the first of His signs, Jesus did at Cana in Galilee, and manifested His glory. And His disciples believed in Him. John 2:11 (Happy)

Jesus wept. John 11:35 (Sad)

And making a whip of cords, He drove them all out of the temple, with the sheep and oxen. And He poured out the coins of the money-changers and overturned their tables. And He told those who sold the pigeons, "Take these things away; do not make My Father's house a house of trade." John 2:15–17 (Angry) ✑

*A*s you read the following the devotion for today, put in the missing words.

Dear (word for Jesus), today I feel (happy, sad, angry). It has been such a (word to describe your feeling) day. Let me tell You what happened. (Share an experience from your day.)

I know You understand, (word for Jesus). When You lived here on earth, You felt (word to describe your feeling) too.

Read the Bible reference that goes with the feeling you experienced today.

I am glad to know You rejoice with me when I feel happy. It comforts me that You know what it's like to feel sad. And I am thankful that You know my feelings of anger.

Dear (word for Jesus), I also know there is a big difference between my feelings and Your feelings. Many times my feelings are the result of my own wrongdoing, but You never did anything wrong.

Dear (word for God), I am so thankful that You sent Your Son, Jesus, to (what Jesus did for us) for me and all other people. I'm glad You also understand my feelings of sorrow when I have done something wrong. You understand, and You forgive. For this I am very grateful.

_____Let's talk: Read John 2:1–11, 13–17; 11:21–36. These stories tell how Jesus felt about some things that happened in His life. Knowing how Jesus felt and what He did, how might you respond the next time you feel happy, angry, or sad?

_____Let's pray: Dear Jesus, we're glad You understand how we feel. We're especially glad You suffered and died to take away our sins and the feelings of guilt and sadness they bring. Thank You for loving and forgiving us. Help us share this forgiveness with others. Amen.

J. W.

Freedom for All

Read from God's Word

The Spirit of the Lord God is upon me, because the Lord has anointed me to bring good news to the poor. He has sent me to bind up the brokenhearted, to proclaim liberty to the captives, and the opening of the prison to those who are bound; to proclaim the year of the Lord's favor, and the day of vengeance of our God; to comfort all who mourn; to grant to those who mourn in Zion—to give them a beautiful headdress instead of ashes, the oil of gladness instead of mourning, the garment of praise instead of a faint spirit; that they may be called oaks of righteousness, the planting of the Lord, that He may be glorified.
Isaiah 61:1-3 ⌀

You may have read about Martin Luther King Jr. in your history book. He is one of the most famous African Americans. At the time he grew up, blacks had to sit at certain tables in restaurants. They had to sit at the back of buses. They did not have equal opportunities for education or jobs.

Martin Luther King Jr. began a peaceful movement to change the way African Americans were treated. Many people helped him. But some people disagreed with him. Today is the anniversary of the day one of these people shot and killed him.

Martin Luther King Jr. died, but as a result of his work, the laws of the United States were changed to guarantee equal rights for all citizens.

There is a bigger champion for freedom than Martin Luther King Jr. You won't read about Him in most history books. That person is Jesus, God's Son. He came to earth to make all people free.

The Bible tells us that all people are slaves to sin and are doomed to spend eternity in hell. Jesus came from heaven to live a perfect life for us. He died to take the punishment for our sins. Through faith in Jesus we have forgiveness of all our sins and new life. Now that's real freedom!

_____Let's talk: What would life be like without the earthly freedoms we enjoy? What would life without Jesus be like? Give praise and thanks to God for all He has done for you.

_____Let's pray: Sing or say the following words (tune: "There Is a Green Hill Far Away"): He died that we might be forgiv'n, He died to make us free, That we might live with Him in heav'n For all eternity.

J. W.

It's Hard to Believe

Jessica and Rick couldn't believe their eyes when they looked outside. It looked like someone had made snowballs in the yard, but there were no footprints. Puzzled, Rick told his dad about it.

Mr. Arnold chuckled. It had been years since he had seen "snow rolls." He told Rick and Jessica that these unusual shapes form on level ground when wind blows wet snow into shapes that look like giant cinnamon rolls.

Jessica was so excited she had to call Grandma Wolsky and tell her. At first Grandma thought her granddaughter was making up the whole story. But Jessica said, "Really, Grandma!" And to prove they were telling the truth, Rick and Jessica took a picture of the snow rolls and sent it to Grandma.

In the Bible reading for today, Thomas had a hard time believing something. He just couldn't believe that Jesus, who had been crucified,

Read from God's Word

Now Thomas, one of the Twelve, called the Twin, was not with them when Jesus came. So the other disciples told him, "We have seen the Lord." But he said to them, "Unless I see in His hands the mark of the nails, and place my finger into the mark of the nails, and place my hand into His side, I will never believe." Eight days later, His disciples were inside again, and Thomas was with them. Although the doors were locked, Jesus came and stood among them and said, "Peace be with you." Then He said to Thomas, "Put your finger here, and see My hands; and put out your hand, and place it in My side. Do not disbelieve, but believe." Thomas answered Him, "My Lord and my God!" John 20:24–28 ✎

was alive. Jesus appeared to Thomas and showed that He was truly alive. He said to Thomas, "Put your finger here, and see My hands; and put out your hand, and place it in My side. Do not disbelieve, but believe." Then Thomas knew that Jesus, who had died for the sins of all people, had risen from the dead. Really!

_____Let's talk: Do you believe that Jesus, God's Son, lived, died, and came alive again for you? Why do you believe in Him? Thank God for His gift of faith.

_____Let's pray: Dear God, thank You for the Holy Spirit, who gives me faith to believe in You. In Jesus' name. Amen.

J. W.

Read from God's Word

"Therefore I tell you, do not be anxious about your life, what you will eat or what you will drink, nor about your body, what you will put on. Is not life more than food, and the body more than clothing? ... O you of little faith? Therefore do not be anxious, saying, 'What shall we eat?' or 'What shall we drink?' or 'What shall we wear?' For the Gentiles seek after all these things, and your heavenly Father knows that you need them all. But seek first the kingdom of God and His righteousness, and all these things will be added to you. Therefore do not be anxious about tomorrow, for tomorrow will be anxious for itself. Sufficient for the day is its own trouble." Matthew 6:25–34 ✍

We Depend on God

Sid was puzzled. Every time he saw the new neighbor, Mr. Golds, he was wearing a backpack. He wore it when he went walking, when he mowed the lawn, and even when he washed his car.

When Sid finally met his neighbor, he could see there was a small, plastic tube coming from the backpack to Mr. Golds's nose.

Mr. Golds told Sid he had emphysema, a disease that prevents the lungs from taking in enough oxygen. He received extra oxygen from a small tank of oxygen in the backpack.

Sid told his mom he was glad he didn't have to depend on a tank of oxygen in order to stay alive. Mom agreed, but she told Sid, "We depend on God to keep us alive. God gives us air to breathe, water and food, and everything else we need."

God also wants us to live with Him forever in heaven, but our sinfulness made this impossible. So Jesus came from heaven and lived a perfect life for us. He also took our punishment for all our sin and died on the cross. But Jesus came alive again. Because of what our Savior did, we can depend on God to take us to heaven to live with Him.

_____Let's do: Reread Matthew 6:25–34. How many blessings (all the things God gives us) can you find in the Bible reading?

_____Let's pray: Make up a responsive prayer using each blessing you named. After each one, tell God you are thankful with the words "O give thanks to the Lord, for He is good." Remember to thank God for sending His Son, Jesus, to be our Savior.

J. W.

Members of Two Families

Read from God's Word

For in Christ Jesus you are all sons of God, through faith. For as many of you as were baptized into Christ have put on Christ. Galatians 3:26–27 ✍

Jeremy is part of a special family. He lives with his mother, father, and two brothers. He and his brother Jeff play Nintendo games, go swimming, and share funny jokes. Jeremy and his brother Jason enjoy each other's company too. Sometimes Jason takes Jeremy fishing! The members of Jeremy's family love each other and help each other.

Jeremy is part of another family too. So are you and I. We are part of the Christian family with lots of brothers and sisters. We became part of God's family at our Baptism.

Our Christian family does things together too. We worship together and enjoy potlucks and picnics. We meet together to study God's Word. We learn that God sent His Son, Jesus, to live, suffer, and die for our sins so that we could become children of God. At church we sing praises, telling God how wonderful He is. We ask Him to help us live as His children. God has a special plan for His family—we will all live with Him in heaven.

Isn't it wonderful to be part of two families, the family with whom you live and the family with whom you'll live forever—God's family!

_____Let's do: What do you like about the family God has given you? Think of something you like about each member, write it down, and share it with him or her.

_____Let's pray: Dear God, we thank You for the family You have given us. We thank You especially for making us part of Your Christian family. Help us live as Your children every day. In the name of our Savior and Brother, Jesus, we pray. Amen.

J. W.

Read from God's Word

"You are the light of the world. A city set on a hill cannot be hidden. Nor do people light a lamp and put it under a basket, but on a stand, and it gives light to all in the house. In the same way, let your light shine before others, so that they may see your good works and give glory to your Father who is in heaven." Matthew 5:14–16 ⤸

The Light of the World

One evening Scott and his family were sitting at home when the lights, TV, clocks, and everything electric went off.

"Power failure!" his sister Darla called out.

His mom brought a lantern out of the kitchen, and his dad turned on a battery-operated radio. It wasn't very late yet, so there was still some light coming in through the windows. Still, Scott was nervous. What if the power stayed off for a long time? The lantern didn't give off enough light to read and it threw spooky shadows on the walls.

What if they woke up in the morning and there were still no lights? There wasn't even a window in the bathroom. How would he brush his teeth? How would he get ready for school? Thankfully, just when Scott was really getting ready to panic, the power came back on!

There is one light that never goes out—the light of God's love that shines through us. The Bible tells us that Christians are the "light of the world." Sin throws darkness over the world. But God showed us the brightness of His love through the death and resurrection of Jesus. Now, God's love and that brightness live in your heart. Every day is a new chance to share that light with others!

_____Let's talk: What are some ways that the light of God's love can shine through you today?

_____Let's pray: Dear God, thank You for shining the light of Your love through the darkness of sin. Please use me today to shine Your love on others. In Jesus' name. Amen.

J. L. A.

God Still Speaks

Read from God's Word

For the word of God is living and active, sharper than any two-edged sword, piercing to the division of soul and of spirit, of joints and of marrow, and discerning the thoughts and intentions of the heart. Hebrews 4:12 ❧

Jenny likes to take part in plays. Whenever she finishes a performance, she has the same dream. In the dream it's a few days later, and the director has come to her and said they're doing the play again. But she can't remember any of her lines and someone has hidden her costume. Jenny has had this dream over and over for so many years that now she's not surprised anymore when she has it.

God used dreams to speak to people. In the Old Testament we read how God used Joseph to interpret the dreams of Pharaoh (Genesis 41). In the New Testament God spoke to another Joseph and told him to take Mary and the baby Jesus to another city and avoid danger (Matthew 2:19–23).

God could speak to you through a dream too. But the main way God speaks to us is through His Word.

God gave us the Bible so we can always have His Word close at hand. He wants us to know how much He loves us. He wants us to know that we are assured of eternal life with Him through the blood of His precious Son, Jesus. And He wants us to know that we can always speak to Him through prayer.

_____Let's talk: What are some ways God has spoken to you?

_____Let's pray: Dear Lord, thank You for the many ways You speak to me. Please be with me and help me to recognize Your voice throughout my day. In Jesus' name. Amen.

J. L. A.

A Walk on the Water

Read from God's Word

I can do all things through Him who strengthens me.
Philippians 4:13 ✍

L ittle green lizards called "basilisks" live along Costa Rican rivers. These lightweight lizards can run so fast that they skim across the water, making it look like they are walking on water. The first person who ever saw one of these lizards must have been shocked!

Now, imagine how shocked you would be to see a full-grown man walking on water. Jesus' disciples had that experience. They were out on a boat and saw Jesus walking toward them.

But Peter wanted more proof. So Jesus called to Peter, and he stepped out on the water and started walking toward the Lord. He was actually walking on the water until he looked away from Jesus and saw the waves and the wind. Peter was very scared, and then he began to sink. Jesus reached out and saved Peter by bringing him back into the boat. (You can read the whole story in Matthew 14:25–33.)

Jesus performed many miracles. The greatest miracle of all was rising from the dead after paying for our sins on the cross. It was His greatest act of love.

We can do everything with Jesus' strength. Peter was doing fine until he took his eyes off the Lord. The strength of Jesus rescued him when he was sinking. The strength of Jesus is with you, too, in everything.

_____Let's do: Write about a time when Jesus helped you through a difficult situation.

_____Let's pray: Dear Jesus, please be with me today. Help me in times of trouble. I pray in Your name. Amen.

J. L. A.

Cookie-Cutter People

Jamie and her little sister, Rachel, were making gingerbread cookies.

Rachel made glasses for her cookie out of frosting. She also turned her cookie into a gingerbread woman by creating an elaborate frosting dress.

"What are you doing?" Jamie cried. "You're ruining it!"

"No, I'm not," Rachel answered. "I'm just making it different."

"But they're all supposed to be the same!" Jamie insisted.

"Says who? Are all the kids at your school the same?"

Rachel had a good point, didn't she? Not all kids are alike, even if they look alike on the outside.

Sometimes we're uncomfortable around people who aren't the same as we are. It can be hard to get to know people, especially if we don't understand their background or customs. Once we get to know them, though, their differences might be what we like the best.

Read from God's Word

Then God said, "Let us make man in our image, after our likeness. And let them have dominion over the fish of the sea and over the birds of the heavens and over the livestock and over all the earth and over every creeping thing that creeps on the earth." So God created man in His own image, in the image of God He created him; male and female He created them. Genesis 1:26–27

As Christians we have something in common. God created all people in His own image. His Spirit lives in us. God loves all His children, no matter what country they come from or if they have a handicap or whether they are rich or poor. Jesus Christ paid the price for the sins of all people around the world. He helps us to love Him and each other.

_____Let's talk: Think about some of your friends. In what ways are you different? In what ways are you alike?

_____Let's pray: Dear Father, thank You for making so many different kinds of people. Let Your Spirit shine through me today and touch someone who may not know You. I pray this in Jesus' name. Amen.

J. L. A.

God's Directions

Read from God's Word

You make known to me the path of life; in Your presence there is fullness of joy; At Your right hand are pleasures forevermore. Psalm 16:11

Joel's family was moving from Pennsylvania to California. At first, Joel wasn't 100 percent sure that he wanted to move. But the more his family talked about it and planned, the more excited he became.

Joel's family had prayed that God would show them what city to move to, when to move, even what route to take to California. After the prayers they made lists, looked at maps, and planned everything for their big mission.

Jesus came to earth for a big mission. He needed to die for the sins of all people and rise again in victory over the devil. He was true God, but He was also true man. He knew what pain and humiliation He would experience. So He prayed to ask God if there was any way out of the situation. Of course, God the Father knew best. Jesus was the sacrificial Lamb, and He followed the course God set out for Him.

Sometimes you may face things you don't want to do. It's okay to ask God for another way. Sometimes He may show you another way. Other times you will know you have to follow the path God has put in front of you. Take comfort in knowing that God is at your side. With His help you will never get lost!

_____Let's talk: Have you ever gotten lost? How did it make you feel? How did you feel when you'd found your way again?

_____Let's pray: Dear heavenly Father, I'm so glad You have a plan for my life. Help me to follow You. In Jesus' name I pray. Amen.

J. L. A.

Not Too Young for God

Read from God's Word

Then children were brought to Him that He might lay His hands on them and pray. The disciples rebuked the people, but Jesus said, "Let the little children come to Me and do not hinder them, for to such belongs the kingdom of heaven." And He laid His hands on them and went away. Matthew 19:13–15

"You're too young." Has anyone ever said something like that to you? Sometimes it can be discouraging. You might even think that because you're a kid, you're not very important. But did you know that God worked through young people to do some of the greatest things in the Bible?

When Samuel was a boy, God spoke to him and used him to teach all of Israel. David was very young when he fought Goliath with a slingshot and a stone and, through the Lord's might, won. Mary was probably a teenager when the angel Gabriel told her she would give birth to a Son who would be the Savior of the whole world.

In the Bible reading for today, some parents brought their children to Jesus so He could bless them. The disciples thought Jesus had more important things to do, so they told them to go away. But Jesus stopped them. He told the disciples just how important the children were and He blessed them all.

Jesus won victory over death for people of all ages who believe in Him, not just adults. The next time you feel you're too young for God to work through you, think of how much God loves you and how He has had a plan for your salvation since before you were born!

_____Let's talk: In what ways has God worked through you in the past? Think of some ways He can work through you today.

_____Let's pray: Dear Father, thank You for loving me before I was born. Help me to share Your love with others. In Jesus' name. Amen.

J. L. A.

Read from God's Word

The next day the large crowd that had come to the feast heard that Jesus was coming to Jerusalem. So they took branches of palm trees and went out to meet Him, crying out, "Hosanna! Blessed is He who comes in the name of the Lord, even the King of Israel!" And Jesus found a young donkey and sat on it, just as it is written, "Fear not, daughter of Zion; behold, your King is coming, sitting on a donkey's colt!" John 12:12–15

Ordinary or Special?

Sebastian and Angela spent a day at the zoo. Big cats prowled, giraffes stretched, and bright jungle birds squawked. Angela liked the farm animals inside the zoo, especially the donkeys.

"I like the donkeys the best," Angela told her brother.

Sebastian was surprised. "You gotta be kidding!" he said. "Out of all these beautiful, smart, and interesting animals, you pick *donkeys?*"

Donkeys usually aren't thought of as beautiful or smart. They don't have colorful coats and they don't do tricks. There's nothing very special about them.

But when Jesus, King of the world, rode into Jerusalem on Palm Sunday, He didn't choose a magnificent horse to ride. In John 12:15 we read what Jesus did choose. "Behold, your King is coming, sitting on a donkey's colt!" This was a triumphant ride into Jerusalem. Jesus was coming to die for the sins of all people.

Do you sometimes feel like the donkey—not too special? Do you feel like other kids are more spectacular? No matter how spectacular you think you are—or aren't—the most important thing is to know that even before you were born God loved you. You are so important to Jesus that He died for you! He wants you to live with Him forever. That's not ordinary—that's extraordinary!

_____Let's talk: You are special to God. How does He show that to you?

_____Let's pray: Thank You, Jesus, for loving me so much You died to save me from my sins. I pray in Your name. Amen.

J. D.

Transformed

It was a cool, sunny morning, and Marie was walking through the school parking lot. She saw something shining. It certainly did sparkle! The sun was bouncing off it and sending brilliant rays in every direction.

Maybe it was a diamond wedding ring and one of the teachers had lost it. She could take it to the office and become a hero for finding such a sentimental piece of jewelry. Or maybe there would be a reward. She started thinking of all the things she could buy with the reward money.

Finally, she got close enough to see that it was a leaf—just a plain, yellowish-brown dried-up leaf! Rainwater had collected in the leaf and was reflecting rays of sunlight in different directions. Marie was amazed. Two things in God's creation had been turned into something beautiful by the light of the sun shining on it.

You know, we are a lot like that leaf. On our own we are ordinary. Sin keeps us lifeless. But when the light of God's love shines on us, especially through the waters of Holy Baptism and through the Bible, we are transformed. Jesus paid the price to deliver us from the darkness of sin. His precious blood changes us into new beings. We reflect His image as we bask in His love.

Read from God's Word

Therefore, if anyone is in Christ, he is a new creation. The old has passed away; behold, the new has come. 2 Corinthians 5:17

_____Let's talk: How has God's love transformed you?

_____Let's pray: Dear God, thank You so much for Your love. Please help me be a reflection of You today. For Jesus' sake. Amen.

J. L. A.

A Special Family

Families are different. There are two-parent families and single-parent families. There are blended families and families with adopted children. Some families may include grandparents. All of these families are alike in lots of ways.

Being part of a family carries certain responsibilities. Every member needs to do his or her share of work. They should respect each other and get along together.

There are also privileges that families share. They encourage each other, cooperate on tasks, and love each other in spite of differences. Families stick together when things go bad.

God tells us that we also belong to a second family. It is called the family of faith. God the Father is the Head. Jesus is our perfect Brother, and all of those who believe in Jesus as the Savior are brothers and sisters.

Being in God's family has responsibilities and privileges too. We are responsible to God for our behavior. When we sin, we are accountable. One of the greatest privileges is receiving the full forgiveness of sin for Jesus' sake. Many other spiritual blessings touch our lives as well, as the Holy Spirit enables us to receive and enjoy them.

So we look forward to life together in the family of faith and the family reunion on the Last Day.

_____Let's talk: What is special about your family?

_____Let's pray: Dear God, thank You for putting me in my family. Help me to be a caring member. In Your Son's holy name I pray. Amen.

J. D.

Watch and Pray

Have you ever done something familiar that seemed different? Maybe that's how the disciples felt on that last Thursday night they spent with Jesus before He died.

Before supper Jesus washed their feet. Servants were supposed to do that! But Jesus said they were to serve one another. During the meal Jesus took the bread and the wine and said, "This is My body, which is given for you. ... This cup [wine] that is poured out for you is the new covenant in My blood" (Luke 22:19–20). The disciples didn't quite understand what Jesus was saying. Now we understand that through this meal—which we call the Lord's Supper—Jesus brings forgiveness and strengthens our faith.

After supper they all went to Gethsemane. The disciples could tell that Jesus was suffering as He prayed. They were so upset and exhausted they fell asleep. Jesus woke the disciples and told them to "pray that you may not enter into temptation."

Jesus tells us to "watch and pray" too (Matthew 26:41). We have many things that tempt us to not follow Jesus. We can't overcome the temptations by ourselves. God hears our prayers and helps us. God does this out of love—the same love that sent Jesus to the cross to die for our sins. In Him we have forgiveness and strength.

Read from God's Word

And He came out and went, as was His custom, to the Mount of Olives, and the disciples followed Him. And when He came to the place, He said to them, "Pray that you may not enter into temptation." And He withdrew from them about a stone's throw, and knelt down and prayed, saying, "Father, if You are willing, remove this cup from Me. Nevertheless, not My will, but Yours, be done." And there appeared to Him an angel from heaven, strengthening Him. And being in an agony He prayed more earnestly; and His sweat became like great drops of blood falling down to the ground. And when He rose from prayer, He came to the disciples and found them sleeping for sorrow, and He said to them, "Why are you sleeping? Rise and pray that you may not enter into temptation."
Luke 22:39–46 ᔆ

_____Let's do: What tempts you? Watch and pray for God's help.

_____Let's pray: Dear Jesus, thank You for all You suffered for me. Help me to watch and pray. In Your name I pray. Amen.

J. D.

The Wondrous Cross

Read from God's Word

After this, Jesus, knowing that all was now finished, said (to fulfill the Scripture), "I thirst." A jar full of sour wine stood there, so they put a sponge full of the sour wine on a hyssop branch and held it to His mouth. When Jesus had received the sour wine, He said, "It is finished," and He bowed His head and gave up His spirit. John 19:28–30 ∽

When Jesus lived on earth, the cross was a place of terrible punishment for the very worst criminals. No one would ever have worn a cross as jewelry or displayed it. It was horrendous to be nailed to a cross and hang there until death. Jesus did this for you and me! Jesus never sinned, so He didn't die because of something He had done. Jesus did it out of love to free us from all of our sins.

The hymn "When I Survey the Wondrous Cross" was written by Isaac Watts. In this hymn Watts pictured himself at the foot of the cross.

At first, people who heard this hymn were angry. They thought it was wrong of Isaac Watts to write in this way. The hymn was criticized as too personal. But Jesus' death *is* personal. He died for each of us—you and me. The hymn survived and is still sung in many churches, especially on Good Friday.

Today the cross has become something beautiful for Christians. Crosses are found in our churches and homes. We may wear a cross around our neck. The cross changed from a horrible thing to a good thing because of Jesus. Now we think of Jesus' love and forgiveness when we see a cross.

_____Let's talk: What do you think of when you see a cross? How can you use a cross to tell others about Jesus?

_____Let's pray: When I survey the wondrous cross On which the Prince of Glory died, My richest gain I count but loss And pour contempt on all my pride. (*LW* 114)

J. D.

The Peep and Tweet Chorus

D o you ever wake up just when it's getting light and hear the "peep and tweet" chorus of birds outside your window?

Some people think the birds are praising God and thanking Him for His care. Next time you hear the bird songs, you can think of Psalm 65:8: "You make the going out of the morning and the evening to shout for joy."

In Matthew 6:25–27 Jesus tells us not to worry about food and clothing. God reminds us that since He takes such good care of the birds, He will take care of us. We are much more valuable than they are. God *does* take care of all our bodily needs all the time. He also takes care of our spiritual needs, especially the greatest need we have: forgiveness of sins and eternal life. Jesus gave those to us when He died for our sins.

When we think about all the things God gives and does for us, we want to praise Him. You don't need to join the "peep and tweet" chorus. It might be hard to perch on a branch and sing at the same time! You can praise God by all you do and say every day.

Read from God's Word

By awesome deeds You answer us with righteousness, O God of our salvation, the hope of all the ends of the earth and of the farthest seas; the one who by His strength established the mountains, being girded with might; who stills the roaring of the seas, the roaring of their waves, the tumult of the peoples, so that those who dwell at the ends of the earth are in awe at Your signs. You make the going out of the morning and the evening to shout for joy. Psalm 65:5–8

_____Let's talk: Think of all the things God does for you. What are some ways you like to thank and praise Him?

_____Let's pray: Praise God, from whom all blessings flow; Praise Him, all creatures here below; Praise Him above, O heavenly host; Praise Father, Son, and Holy Ghost. (*LW* 461)

J. D.

He's Not Here!

Read from God's Word

But on the first day of the week, at early dawn, they went to the tomb, taking the spices they had prepared. And they found the stone rolled away from the tomb, but when they went in they did not find the body of the Lord Jesus. While they were perplexed about this, behold, two men stood by them in dazzling apparel. And as they were frightened and bowed their faces to the ground, the men said to them, "Why do you seek the living among the dead? He is not here, but has risen. Remember how He told you, while He was still in Galilee, that the Son of Man must be delivered into the hands of sinful men and be crucified and on the third day rise." And they remembered His words. Luke 24:1–8

"Hello," Makayla said as she answered the phone.

"Can I speak to Lucas? It's really important. I need to talk to him right now!"

"Sorry, Evan, he's not here," Makayla responded.

Makayla knew Evan was upset with her. But she could do nothing except tell Lucas that Evan had called.

The women on that first Easter morning didn't call ahead. They knew Jesus was dead. They saw His friends place Him in the tomb. The women were coming to add spices to the burial cloths. It was their way of showing love and saying a final good-bye.

Boy, were they in for a surprise! Instead of Jesus' body, the women found two angels. The angels had a message for them, "He is not here, but has risen." (Luke 24:6).

What a wonderful message for the women and for us! Jesus died for the sins of all people. He suffered punishment from God for sin—in our place. But He didn't stay dead. Jesus rose on the third day—just as He said He would. We will die someday, but we will not stay dead. We will be resurrected, just as Jesus was. Then we will live forever with the risen Lord.

He is not here. He has risen! Alleluia! Alleluia! Alleluia!

_____Let's do: Read on in Luke 24. Write a brief summary of what happened when the women told the news to the Eleven and others in verses 9–12.

_____Let's pray: I know that my Redeemer lives! What comfort this sweet sentence gives! He lives, He lives, who once was dead; He lives, my ever-living head! (*LW* 264)

J. D.

Thirsty Again?

M any churches provide food and a place to sleep for homeless people. Often, members of these churches give food to them.

When Matthew visited his grandmother, he went with her to deliver the food and juice she was giving. Matthew asked why she did this. Grandma explained that some people were hungry and thirsty.

The next month, his grandma again set aside food to donate. When Matthew visited, he said, "Oh, no, don't tell me they're thirsty again!"

Matthew didn't understand that we are to help the needy all the time. Jesus loves us and helps us all the time. We show Jesus' love in our lives by loving others and helping them. In Matthew 25:40 Jesus says, "As you did it to one of the least of these [people] My brothers, you did it to Me."

Look at Matthew 25:35–36 to discover some of the ways we can help others. Put the words in the blanks below:

Read from God's Word

"Then the righteous will answer Him, saying, 'Lord, when did we see You hungry and feed You, or thirsty and give You drink? And when did we see You a stranger and welcome You, or naked and clothe You? And when did we see You sick or in prison and visit You?' And the King will answer them, 'Truly, I say to you, as you did it to one of the least of these My brothers, you did it to Me.'"
Matthew 25:37–40 ✍

I was _____ and you gave Me _____.

I was _____ and you gave Me _____.

I was a _____ and you _____ Me.

I was _____ and you _____ Me.

I was _____ and you _____ Me.

I was in _____ and you _____ Me.

Yes, Matthew, they are thirsty again. By His grace Jesus loves us and helps us help them.

_____Let's do: Think of someone who needs help. How can you help him or her?

_____Let's pray: Dear God, let me show Your love by helping those in need. In Jesus' name. Amen.

J. D.

Real Friends

Jasmine was walking home from school when Katie, one of the most popular girls in class, joined her. "Hey, Jas. Want to stop at my house and see something cool?" she asked.

Jasmine was amazed and flattered that Katie was talking to her.

Katie said, "My older brother rented this really neat video—*The Deadly Beast Man.*"

Jasmine thought about Katie's suggestion. "No. Mom doesn't allow me to see that kind of video."

"Oh, come on," urged Katie. "Your mom will never know. Don't you want to be my friend?"

Slowly and regretfully Jasmine shook her head no. "Real friends don't ask you to do things that are wrong," she said.

We all want to fit in. Sometimes friends tempt us to do something wrong. That's why we need to choose our friends wisely. Real friends will help us do what's right.

Jesus talked to His disciples, and to us, about friendship. He encourages us to remain faithful because He is our friend. Jesus tells us, "Love one another as I have loved you. Greater love has no one than this, that someone lays down his life for his friends" (John 15:12–13). Jesus died so we can have forgiveness and eternal life. He will help us when others tempt us to sin. Jesus is a real friend.

_____Let's talk: Which of your friends encourage you to do the right thing? How can you be a "real" friend to someone?

_____Let's pray: Jesus, thank You for being my friend. Please help me be strong when I am tempted to sin. Help me encourage my friends to do the right thing. In Your name I pray. Amen.

J. A. D.

Give Thanks!

onji was obviously upset as she helped her mom with dinner. Before the meal Mom prayed, "Give thanks to the LORD, for He is good, for His steadfast love endures forever" (Psalm 136:1). Sonji just mumbled along.

Sonji sighed and said, "I don't feel thankful. This has been the most rotten day ever! I flunked my math test, I struck out in softball at recess, and Rhonda's mad at me."

Mrs. Woo put her arm around Sonji. "You really did have a bad day. But, you know, God still loves you and cares about you."

Martin Rinckart was a German pastor who lived in the early 1600s. During the Thirty Years' War many people died, including other pastors. In one year he led burial services for 4,480 people!

During this terrible time Pastor Rinckart wrote a hymn. You might think it was a sad hymn, but it wasn't. He wrote "Now Thank We All Our God" to remind us that even in the middle of all the suffering, people could remember how good God is.

Nothing can take God's love from us. God loves us enough to take care of us no matter how terrible things might be. He loved us so much that He sent Jesus to die for our sins. Thanks, God!

Read from God's Word

Oh give thanks to the LORD, for He is good; for His steadfast love endures forever! Let Israel say, "His steadfast love endures forever." Let the house of Aaron say, "His steadfast love endures forever." Let those who fear the LORD say, "His steadfast love endures forever." Out of my distress I called on the LORD; the LORD answered me and set me free. The LORD is on my side; I will not fear. What can man do to me? The LORD is on my side as my helper; I shall look in triumph on those who hate me. Psalm 118:1–7

_____Let's talk: Read Romans 8:35, 37. How was it possible for St. Paul and Martin Rinckart to be thankful in the middle of troubles?

_____Let's pray: Now thank we all our God With hearts and hands and voices, Who wondrous things has done, In whom His world rejoices; Who from our mothers' arms Has blest us on our way With countless gifts of love And still is ours today. (*LW* 443)

J. A. D.

Read from God's Word

Trust in the LORD with all your heart, and do not lean on your own understanding. In all your ways acknowledge Him, and He will make straight your paths. Be not wise in your own eyes; fear the LORD, and turn away from evil. It will be healing to your flesh and refreshment to your bones. Proverbs 3:5–8

God Guides Our Choices

A television game show once gave away shopping sprees. The contestants answered questions for points, and the winner got five minutes to shop. Everything in the cart would be free.

Any item could be chosen and put into the basket. At the end of the shopping spree the prices were totaled at the checkout stand. It was usually hundreds of dollars! At the end of the show the smiling winners were always displayed with the food and cash they had won.

We may not win a chance to choose free food from a grocery store. But we do make choices every day. Sometimes they are little decisions, like which cereal to eat for breakfast. At other times more difficult choices must be made: how to tell a friend that we're sorry or what to do when someone hurts our feelings.

God knows we have decisions to make, and He wants to help. He hears our prayers. His love is so great that He sent Jesus to be our Savior. Because of this we can "trust in the LORD with all [our] heart." We can trust Him to help in the choices we need to make. After all, He chose us in Jesus to be His own.

_____Let's talk: What are some difficult decisions you have made? How did God guide you?

_____Let's pray: Lord God, You chose us to be Your children. How thankful we are! Help us call on You each day. In Jesus' name. Amen.

J. G.

A Name to Remember

Jesse burst in through the kitchen door after school. "Mom, guess what? My name means 'chosen by God.'"

"I know, Jesse. Your dad and I picked it out before you were born. We spent many evenings trying to decide just the right name for you. By the way, since your name means 'chosen by God,' do you know what God's name means?"

"No, I didn't know it had a meaning."

"Oh, yes, a very special meaning. His name means 'I am.'"

"That sounds like a funny name to me, Mom."

"It may seem like a funny name until you know what it means for us. If God were only with us yesterday or tomorrow, He might be called 'I was' or 'I will be.' But He is always with us, so His name is 'I am.'"

"I think I get it. Anytime I want to talk with Him, I know He's there to listen."

"That's right. Even when we forget to talk with Him, He still watches over us. God loves us and wants the best for us. That's why He sent Jesus to take away our sins. Now we can go directly to God in prayer. He really does have a name to remember."

Read from God's Word

But Moses said to God, "Who am I that I should go to Pharaoh and bring the children of Israel out of Egypt?" He said, "But I will be with you, and this shall be the sign for you, that I have sent you: when you have brought the people out of Egypt, you shall serve God on this mountain." Then Moses said to God, "If I come to the people of Israel and say to them, 'The God of your fathers has sent me to you,' and they ask me, 'What is His name?' what shall I say to them?" God said to Moses, "I AM WHO I AM." And He said, "Say this to the people of Israel, 'I AM has sent me to you.'" Exodus 3:11–14

_____Let's talk: What help did God give Moses to overcome his fear of leading in Exodus 3:5–8? How does He do the same thing for you?

_____Let's pray: Dear God, thank You for letting us know by Your name that You are with us. Keep our faith strong and help us grow in wisdom by putting You first. In Jesus' name we pray. Amen.

J. G.

Jesus, the Bread of Life

Read from God's Word

Jesus then said to them, "Truly, truly, I say to you, it was not Moses who gave you the bread from heaven, but My Father gives you the true bread from heaven. For the bread of God is He who comes down from heaven and gives life to the world." They said to Him, "Sir, give us this bread always." Jesus said to them, "I am the Bread of life; whoever comes to Me shall not hunger, and whoever believes in Me shall never thirst. ... I am the living bread that came down from heaven. If anyone eats of this bread, he will live forever. And the bread that I will give for the life of the world is My flesh." John 6:32–35, 51

Fresh bread is an important part of every meal in France so people buy it every day. With such a daily demand there are many bakeries. Boys and girls often help their parents by running to the bakery to buy bread for breakfast.

Getting the daily bread could be a big problem, all because of another French tradition—long summer vacations. Even bakeries close for a whole month while the owners go on vacation. Imagine being hungry for some bread, only to find out that your favorite bakery is closed for a month. It may take a lot of searching before you find another bakery that is open.

Praise God that our "bread of life," Jesus Christ, doesn't go on vacation. He is always available to us by the power of the Holy Spirit. Through His Word our hungry souls are fed.

Unfortunately, we sometimes go on vacation from Jesus when we neglect His Word or stop going to church. It is good to know that He never gives up on us! He is always ready to feed us with His Word, to forgive all our sins, and to guide us on the way to heaven.

_____Let's talk: Why is bread important to you? Why is Jesus important to you? Why do we say Jesus is the bread of life?

_____Let's pray: Lord Jesus, when we go "on vacation" from listening to Your Word, please forgive us. Send Your Holy Spirit to guide us back to You, the true bread of life. In Your name we pray. Amen.

J. D.

Fearfully and Wonderfully

Have you ever been to a carnival or a fair where they have a house of mirrors? When you walk inside, you see yourself reflected and distorted in lots of shaped mirrors. It can be very funny, especially when you make a face in the mirrors.

Sometimes we have a distorted view of ourselves, even without those strange mirrors. Perhaps someone has made fun of our nose or ears, or of how tall or short we are. We begin to think that we're ugly. Those lies sound like the truth to us.

Then we need to hear the real truth. In Psalm 139:14 David said, "I praise You [God], for I am fearfully and wonderfully made. Wonderful are Your works; my soul knows it very well."

Because you and I were made by our heavenly Father, we, too, are "wonderfully made." Remember that God doesn't make mistakes. He loves us the way we are. He wants us to love ourselves and to love one another.

Read from God's Word

I praise You, for I am fearfully and wonderfully made. Wonderful are Your works; my soul knows it very well. My frame was not hidden from You, when I was being made in secret, intricately woven in the depths of the earth. Your eyes saw my unformed substance; in Your book were written, every one of them, the days that were formed for me, when as yet there were none of them. How precious to me are Your thoughts, O God! How vast is the sum of them! If I would count them, they are more than the sand. I awake, and I am still with You.
Psalm 139:14–18

God cared enough to send His only Son to die for us on the cross so one day we can live forever with Him. Do you know that if you were the last person on earth, Jesus would still want you as His own? That makes you a very wonderful person, doesn't it?

_____Let's talk: What are three things you like about yourself?
How can you give God the credit for these blessings?

_____Let's pray: Heavenly Father, when I start to believe the lies that say I'm a piece of junk, remind me that everything You make is wonderful, including me. Thank You for loving me so much and sending Your Son to die for me! In Jesus' name. Amen.

J. D.

Where's the Evidence?

Read from God's Word

Do not be unequally yoked with unbelievers. For what partnership has righteousness with lawlessness? Or what fellowship has light with darkness? What accord has Christ with Belial? Or what portion does a believer share with an unbeliever? What agreement has the temple of God with idols? For we are the temple of the living God; as God said, "I will make My dwelling among them and walk among them, and I will be their God, and they shall be My people. Therefore go out from their midst, and be separate from them, says the Lord, and touch no unclean thing; then I will welcome you, and I will be a father to you, and you shall be sons and daughters to Me, says the Lord Almighty."

2 Corinthians 6:14–18

Imagine you are on trial for being a Christian. Would your accusers be able to prove you are guilty of being a Christian? Or would they look at the way you talk back to your parents and the way you treat your little brother and realize they have no case?

Thankfully it is not a crime to be a Christian. And, in truth, our lives will at times contradict our Christianity because of our sinful nature. Do we show love to the people we meet? Do we honor Jesus by the movies we watch and the magazines we read? Does our love for Jesus show in the language we use?

If we are truly honest with ourselves and with our Lord, we know that many times there isn't much evidence of Christian faith in our lives. But we are led to confess our sins to the Lord, and He forgives us. God helps us to act in ways that show His power at work inside us.

Christ gave Himself to redeem us (buy us back) from all impurity and to make us eager to do what is good. By God's grace we are free in our daily lives to serve one another.

_____Let's talk: What are some ways you can reflect God's love?

_____Let's pray: Lord Jesus, we confess that we are sinners in need of Your forgiveness. Help us live lives that show we truly love You. In Your name we pray. Amen.

J. D.

A Clean Piece of Paper

Read from God's Word

But this I call to mind, and therefore I have hope: The steadfast love of the LORD never ceases; His mercies never come to an end; they are new every morning; great is Your faithfulness. "The LORD is my portion," says my soul, "therefore I will hope in Him." Lamentations 3:21–24 ✍

When Jeanne was in elementary school, she felt very important being allowed to use a fountain pen (a special pen with a point that is fed from a reservoir filled with ink). Sometimes her fountain pen would leak, and her paper would be a mess. Then Jeanne would have to ask her teacher for another piece of paper. He might say yes, but sometimes he said no because she had already asked too often or he had run out of nice paper.

Jesus is more consistent than that. Every day we get a "clean piece of paper" that has no marks on it. And every day we sin. Sin makes marks on the clean sheet.

Every night, when it's time for bed, we know that the paper of our life is stained and blotted with the ink of sin. Our life gets messed up by our actions and by our sinful nature. Yet Jesus forgives us. He never gives up or runs out of patience. His love and mercy never end. Jesus does not run out of forgiveness either. He is always ready to forgive and to give us another chance.

That's Good News for anyone who is plagued by sin—for all of us. It gives us a reason to praise our Savior every day.

_____Let's talk: What is a good prayer to say each night when you go to sleep?

_____Let's pray: Lord Jesus, help us confess our sins and turn to You for forgiveness. We pray in Your name. Amen.

J. D.

Ambassadors for Christ

Read from God's Word

All this is from God, who through Christ reconciled us to Himself and gave us the ministry of reconciliation; that is, in Christ God was reconciling the world to Himself, not counting their trespasses against them, and entrusting to us the message of reconciliation. Therefore, we are ambassadors for Christ, God making His appeal through us. We implore you on behalf of Christ, be reconciled to God. For our sake He made Him to be sin who knew no sin, so that in Him we might become the righteousness of God.
2 Corinthians 5:18–21 ↶

What is an ambassador? Ambassadors are people chosen to represent their home government before the government of a foreign country.

Being an ambassador is hard work. People are always watching you and listening to you. Everything you do may be taken as the official action of your country. If you say or do something mean, your host country may believe that your country is mean—and all your fellow citizens too.

Every Christian is an ambassador, but you do not work for a government. Those who love Jesus are His messengers. We represent Jesus and His message of love and forgiveness to all the people around us. That's what Paul says in our Bible reading: "Therefore, we are ambassadors for Christ, God making His appeal through us. We implore you on behalf of Christ, be reconciled to God. For our sake He made Him to be sin who knew no sin, so that in Him we might become the righteousness of God."

As Jesus' ambassadors we need to be sure His message of love and forgiveness comes through loud and clear. This is not an easy thing to do. Many times we fail, or we think we fail. But every day Jesus forgives us. He sends the Holy Spirit to help us be His faithful ambassadors.

_____Let's talk: To whom can you be Jesus' ambassador? What is the first message you could deliver?

_____Let's pray: Lord Jesus, help me to be a faithful ambassador. Forgive me when I fail. In Your name. Amen.

J. D.

may

Contributors for this month:

LaVerne Almstedt

Eunice L. Graham

Ed Grube

Mary Jane Gruett

Beverly J. Soyk

Read from God's Word

"Be strong and courageous. Do not fear or be in dread of them, for it is the LORD your God who goes with you. He will not leave you or forsake you." Then Moses summoned Joshua and said to him in the sight of all Israel, "Be strong and courageous, for you shall go with this people into the land that the LORD has sworn to their fathers to give them, and you shall put them in possession of it. It is the LORD who goes before you. He will be with you; He will not leave you or forsake you. Do not fear or be dismayed."
Deuteronomy 31:6–8 ✒

The Toughest Foe

Marcy had planned to graduate college, play professional basketball in Europe for a year, and then teach math in high school.

All these plans changed when Marcy found out she had Hodgkin's disease, a type of cancer. On the court she had faced many opponents and won, but this was her toughest opponent yet.

Instead of going to Europe, Marcy went to the hospital for radiation treatments. They helped. There are no traces of the cancer. This opponent has been defeated—for now.

What is your toughest foe? Is it living in peace with your brother or sister? putting up with the bully at school? trying to find peace in a family that seems to be breaking apart? telling your friend about Jesus?

Joshua could have been overwhelmed with fear. He was taking over leadership of the unruly Israelites. They wouldn't obey Moses; why would they obey him? He had an enormous task: to drive out the Canaanites so Israel could take over their land. There were many walled cities and strong enemies to conquer.

But God promised Joshua, "The LORD your God ... goes with you." We have that promise too, no matter how tough our foes. Through faith, given by the Holy Spirit, Jesus lives in us, forgives our sins, and strengthens us to face every foe.

_____Let's do: Where does God give help to face our toughest foes?

_____Let's pray: Dear Father, give us Your courage and strength to face every foe. Help us remember that You will be with us. In Jesus' name. Amen.

M. J. G.

Giant Steps

Jason, age 11, has cerebral palsy, and the doctors said he would never walk or talk. Now he is doing math and writing letters, all through much hard work. Recently he was honored by his special school with a "Giant Step" award.

Steve, who attends high school, is helping others by tutoring students with drug problems. He has trouble hearing and talking, but he can show love to others. That's surely a giant step!

Our Bible reading tells us we are to love one another. The love we show may not receive an award. But by simple, kind acts we can support other people and show that the Lord lives in our hearts.

Love means visiting Grandma in a nursing home even if she doesn't know who we are. Love means inviting friends to church and helping them during the service. Love means offering to help mow the lawn—for nothing. These are giant steps of kindness.

We can share ourselves with others because God loves us so much. He sent Jesus to take away our sins of being unloving and unlovable. We look to the cross and are filled with joy because of what our Savior did for us. Having experienced His mercy and forgiveness, we turn to others to see how we can pass on our joy to them.

Read from God's Word

Beloved, let us love one another, for love is from God, and whoever loves has been born of God and knows God. Anyone who does not love does not know God, because God is love. In this the love of God was made manifest among us, that God sent His only Son into the world, so that we might live through Him. In this is love, not that we have loved God but that He loved us and sent His Son to be the propitiation for our sins. Beloved, if God so loved us, we also ought to love one another. No one has ever seen God; if we love one another, God abides in us and His love is perfected in us. 1 John 4:7–12

_____Let's talk: Look at the Bible reading again. Who loves? Who does not love? How does God show His love for us?

_____Let's pray: Dear Father, help me to be more loving. Thank You for loving me even when I fail to love others. In Jesus' name. Amen.

L. A.

Read from God's Word

When Joseph's brothers saw that their father was dead, they said, "It may be that Joseph will hate us and pay us back for all the evil that we did to him." ... But Joseph said to them, "Do not fear, for am I in the place of God? As for you, you meant evil against me, but God meant it for good, to bring it about that many people should be kept alive, as they are today. So do not fear; I will provide for you and your little ones." Thus he comforted them and spoke kindly to them. Genesis 50:15–21

God Has a Plan

A family of Dutch immigrants was about to board a steamship in 1847. Winter was coming. The last steamer of the season was leaving that day. Suddenly they realized the bag containing the family Bible was missing. They decided to search for it.

When they returned to the wharf, the steamship had sailed. They were stranded—friendless, penniless, and homeless. Perhaps the family felt that God had abandoned them. The father was able to find work, however, and they planned to go west in spring.

About a month later, they heard the steamship had burned and sunk in Lake Michigan. Most of the passengers and crew died in the fire or drowned in icy waters.

Sometimes we may feel abandoned by God. We have plans for our future, but everything is going wrong. We wonder, "Where is God?"

Joseph may have wondered the same thing. He had no plans for slavery, false accusations, and prison in a foreign country. But God had a plan, as He always does. Joseph was to rescue his family from the coming famine.

God may be taking you through some hard times right now. As in Joseph's life, God can take the bad and use it for good. Through the faith the Spirit gives, you can be sure He has a plan for you too.

———Let's talk: Read Genesis 50:15–21 in your Bible. How was Joseph able to put up with all the troubles he had to endure? What is your source of strength when troubles come?

———Let's pray: Father, make us strong for the troubles we face. Help us find strength in You. In Jesus' name. Amen.

M. J. G.

Tricks and Traps

Read from God's Word

"Behold, I establish My covenant with you and your offspring after you, ... that never again shall all flesh be cut off by the waters of the flood, and never again shall there be a flood to destroy the earth." And God said, "This is the sign of the covenant that I make between Me and you and every living creature that is with you, for all future generations: I have set My bow in the cloud, and it shall be a sign of the covenant between Me and the earth. When I bring clouds over the earth and the bow is seen in the clouds, I will remember My covenant that is between Me and you and every living creature of all flesh. And the waters shall never again become a flood to destroy all flesh. Genesis 9:8–15 ↩

anny, get into the house before the serpent takes you away!" The grandmother who shouted this warning had just seen a rainbow in the sky. She is a member of a group who haven't heard the Gospel. These people fear the rainbow and call it a serpent.

Who could trick someone into believing the rainbow is evil? The devil can. He is a master at turning God's creation into something evil or something to be feared.

Paul tells us in 2 Corinthians 11:14 that the devil can change himself to look like an angel of light. The devil can twist things so wrong looks right, evil seems good, and a rainbow becomes something frightening for people who don't know God and His Word.

Would we ever fall into the devil's traps? One of his tricks is to suggest that God's commandments are old-fashioned. He'd like us to believe those rules were for believers long ago, but not for us. He'd like us to believe that we do not sin or need Jesus.

How can we escape the traps of the devil? God gives us help in His Word and Sacraments. Our faith is in Jesus Christ, who died, rose again, and lives in our hearts.

_____Let's talk: Look up 1 Peter 5:8–9. What help has God given you to resist the devil?

_____Let's pray: Dear Father, thanks for sending Jesus to forgive our sins and strengthen us. Help us listen to Your Word. In Jesus' name we pray. Amen.

M. J. G.

It's Not Fair!

Read from God's Word

The LORD has heard my plea; the LORD accepts my prayer. All my enemies shall be ashamed and greatly troubled; they shall turn back and be put to shame in a moment. Psalm 6:9–10 ✍

I don't want Sukie to go shopping with us," Monique whispered to Jo Beth. The two girls went shopping without Sukie.

"How can my friends do this to me?" Sukie cried when she found out later. "This isn't fair!" Sukie attended Sunday school regularly, and had invited Monique to come with her. Now Monique had taken away her best friend. "God, I did Your will and look what's happened. I don't think You really care," Sukie complained in her prayers.

Elijah, the prophet, felt like Sukie. He faithfully did God's will. He worked very hard for the Lord. Elijah was rewarded with threats against his life (1 Kings 19:10). He ran away and felt sorry for himself. In the middle of his self-pity, he told God how he felt. As they talked, God straightened things out. Then Elijah was ready to do God's work again.

Sukie felt terrible when her friends betrayed her. Like Elijah, she talked to God and did not hide her feelings.

We can tell God how we feel. He will hear us. He may not take the problem away, but He will help us get through the problem. Just as the Lord heard the psalmist's cry for deliverance (Psalm 6:9), so He answers our prayers.

_____Let's talk: How do you respond when you are treated unfairly? What can you do differently next time?

_____Let's pray: Father, thanks for being there to listen when we think we've been treated unfairly. Lead us to talk to You and trust in You. In Jesus' name. Amen.

M. J. G.

Open My Eyes

Read from God's Word

Blessed are those whose way is blameless, who walk in the law of the LORD! Blessed are those who keep His testimonies, who seek Him with their whole heart, who also do no wrong, but walk in His ways! ... How can a young man keep his way pure? By guarding it according to Your word. With my whole heart I seek you; let me not wander from Your commandments! I have stored up Your word in my heart, that I might not sin against You. ... I will not forget Your word. Deal bountifully with Your servant, that I may live and keep Your word. Open my eyes, that I may behold wondrous things out of Your law. Psalm 119:1–3, 9–18

How many Bibles do you own? There are dozens of translations, sizes, and prices to choose from when we go Bible shopping. That's not how it always has been.

In the early history of America, Bibles were expensive and few in number. Still, most immigrants had God's Word in their hearts, if not in their hands.

The first Bible printed in the United States was a new translation and not in English. In 1663 a pastor named John Eliot worked with the Algonquin Indians in Massachusetts. He wanted them to be able to read the Bible for themselves, so he translated it into their language.

Christians in China are persecuted. Their Bibles are taken away. An older woman's hands were badly beaten by soldiers because she would not give up her only Bible.

The writer of Psalm 119 loved God's Word. He wrote 176 verses to remind us how wonderful it is. God's Word directs and guides us. It shows us how to live life to its fullest. It gives us comfort in times of trouble. But more than that—God's Word shows us salvation through Jesus Christ. It describes all He did to win forgiveness for our sins, and it promises eternal life with God to all who believe. That's Good News!

_____Let's talk: What is your favorite passage from the Bible? How can we show that we love God's Word?

_____Let's pray: Dear God, thank You for Your Word. It shows us how much You love us. In Jesus' name. Amen.

M. J. G.

Read from God's Word

For by works of the law no human being will be justified in His sight, since through the law comes knowledge of sin. But now the righteousness of God has been manifested apart from the law, although the Law and the Prophets bear witness to it —the righteousness of God through faith in Jesus Christ for all who believe. For there is no distinction: for all have sinned and fall short of the glory of God, and are justified by His grace as a gift, through the redemption that is in Christ Jesus. Romans 3:20–24

Rescued!

"Dog Saves Woman's Life" was the newspaper headline. You may have heard of a dog barking to awaken its master when the house is on fire. But this dog, an Irish setter, dialed 911 and saved a life.

The owner slept with an oxygen mask over her face. As she slept, the breathing machine's plug fell out, and oxygen was cut off. She could have died.

But the dog remembered her training. She heard the oxygen alarm and first tried to awaken her mistress. When the woman did not respond, the dog knocked the receiver off a telephone and bumped a button programmed to dial 911. Help arrived in time; her owner's life was saved.

Our rescue by God is even more amazing. Why should a holy God rescue people who had turned their backs on Him? (Romans 3:10–12).

Because of His great mercy, God provided a way for us to be freed from sin's curse. His Son, Jesus, paid the debt we owed for sin. Through Him we are restored to God, made part of His family.

And there's even more to this rescue. Although we sin daily, God freely forgives us. He cares for us (1 Peter 5:7) and promises to never leave us (Hebrews 13:5). That's truly amazing love!

_____Let's talk: What price did Jesus pay to rescue us from sin?
What are some good things about being part of God's family?

_____Let's pray: Thank You, Jesus, for rescuing us from sin.
Be with us always. In Your name we pray. Amen.

M. J. G.

Overflowing Love

Read from God's Word

There is no fear in love, but perfect love casts out fear. For fear has to do with punishment, and whoever fears has not been perfected in love. We love because He first loved us. 1 John 4:18–19

In amazement, Paul watched the bubbles in the sink slowly rise to the top. He had used just a small amount of soap, yet the sink was filled with bubbles. He couldn't even see any water. Turning the water off, Paul swished his hands inside the bubbles. He could feel the water beneath. Blowing gently, he parted the bubbles and exposed the water.

Just a small amount of concentrated soap will produce many bubbles. It works the same with love. Just a small act of kindness can bring many smiles to another's face.

God started it all. He loved us first. In sending His Son to save us, God showed us His great love. We did nothing. He did it all. He loved us, and now we are able to love others. It is God's love in us that others see. His love in us overflows to others.

How does God show His love? He created us. He cares for us. He forgives us. He gave us His own Son as our Savior from sin and death.

When someone has been mean to you, it would be easy to be mean right back. But because God has loved us, He helps us reflect His love in the lives of others. Like bubbles on the water, His love will spread.

_____Let's do: Draw some bubbles. Fill them with words that describe (or pictures that show) ways God can use you to spread His love.

_____Let's pray: Heavenly Father, thank You for loving me. Thank You for Your perfect love that chases away all fears. Fill me with Your love so I can love others. In Jesus' name. Amen.

B. J. S.

Read from God's Word

There is a way that seems right to a man, but its end is the way to death. Proverbs 14:12 ❧

The Surprising End

The spiral staircase wound around the front of the old sanctuary into the unknown. Emily and her sister, Elizabeth, couldn't resist exploring it.

What secrets would they find at the bottom of the forgotten staircase? They began to follow the darkened stairs around and around, down, down, down.

Finally they reached the bottom where they found ... a boarded-up door. There were no exciting secrets— just a dead end. What seemed right was no good in the end.

Have you ever had an experience like this? Did you try to practice the clarinet with new braces? Ouch! Did you cram for 20 minutes before taking a test and end up with a D? Did you try to run three miles at the track meet although you skipped the last week of practice?

Even if we could do everything right, we would still be sinful because we were born sinful. And all that sin leads us to a spiritual dead end.

But God wants to lead us to eternal life with Him now and forever. Jesus, the sinless Son of God, made all the right choices. Then He died for our sin and rose again to give us new life. Now we are free to serve others in every twist and turn in our lives.

_____Let's talk: How does God help us according to Psalm 119:104–106?

_____Let's pray: Dear God, please stay with me and show me the way to go in my life. In Jesus' name. Amen.

E. L. G.

Can I Pray for Me?

Many years ago Laura Ingalls lived with her family in the Dakota Territory. Their little town of De Smet once went through a very long, hard winter. The trains couldn't get through and food began to run out. Finally, two young men set out to find food.

Laura and her sister prayed very hard for the safety of these young men. They worried the men might easily get lost in a blizzard and freeze to death. The girls didn't think they should pray for food because it would be selfish to pray for their own needs.

Laura and her sister were wrong. God wants us to tell Him what we need and want, just as any loving father does. He invites us to thank and praise Him. God promises to listen and to answer us in the best way.

God heard the prayers of Laura and her sister. The young men returned to the town safely, bringing enough food so no one starved to death that winter.

God hears our prayers too. He hears them for Jesus' sake. Jesus suffered more than a harsh winter to rescue us from sin and death through His death and resurrection. He opened the way for us to talk to our heavenly Father about everything and anything—even our own needs.

Read from God's Word

Do not be anxious about anything, but in everything by prayer and supplication with thanksgiving let your requests be made known to God. And the peace of God, which surpasses all understanding, will guard your hearts and your minds in Christ Jesus. Philippians 4:6–7

_____Let's talk: Is there anything on your mind right now that you'd like to pray about? God is ready to listen!

_____Let's pray: Dear God, thank You for hearing all of our prayers. In Jesus' name. Amen.

E. L. G.

Change the Towels

Read from God's Word

I will sprinkle clean water on you, and you shall be clean from all your uncleannesses, and from all your idols I will cleanse you. And I will give you a new heart, and a new spirit I will put within you. And I will remove the heart of stone from your flesh and give you a heart of flesh. And I will put My Spirit within you, and cause you to walk in My statutes and be careful to obey My rules. Ezekiel 36:25–27

Have you ever read about the maid, Amelia Bedelia? She does exactly what she's assigned, whether it makes sense or not! Once she was told to *change* the towels in the bathroom. Most people would put the old towels in the wash and replace them with clean ones. But not Amelia Bedelia! She cut shapes and patterns out of the towels. She *changed* the way the towels looked.

We hope we would never make a mistake quite that bad! But some people make an even more serious mistake when it comes to life with God. They take their hearts, dirty with sin, and try to change them themselves. They think they can make their hearts better if they just follow some of God's rules or try to be kind and loving to people. But our old hearts are sinful no matter what we do.

Only God gives brand new hearts in place of the old ones. He does this through the blessings of Baptism, through the faith we receive as a gift through the Holy Spirit in His Word. God does this for us because Jesus died for the sins of all. His resurrection opened the way to God's love and help. Now all who believe in Jesus have hearts and lives that are changed.

_____Let's do: Write a thank-You note to God in the shape of a heart for the new heart He's given you.

_____Let's pray: Dear Jesus, thank You for giving me a new heart. Amen.

E. L. G.

Safety Zones

Where can you find a safety zone? In a game, it's the place where you can't be tagged, be "it," or be out. In a school, it's all the property. No weapons or drugs are allowed there. Some cultures, such as in Polynesia, had safety zones. People in danger could run to this place and no one could hurt them within the boundaries.

Do *you* need the security of a safety zone? Your day-to-day life is like a game with dangers you can see and dangers you cannot see.

What are some of those dangers? The devil is one. He would love to get us away from God and he uses all kinds of tricks to separate us from God. Another danger is that the world that doesn't know God wants to call us away to other ideas. We sometimes feel a pull to run away from God because we have a sinful nature.

God's safety zone is "the love of God in Christ Jesus our Lord." He promises to keep us in this one true faith through His Spirit. His Word and Sacraments offer us God's peace and hope in the death and resurrection of Jesus. God is always watching over us, for Jesus' sake. We are in His safety zone, here and in heaven.

Read from God's Word

For I am sure that neither death nor life, nor angels nor rulers, nor things present nor things to come, nor powers, nor height nor depth, nor anything else in all creation, will be able to separate us from the love of God in Christ Jesus our Lord. Romans 8:38–39

_____Let's do: Draw a rectangle. Label it "Safety Zone."
Inside list the opportunities God will give
you this week to learn more about Him.

_____Let's pray: Dear heavenly Father, please keep me safe
in Your care always and take me to heaven
to be with Jesus, in whose name I pray. Amen.

E. L. G.

Read from God's Word

Now the tax collectors and sinners were all drawing near to hear Him. And the Pharisees and the scribes grumbled, saying, "This man receives sinners and eats with them." So He told them this parable: "What man of you, having a hundred sheep, if he has lost one of them, does not leave the ninety-nine in the open country, and go after the one that is lost, until he finds it? And when he has found it, he lays it on his shoulders, rejoicing. And when he comes home, he calls together his friends and his neighbors, saying to them, 'Rejoice with me, for I have found my sheep that was lost.' Just so, I tell you, there will be more joy in heaven over one sinner who repents than over ninety-nine righteous persons who need no repentance." Luke 15:1–7

The Corn Maze

Tim and Amanda had come to test their skill in Farmer Will's corn maze. It had been advertised as the most "cornfusing" maze in the state, boasting over 10,000 feet of trails. Helpers, dressed in yellow shirts, kept Tim and Amanda from making early mistakes.

It was fun for the first hour and sort of fun the second hour, but then the comforting noise of other wanderers stopped. Tim noticed that the sun was setting. Amanda panicked because she couldn't find anyone in a yellow shirt. It seemed as if the more they tried to get out of the maze, the more they were going around in circles, getting nowhere.

Finally, just when they were about to give up, a yellow-shirted expert found them. He had gotten word that two visitors had not finished the maze. Once he found them, he was able to lead them out. Scattered applause accompanied smiles and hugs at the exit. The lost had been found.

God is like the expert in the yellow shirt. He knew we were lost in a maze of sin. He knew we could never find our way out. So He sent Jesus to our rescue. Jesus' perfect life, death, and resurrection offer us new life with Him now, in our earthly maze, and forever. What a rescue to celebrate!

_____Let's do: Draw your own maze in the shape of a cross.

_____Let's pray: Dear Jesus, thank You for looking for me and finding me when I was lost. Amen.

E. L. G.

Victory!

O nce upon a time there were townspeople under the power of an evil knight. The knight kept a dragon outside the town gates. The king, hearing of this problem, sent messages of hope to his subjects.

One day a baby boy was found in the town square. No one knew where this baby had come from. The boy grew up and became a man.

This mysterious man was not afraid of the dragon or the knight, and he challenged the knight to a battle. The knight threw him to the dragon. As the townspeople watched in horror, the dragon breathed fire on the man, killing him.

Strangely, the man came back to life. He battled the evil knight and won. The knight was banished from the kingdom forever.

Then the townspeople recognized the hero. "It's our king!" they shouted. The king loved his people so much that he had come among them. Now he promised to stay with them always.

This story is a fairy tale but it gives us a picture of what Jesus did for us. We had sinned and fallen under the power of the devil, our sinful nature, and the world. Jesus was born into our world and remained sinless. He battled sin, death, and the devil. Jesus won! Now He offers His victory to us.

Read from God's Word

"O death, where is your victory? O death, where is your sting?" The sting of death is sin, and the power of sin is the law. But thanks be to God, who gives us the victory through our Lord Jesus Christ. 1 Corinthians 15:55–57 ✍

_____Let's do: Read the Easter story in Matthew 28:1–10. List the ways the victory was announced.

_____Let's pray: Dear Jesus, thank You for coming to our rescue. Stay with us and help us to live for You. Amen.

E. L. G.

Read from God's Word

Now Elijah the Tishbite, of Tishbe in Gilead, said to Ahab, "As the Lord the God of Israel lives, before whom I stand, there shall be neither dew nor rain these years, except by my word." And the word of the Lord came to him, "Depart from here and turn eastward and hide yourself by the brook Cherith, which is east of the Jordan. You shall drink from the brook, and I have command-ed the ravens to feed you there." So he went and did according to the word of the Lord. He went and lived by the brook Cherith that is east of the Jordan. And the ravens brought him bread and meat in the morning, and bread and meat in the evening, and he drank from the brook. 1 Kings 17:1–6 ✍

Bird-Feeding

Do you like birds? Some people like birds so much they put bird feed-ers in their yard or tree. Today's Bible reading might make you think that Elijah loved birds. But Elijah didn't feed the birds—the birds fed him!

Elijah worked for God. His job was hard. People often were angry with Elijah because he told them they were living as sinners, which kept them from enjoying life as God's people. He told them how much they needed God. These people thought they were good just being themselves.

God showed the people what life without Him is like. God had Elijah announce that no rain would fall. Without rain, plants and animals would die. But God promised to care for Elijah. He sent Elijah to a place where there was water. Large birds, called ravens, brought food to Elijah. God provided for Elijah.

Some people still don't want to hear about God's love for them. They don't want to admit their sins. Do you know anyone like that? Are you like that sometimes?

All people are sinners. They deserve to die and go to hell. But God sent Jesus to take away sin. God also takes care of you. God always finds ways to help His people—and you are one of His people.

_____Let's do: What amazing thing happened next in the Bible reading? Read 1 Kings 17:7–16 and write about it.

_____Let's pray: Dear God, thank You for taking care of Elijah. Thank You for all You give me. I especially thank You for sending Jesus to take away my sins. Amen.

E. G.

What Are You Worth?

To answer the question in the title, you might say how much money you have. Do you own anything else? Did you count the sports car, the home theater system, your personal maid or butler, pets, computer, books, summer vacation home, and so forth?

Okay, so it's possible you actually own none of these things.

What would your family say if they were asked what you are worth? Aside from a few silly comments, your family might consider you worth more than any amount of money. But maybe you don't always feel worth much. An angry family member, a friend who turns against you or a poor grade in English might make you feel worthless.

What would Jesus answer if He were asked what you are worth? If you didn't know Jesus as your Friend, you might think He would say you're worth nothing. After all, you do sin at times, right? Maybe you sin often. Would He be angry because your sins helped to send Him to suffer on the cross? No, Jesus would not think that way.

Jesus loves you. Willingly He suffered, died, and rose from the grave to take away all your sins. To Jesus you are worth more than any amount of money.

Read from God's Word

And He sat down opposite the treasury and watched the people putting money into the offering box. Many rich people put in large sums. And a poor widow came and put in two small copper coins, which make a penny. And He called His disciples to Him and said to them, "Truly, I say to you, this poor widow has put in more than all those who are contributing to the offering box. For they all contributed out of their abundance, but she out of her poverty has put in everything she had, all she had to live on." Mark 12:41–44 ∽

_____Let's do: Choose one surprising fact from Mark 12:41–44 to write about.

_____Let's pray: Dear Jesus, thank You for making me worth more than anything else in the world. Help me tell others that You did the same thing for them. Amen.

E. G.

Read from God's Word

How beautiful upon the mountains are the feet of him who brings good news, who publishes peace, who brings good news of happiness, who publishes salvation, who says to Zion, "Your God reigns." Isaiah 52:7 ∽

God, the Podiatrist

D on't let the title scare you. If you don't know how to pronounce *podiatrist*, here's how: po-di-a-trist.

A podiatrist is a foot doctor. Why would anyone think of God as a podiatrist? When you read Isaiah 52:7, you have a clue.

In that Bible verse God speaks to you and everyone else who believes in Jesus. Did you hear what He said about your feet? They are beautiful! It's important to know how they got that way.

Imagine you are walking barefoot through mud. (Don't try this at home.) As you squish through the mud, you step on a stem from a rose bush. Ouch! As you hop around in pain, you accidentally kick a rock with your other foot. Bigger ouch! Now you can only limp around with muddy, bloody, stubby feet.

Before Jesus made our feet beautiful, they looked like the feet in your imagination. Sin makes us ugly, dirty, bruised, and messed up—kind of like those feet. But Jesus cleaned us up. By dying on the cross and rising from the dead, Jesus took away our sins and made us clean—including our feet. Now He helps us to use our beautiful feet to walk around and tell others that Jesus made them and their feet clean too.

_____Let's do: Draw a picture of your beautiful feet standing next to the feet of someone who doesn't yet know Jesus. (Don't just stand there! Tell him or her the Good News about Jesus.)

_____Let's pray: Dear Jesus, help me use my beautiful feet to tell others about You wherever I go. Amen.

E. G.

Let God Know

L onnie shivered. His eyes darted left and right. He bent over until he was half his size. Then he rocked himself back and forth, back and forth, eyes tightly shut and teeth clamped against each other. Lonnie was reacting to fear.

Fear of getting hit by a truck causes us to look both ways before crossing streets. Fear of pain keeps us from putting our hand in the fire. Fear of strangers stops us from getting into the car of someone we don't know. Fear of the devil is good because the devil only wants to hurt us. Fear can be good—a gift from God. But not all fear is good.

When faced with scary things we cannot avoid, God wants us to trust in Him. Of course, God knows that everyone is afraid at some time. God tells us what to do when we are afraid. Our Bible passage reminds us to pray, to look to God for help.

Read from God's Word

I sought the LORD, and He answered me and delivered me from all my fears. Those who look to Him are radiant, and their faces shall never be ashamed. This poor man cried, and the LORD heard him and saved him out of all his troubles. The angel of the LORD encamps around those who fear Him, and delivers them. Psalm 34:4–7

God loves us. He sent Jesus to take away our sins. Jesus will not allow anything to take us away from Him. He wants us to talk to Him when we are afraid and tell Him what we fear. Most of all, Jesus wants us to know that He loves us and will always be with us.

_____Let's do: Pretend you know someone who is afraid that
            God doesn't love her. Tell her why she doesn't
            need to be afraid.

_____Let's pray: Dear Jesus, let me tell You what scares me.
            (Tell Jesus about your fears.) Please, dear Jesus,
            take care of me. Help me remember that You
            will always love me. Amen.

E. G.

Read from God's Word

For He will command His angels concerning you to guard you in all your ways. On their hands they will bear you up, lest you strike your foot against a stone. Psalm 91:11–12

Help You Can't See

Today's psalm seems to say that angels keep you from falling or protect you from stubbing your toe. But is that true? You might wonder what the angels were doing the last time you fell off your skateboard or hit your toe on the leg of a chair.

We don't know why God's angels don't protect us from all accidents, sickness, or pain. We just trust that God does what is best for us because He knows everything about everything. We also trust that God sends angels to protect us from harm and danger we can't see.

The Bible says the devil is loose in this world like a hungry lion trying to hurt us. He would like to drag us away from Jesus and keep us from getting to heaven. Thank God for angels! They chase away the devil.

As important as angels are, Jesus is even better. Jesus saved us from going to hell for our sins. He saved us when He died on the cross and rose from the grave. Someday we'll see Jesus in person. Do you think He might introduce us to the angels who are protecting us right now?

_____Let's do: Draw or write about an angel doing one of the jobs angels do. Use a Bible index to help you find references.

_____Let's pray: Thank You, dear God, for sending angels to protect me. Thank You even more for sending Jesus to save me. Amen.

E. G.

The End?

How do you feel when you come to the end of the school year? You may feel like you accomplished a lot and are much smarter now than you were when school began. Of course, after taking a vacation break, school starts again. The end really isn't the end.

The Bible talks about the end. God tells us that Jesus will return to earth like a hero. On that day, life as we know it will end. Those who believe Jesus took away their sins will go to heaven to live with God. So you see, the end really isn't the end.

Many people fear death. They might be afraid of seeing Jesus come again. People are afraid because they know they are sinners. They might fear that God doesn't love them or that they have done too many bad things and not enough good things.

The only thing that really ends for believers is life as a sinner. Jesus took away our sins. When Jesus comes to take us to our new home, every pain, sorrow, and evil will end—really! The end will be the end of sin. But all who believe in Jesus will live forever.

Read from God's Word

For the Lord Himself will descend from heaven with a cry of command, with the voice of an archangel, and with the sound of the trumpet of God. And the dead in Christ will rise first. Then we who are alive, who are left, will be caught up together with them in the clouds to meet the Lord in the air, and so we will always be with the Lord. Therefore encourage one another with these words.
1 Thessalonians 4:16–18 ✑

_____Let's do: Write what you think you will like best about life with Jesus in heaven.

_____Let's pray: Dear God, thank You for sending Jesus to end the devil's power to send us to hell. We look forward to the end of life on earth and the start of endless life in heaven. Amen.

E. G.

Read from God's Word

Do you not know that you are God's temple and that God's Spirit dwells in you?
1 Corinthians 3:16 ✎

God's House

M any years ago, God's people built Him a house. To be truthful, it was more like a mobile home. The tabernacle was a tent-church. Since God's people moved around a lot, a tent-church was a good idea.

Once God's people settled down in one spot, God directed Solomon to build Him a new house. This one was made of stone. They decorated God's house with beautiful wood and gold. Many artists, carpenters, stonecutters, and other skilled people used only the best materials to make God's house beautiful.

Where does God live today? Some people call church buildings God's house. By the number of churches you see during a drive in the city, you might think that God moves around a lot. God is everywhere!

Today's Bible reading tells you about God's newest home. The verse says, "You are God's temple." *Temple* is another word for church. Can you imagine that? You are God's house. His Holy Spirit lives in you and in all believers. God is back in His mobile home again!

God didn't choose to live in you because you're so good. God lives in you because Jesus made you a great place to live. Jesus made you clean from sin so God could live in you. God is with you everywhere.

_____Let's do: Write a thank-You note to God, thanking Him for moving into you.

_____Let's pray: Don't ever move away from me, dear God. Make me a good house for You. In Jesus' name I pray. Amen.

E. G.

A Spiritual Sandwich

Read from God's Word

Oh how I love Your law! It is my meditation all the day. Your commandment makes me wiser than my enemies, for it is ever with me. I have more understanding than all my teachers, for Your testimonies are my meditation. I understand more than the aged, for I keep Your precepts. I hold back my feet from every evil way, in order to keep Your word. I do not turn aside from Your rules, for You have taught me. How sweet are Your words to my taste, sweeter than honey to my mouth! Through Your precepts I get understanding; therefore I hate every false way. Psalm 119:97–104 ✍

What's your idea of a perfect sandwich? Does it have turkey, cheese, and lettuce? Or do you go for more exotic ingredients such as popcorn, apples, gingersnap cookies, candy sprinkles, and chocolate syrup on a bun.

This recipe was among those created by elementary school chefs who entered a contest. Some of the sandwiches were more healthful, like a tomato with cheese, lettuce, chicken, apple, dill pickle, and grapes on wheat bread.

If you wanted to make a *spiritually* healthful, nourishing sandwich, what ingredients would you include? Perhaps you would start with God's Word. Does eating God's Word sound strange? The writer of Psalm 119 rejoices in the tasty sweetness of God's Word. The prophet Jeremiah speaks of eating God's Word (Jeremiah 15:16). Ezekiel was told to digest the Word and then speak it to the Israelites (Ezekiel 3:1–4).

Through digestion, the physical food we eat becomes part of us. Likewise, the spiritual food we take in also becomes part of us.

So let's enjoy that *spiritually* nourishing sandwich. Put reading God's Word as the first layer. Then add memorizing a Bible verse and singing Scripture songs. Mix in some time to be led by God to share a smile or a kindness with others. Now top the sandwich with prayer. There it is—spiritual food—and God provided it all!

_____Let's talk: Why do we need *spiritual* nourishment every day? What plan could you make to get spiritual food every day?

_____Let's pray: Father, help us get our spiritual food every day. In Jesus' name we pray. Amen.

M. J. G.

Warnings and Promises

Read from God's Word

But this command I gave them: "Obey My voice, and I will be your God, and you shall be My people. And walk in all the way that I command you, that it may be well with you." But they did not obey or incline their ear, but walked in their own counsels and the stubbornness of their evil hearts, and went backward and not forward. From the day that your fathers came out of the land of Egypt to this day, I have persistently sent all My servants the prophets to them, day after day. Yet they did not listen to Me or incline their ear, but stiffened their neck. They did worse than their fathers. Jeremiah 7:23–26 ∽

The O'Brien family heard a loud beeping noise coming from the stairway wall. The beeping was getting louder. Sometimes it kept them awake at night. What was that noise?

Then the youngest O'Brien child heard the beeping sound and knew it came from a smoke detector in the hallway. The instructions said that a beeping noise would warn when the battery was weak. To keep the smoke detector working, you have to pay attention to the warning sound.

The prophet Jeremiah gives a warning in our Bible reading that the people didn't listen to. We don't always listen to God either. Do computer games take most of our time? Are we too busy at work or play to listen to God? Jeremiah is speaking to us.

Yet with every warning from God Jeremiah also gives great hope. He points us to Christ as the Branch who will be called "The LORD is our righteousness" (Jeremiah 33:16). Listen to this message of love from God: "I will cleanse them from all the guilt of their sin" (Jeremiah 33:8). With the warning came the promise of forgiveness.

God gives us parents, pastors, and teachers to guide us. How God loves us! Listen to His warnings and promises and, with His help, follow His way. It's the way of forgiveness and hope.

_____Let's do: Whom has God sent into your life to teach you His way? Write about a way you would like to thank God for each one.

_____Let's pray: "Give thanks to the LORD of hosts, for the LORD is good, for His steadfast love endures forever!" (Jeremiah 33:11).

L. A.

Victory over Death

Read from God's Word

But in fact Christ has been raised from the dead, the first-fruits of those who have fallen asleep. For as by a man came death, by a man has come also the resurrection of the dead. For as in Adam all die, so also in Christ shall all be made alive.
1 Corinthians 15:20–22 ⤶

Next to LaMoine's backyard is a cemetery. One day a friend walked out the back door and started to laugh. "I'll bet your neighbors don't give you any trouble," he said.

"No," LaMoine replied, "they're a quiet bunch."

When we see a cemetery, it's tempting to make a joke. We may joke about death because it's a hard subject to think about. Burying someone we love is painful. Thinking about our own death isn't easy.

Jesus knows how we feel. He wept at the grave of His friend Lazarus. But Jesus also gives us confidence to face death. We can look death in the face and know for sure that Jesus has taken care of this enemy for us.

Today's Bible reading tells us that because of Christ's resurrection, "all will also live." Because of His lonely death on the cross, our Savior assures us of eternal life with Him. The enemy, death, has been defeated.

When you die with faith in Jesus, you will join Him in heaven, where He waits for you. How does that make you feel? You may still be concerned about dying. You may still feel very sad and cry when a grandparent dies. But you can be sure that you have the victory over death.

_____Let's talk: Why can you feel happy when someone who loves Jesus dies? Why do you also feel sad?

_____Let's pray: Father of life, we pray that You will be with us now so we know we will live with You in eternity. Thank You for the victory we have over death in Christ, our Savior. In His holy name we pray. Amen.

L. A.

Read from God's Word

Anyone whom you forgive, I also forgive. What I have forgiven, if I have forgiven anything, has been for your sake in the presence of Christ, so that we would not be outwitted by Satan; for we are not ignorant of his designs.
2 Corinthians 2:10–11 ✍

Don't Be Deceived

One day a large tarantula fell on Rosita's head. Pastor Gruel put his finger to his lips to tell everyone to be quiet.

"Rosita," he said, "a beautiful bird has landed on your head. Do not move, or you will frighten it away." The girl sat very still. Pastor Gruel walked over to Rosita and brushed the spider off her head.

Pastor Gruel deceived Rosita to help her. But the Bible tells us of a great deceiver who wants to trick us for an evil purpose. The devil tries to turn us away from God.

Can you spot some of those tricky turns? Your friend Sydney says it's all right to take money from the teacher's desk. Your classmates invite you to pull a trick on that fifth grader who wears funny shoes. You wake up on Sunday thinking, *Why go to church? I should rest for my soccer game at noon.* In each case, the devil seeks to deceive.

Because God loves us, He sent Jesus to defeat the devil. Jesus died on the cross for our sins and rose from the grave. This was a victory over the devil and sin.

With God's power we can turn away from the devil, who makes sin feel good. We can turn to God and live for Him!

_____Let's talk: Why does the devil lie to us? What strong weapon does God give us to fight the devil?

_____Let's pray: Dear Father in heaven, deliver me from the power of the devil. Thank You for sending Your Son to defeat Satan. Help me live the strong, victorious life Jesus won for me. In His name. Amen.

L. A.

Lemon-Head Awards

A radio station was giving an award called the "Lemon-Head Award." It was for the person who did a dumb thing and could laugh about it.

We all make foolish mistakes. In the Alvarez family, Dad couldn't find his glasses because they were perched on top of his head! Mom meant to take out the garbage, but she absentmindedly put it in the dryer. Steve studied hard for a test, but he studied the wrong chapter.

God knows we are lemon heads—but He turns us into lemonade. How? He loves us and sent Jesus to die for all our sins. Jesus lived a perfect life and then died on the cross in payment for our sins. Now God in His love sees Christ's perfection instead of our sin.

Our Bible reading says we are "children of God." We have been chosen by God to be His. God knows we are not perfect, yet He calls us His children. We are greatly loved! We can talk to Him in prayer. We can praise Him in worship. We can reach out to our family and friends in love. Best of all, in everything we say or do we have the forgiveness of Jesus every day. No lemons in this bunch!

Read from God's Word

See what kind of love the Father has given to us, that we should be called children of God; and so we are. The reason why the world does not know us is that it did not know Him. Beloved, we are God's children now, and what we will be has not yet appeared; but we know that when He appears we will be like Him, because we shall see Him as He is. And everyone who thus hopes in Him purifies himself as He is pure. 1 John 3:1–3

_____Let's talk: When was the last time you deserved a lemon-head award? What did you do about your error? How does God's love for you make you feel better?

_____Let's pray: Loving Father, thank You for the joy of being Your chosen child. Help me live for You and give Your joy to others. In Jesus' name. Amen.

L. A.

Unusual Names

Read from God's Word

The nations shall see Your righteousness, and all the kings Your glory, and You shall be called by a new name that the mouth of the LORD will give. You shall be a crown of beauty in the hand of the LORD, and a royal diadem in the hand of your God. Isaiah 62:2–3

The Miller family drove west to California to see Grandma in a nursing home. It was a long trip. To pass the time, they looked for unusual road names. Some of the names told us about the country around us.

In Kansas the Millers saw Maple Valley Road and looked at maple trees. In Colorado they kept an eye out for dinosaurs on Dinosaur Trail Road. They saw large black rocks in Arizona as they crossed Black Rock Road. The family looked hard for rabbits in New Mexico at Rabbit Ear Road, and there were no gooseberries around Utah's Gooseberry Road. When they drove by Rainbow Valley Boulevard, everyone in the car was glad to reach the journey's end.

We have been given an unusual name—*Christian*. This name tells something about us: we are like Christ. Through Baptism, He lives in us and makes us like Him. Although by nature we sin, our name *Christian* reminds us we are forgiven. Jesus forgives our sins of being unloving and unkind. Jesus took our sins upon Himself, and that gives us our name. It's a victorious name. In faith we share in Christ's triumph over death through the empty tomb.

Walk the road of life with your new name. You are one of Christ's own.

_____Let's talk: What other words tell what a Christian is?
How does God help us to be more Christlike?

_____Let's pray: Be with me, Jesus, as I walk the road of life.
Help me carry Your name and give Your love
to others. Thank You for the forgiveness You
won for me. Amen.

L. A.

A T-Shirt Witness

Read from God's Word

For I am not ashamed of the gospel, for it is the power of God for salvation to everyone who believes, to the Jew first and also to the Greek. For in it the righteousness of God is revealed from faith for faith, as it is written, "The righteous shall live by faith." Romans 1:16–17 ᴄᴈ

Madison's favorite T-shirt made people think. At a church youth program she got a shirt proclaiming "Look Up to Jesus." Madison was wearing the shirt on a walk in her neighborhood. As she walked, Eric, a neighbor boy, called out, "Here comes that Jesus girl."

Madison was embarrassed and changed her shirt. Mom asked at dinner, "Weren't you wearing your 'Jesus' T-shirt before? I thought it was your favorite."

"I was," said Madison, "but I felt funny wearing something about Jesus."

"Why?" asked Tyler. "That's not a bad word. We don't have to be ashamed of our faith in Jesus."

Mom said, "Let's not point fingers at Madison. We all fail to be God's witnesses. Mrs. Davis called me today about her sick mother. I told her it would work out, but I missed an opportunity to tell her about God's love."

"That's why we need forgiveness," said Dad. "I wish I could talk to my boss about Jesus. He never goes to church. Whatever we do or say can point to Christ. We can pray for courage to share Christ with others. And we can thank God for His forgiveness in Christ when we fail."

"I think I'd like to wear my T-shirt again," said Madison. "This time I'll ask Eric if he knows who Jesus is."

_____Let's do: Write out and then finish this sentence in your journal. "I am not ashamed of Jesus because _____."

_____Let's pray: Dear Savior, I pray for _____, who doesn't know about You. Help me be a witness to Your love. In Your name I pray. Amen.

L. A.

The Masks We Wear

Read from God's Word

God shows His love for us in that while we were still sinners, Christ died for us. Since, therefore, we have now been justified by His blood, much more shall we be saved by Him from the wrath of God. For if while we were enemies we were reconciled to God by the death of His Son, much more, now that we are reconciled, shall we be saved by His life. More than that, we also rejoice in God through our Lord Jesus Christ, through whom we have now received reconciliation. Romans 5:8–11 ✐

The knights of the Middle Ages wore suits of armor and rode into battle on horses. This armor gave protection, but it was also heavy and uncomfortable. Their metal masks made it hard to see and were dark and stuffy inside. These masks protected the face, but they got in the way.

We all wear masks, and they get in the way for us too. Everyone thinks Daemon is cool. He wears cool clothes and tells neat jokes. But Daemon is really unhappy. He has no one to talk to at home. His "cool" mask covers his sadness. Sally is very shy. She doesn't have friends and the other girls at school call her stuck-up. Her mask says she doesn't care, but she cries at home.

God sees through the masks we wear. Our Bible reading tells us the Good News that He loves us. He showed that love by sending Jesus to die for our sins. He knows our false faces and forgives us. He knows our fears, sadness, and pain, and He draws us to Himself.

When no one else understands, God is there. He invites us to come to Him. His love carries us through tough days. Jesus gives us strength to show our best face—praising Him!

_____Let's do: Write about a mask you sometimes wear. Then tell how you can help someone who wears a mask.

_____Let's pray: Dear Lord, thank You for Your great love, which sees through my masks. Help me live in the joy of Your love and forgiveness. Amen.

L. A.

Good Fruit

What fruit is as large as a soccer ball, has a spiky outer shell, and smells like dirty socks? The durian (DURE-ee-un)! This fruit grows on trees in Southeast Asia and weighs about five pounds. Its flesh is sweet, tasting somewhat like a mango, and looks like creamy custard ice cream.

This unique fruit is prized by many in Malaysia and Thailand. Others despise it because of its smell. Some hotels in those countries will not allow the durian to be brought onto their premises.

In contrast, the fruit of the Holy Spirit is available to all Christians and is pleasing to everyone. God works in us through the Holy Spirit to help us be kind, patient, and gentle. He helps us live peaceably with others. He helps us control our thoughts, emotions, and actions. Love, joy, goodness, and faithfulness characterize our lives. This fruit pleases God and others.

Read from God's Word

But the fruit of the Spirit is love, joy, peace, patience, kindness, goodness, faithfulness, gentleness, self-control; against such things there is no law. Galatians 5:22–23

Such fruit is the result of our faith in Jesus Christ. As Jesus lives in us and forgives our sins, He changes us. His fruit grows as our lives are governed more and more by the Holy Spirit. Then we will be like the tree in Psalm 1:3, "yield[ing] its fruit in its season."

_____Let's talk: Give some examples of Holy Spirit fruit that you see in the lives of those around you. What are some examples of Holy Spirit fruit in your life?

_____Let's pray: Father, direct our lives by Your Holy Spirit. Help us bear good fruit. In Jesus' name. Amen.

M. J. G.

Read from God's Word

And God saw everything that He had made, and behold, it was very good. And there was evening and there was morning, the sixth day. Thus the heavens and the earth were finished, and all the host of them. Genesis 1:31–2:1 ✎

God's Good Creation

Native Americans never took food for granted. They respected the sun, rain, and earth. They danced with thankfulness. They saw that the earth is good and were thankful for what it brought them.

God made plants and animals to give us food. He made the sun and the rain to help the earth produce vegetation. And He made people, His final creation, to glorify Him and live for Him.

We do God's will when we worship Him as the Creator. He is the one true God. He declared His creation to be "very good," but He also saw the sins of His people, who did not honor Him as the Creator, thank Him for His gifts, or care for them. He sent Jesus, His Son, into this world. Jesus came to live a perfect life for us. Jesus took our sins to the cross to save us. His Spirit gives us new life.

Now we are moved to thank God for forgiveness in Jesus. We thank God for doctors to heal us, for blankets to keep us warm, for parents who care about us, for delicious strawberries and watermelons to eat. The list goes on and on.

God also moves us to tell others about His goodness. Let others see His goodness through you.

_____Let's do: Look around and thank God for all that you have. Choose a song that you can sing or play on an instrument, such as "God Is So Good."

_____Let's pray: Read Psalm 150.

L. A.

june

Contributors for this month:

Mary Krallmann

Ethel P. Lesh

Glenda Schrock

Malinda Walz

Read from God's Word

Then the angel showed me the river of the water of life, bright as crystal, flowing from the throne of God and of the Lamb through the middle of the street of the city; also, on either side of the river, the tree of life with its twelve kinds of fruit, yielding its fruit each month. The leaves of the tree were for the healing of the nations. No longer will there be anything accursed, but the throne of God and of the Lamb will be in it, and His servants will worship Him. They will see His face, and His name will be on their foreheads. And night will be no more. They will need no light of lamp or sun, for the Lord God will be their light, and they will reign forever and ever.
Revelation 22:1–5 ✐

Perfect Days

It's June! Summer vacation is starting. There are graduations, picnics, camps, trips, weddings, and family reunions. It's time for strawberries, vacation Bible school, and long, warm days. What a great month!

A poem by James Russell Lowell describes how pleasant June can be. The birds are singing and building their nests. Grass, leaves, and dazzling flowers are growing. The breezes are warm. The world of nature is full of light and life.

But even when June days are very nice, unpleasant things may happen. Floods, heat waves, sickness, accidents, crime, and death can all happen.

Because of Jesus we can look past any troubles we have—in June or any other time. Jesus lived a perfect life for us. He died to pay for our sin. He came back to life to guarantee us new life in Him. Jesus lives in us and, at the end of our days, we will live with Him forever.

The Bible tells us that in heaven there will be no more sadness, darkness, pain, or death. Heaven is full of the glory of God. In heaven we will be with God in perfect joy. Enjoy these wonderful days in June, but remember—the best is yet to come!

_____ Let's talk: What do you like best about June? What makes heaven even better?

_____ Let's pray: Dear God, our Creator, You have made this world so beautiful. Let my happiness now remind me of living with You forever. I pray in Jesus' name. Amen.

M. K.

How to Do Your Thing

Read from God's Word

So, whether you eat or drink, or whatever you do, do all to the glory of God. 1 Corinthians 10:31

～

Mary's mother has a special African violet. When it blooms, the first flowers are white. When the plant blooms again, the buds open into dark purple flowers. The next blossoms are partly white and partly purple. Then the plant has white flowers again.

God's people grow and bloom too. Just like the African violet, they produce different good results at different times.

For example, David was once a shepherd. He also fought in wars against enemies of God. David played music and wrote psalms as well. He served God in many ways.

You have different things to do for God. One way to serve Him is learning in school. There are jobs around the house. There are lonely people to visit. You can grow in faith at a church camp or vacation Bible school.

Jesus also had different kinds of work to do. He grew up as a carpenter's son. Around age 30, He started to teach and preach. He healed sick people and did other miracles. Finally, Jesus, who was both God and man, died for our sin and came back to life again.

Because of all the things Jesus did for us, we have a new life. God gives us His Spirit to help us grow and bloom as His people.

_____ Let's talk: How do you plan to grow as a Christian this summer? What are some new ways you can serve your Lord?

_____ Let's pray: Thank You, Lord God, for giving me different ways to live for You. Help me in everything I do. In Jesus' name. Amen.

M. K.

A Raging Python

Read from God's Word

Now the serpent was more crafty than any other beast of the field that the LORD God had made. He said to the woman, "Did God actually say, 'You shall not eat of any tree in the garden'?" And the woman said to the serpent, "We may eat of the fruit of the trees in the garden, but God said, 'You shall not eat of the fruit of the tree that is in the midst of the garden, neither shall you touch it, lest you die.'" But the serpent said to the woman, "You will not surely die. For God knows that when you eat of it your eyes will be opened, and you will be like God, knowing good and evil."
Genesis 3:1–5 ✑

A 12-foot python caused big trouble. The snake attacked Christopher, a young man who had been keeping it for a few days. It also attacked his two dogs. Ken and Tom came to help, but then the python wrapped itself around Tom.

In Genesis 3, the devil appeared in the form of a snake. He was more dangerous than the python. He caused serious trouble for the first humans when they listened to him. They did something God had told them not to do. God said they would have many problems because of sin, and because of sin, they would die.

Since then all people sin and all people die. Evil thoughts and actions wrap themselves around our lives and cause us harm.

But in Genesis 3, God also promised a Savior. Jesus crushed the head of the devil by living perfectly and then dying for our sins. Since Jesus is God, He was too strong for the devil to destroy. Jesus came back to life. He unwrapped the power of evil from our lives.

The devil still attacks us, but the same God who made the whole world defends us. We can always go to Him for help. He gives us strength against temptations and forgives our sins.

_____Let's talk: What sins are wrapped around your life right now? How can you get help?

_____Let's pray: Thank You, God, for freeing us from the devil's power. Rescue us whenever we are in danger from sin. You are the only One who can save us. In Jesus' holy name. Amen.

M. K.

Whither Bound?

It was the day after eighth-grade graduation. Greg's mom and Aunt Paula were talking in the kitchen.

"I think I still remember part of the speech at my high school graduation. The topic was 'Whither Bound?'" said Paula, with a smile.

"'Whither Bound?'" Greg repeated as he came into the kitchen. "What's that supposed to mean?"

"I'll update the question for you," said Paula. "Today we'd probably ask, 'Where are you going in life? What are your plans for the years ahead?'"

That's a good question for all of us, whether we're new graduates or not. Some of our plans are God pleasing but others will lead us to sin. As Christians we have God's Word and we have His help. Through the power of the Holy Spirit we have faith in Jesus. Through His life and death He has rescued us from sin and secured us a future in heaven.

Read from God's Word

And behold, a lawyer stood up to put Him to the test, saying, "Teacher, what shall I do to inherit eternal life?" He said to him, "What is written in the Law? How do you read it?" And he answered, "You shall love the Lord your God with all your heart and with all your soul and with all your strength and with all your mind, and your neighbor as yourself." And He said to him, "You have answered correctly; do this, and you will live." Luke 10:25–28

Take a look at where you are going. Are you headed for whatever feels good? Are you working for good grades, sports awards, and a citizenship certificate? Are you going wherever your friends go, no matter what? What or who is guiding you? If the answers are not God pleasing, reconsider. Ask God's Spirit to lead you in love.

_____Let's talk: Read Luke 10:29 in your Bible and think about the expert's question. How does Jesus answer it? What quality did the Samaritan have that made him a real neighbor? How can you show it?

_____Let's pray: Heavenly Father, help us live the way You want us to. Forgive us when we fail. Keep us in faith on the way to heaven. We pray this in Jesus' name. Amen.

M. K.

Read from God's Word

Not that I am speaking of being in need, for I have learned in whatever situation I am to be content. I know how to be brought low, and I know how to abound. In any and every circumstance, I have learned the secret of facing plenty and hunger, abundance and need. I can do all things through Him who strengthens me. Philippians 4:11–13 ✎

Too Much or Too Little

Erica said, "This summer I have softball games, swimming lessons, vacation, babysitting, and trombone practice. When will I ever get a break?"

Lance's complaint was different. "Boring time is here again. There aren't enough summer sports for kids. I'm tired of school, but this isn't any better. Where's the excitement?"

"It's going to be a zoo around here," said Brad. "My older brother will be home from college, so I'll have to sleep in my little brother's room. My aunt, uncle, and cousins are coming for a week. When can I have some time alone?"

Heather said. "It's lonely in the summer. No one else my age lives in the neighborhood. My parents are busy with their jobs. Who can I talk to?"

We are all hard to satisfy. Whether we have a lot of activity and friendship or very little, we're often discontented.

The apostle Paul learned to live with having a lot and a little. He said he could be content either way. So can we, through Christ, who gives us strength.

Jesus did not grumble at the cost of being our Savior. Because of His great love for you and for me, He accepted His Father's will, even though it led to death for our sins. Through Him we have new life with new opportunities.

_____Let's do: Read Hebrews 13:5–6 and look for other reasons to be content. Write down one that you want to remember.

_____Let's pray: Lord, my life comes from You. You know what is best for me. Help me trust You in all things. Amen.

M. K.

Quiet Times

One summer I visited a college friend I hadn't seen for seven years. It was an exciting trip and included flying to another state. It was fun to eat out, talk, and see her new house.

I enjoyed those special activities, but I also remember just getting away. My friend had an exercise bicycle. Before supper each day, I would retreat to the basement to pedal a few miles. Outside it was 100 degrees, but inside it was comfortable. I liked the quiet, peaceful time.

In today's Bible reading Jesus and His followers had been very busy. Jesus had sent His disciples to travel around to different villages and teach. Then the disciples came back and reported what they had done. Many people kept coming to see Jesus. Finally He told His disciples to come away and rest for a while.

Jesus Himself spent many hours alone with His heavenly Father. He often went away from even His closest friends to pray.

Read from God's Word

The apostles returned to Jesus and told Him all that they had done and taught. And He said to them, "Come away by yourselves to a desolate place and rest a while." For many were coming and going, and they had no leisure even to eat. And they went away in the boat to a desolate place by themselves. Mark 6:30–32 ✍

We also need time to be alone with God. We get too busy with other things. Sin can wear us out. We can use quiet times to reflect on God's love and forgiveness, to pray, and to study God's Word so we grow more able to live as God's people.

_____Let's talk: When can you have quiet times with God during vacation?

_____Let's pray: Lord Jesus, I'm sorry I don't always take time for prayer and reading Your Word. Thank You for opportunities to be alone with You. Amen.

M. K.

Brothers

My brother was born 40 years ago on June 7. Our parents named him John, which means "God is gracious."

God truly was gracious (kind) in giving me a brother. Because of John, there was someone for me to play with at home. Having a brother around made me feel safer when I tried scary things. John was there when I nervously climbed along the "rainbow bridge"—a bent-over tree. However, human brothers aren't perfect, and they aren't always around.

God has given us Christians a heavenly Brother. His name is Jesus, which means "Savior." Jesus is always kind to us, and He is always there. He knows more and is stronger and more loving than any human brother. He is God the Son.

God sent Jesus to be born as a human and live on earth like us. He died for our sins. When we believe in Jesus and are baptized, we become children of God. That makes Jesus our Brother because we have the same heavenly Father.

With Jesus as our Brother, our lives are full of God's blessings. The Holy Spirit lives in our hearts, and our sins are forgiven.

_____Let's talk: What blessings has God given you through a brother, sister, or friend? What special blessings do you receive from Jesus, your heavenly Brother?

_____Let's pray: Thank God for the blessings you named.

M. K.

The Power of God

Read from God's Word

For the word of the cross is folly to those who are perishing, but to us who are being saved it is the power of God.
1 Corinthians 1:18 〰

Bailey told Elise, "I liked hearing about when Jesus raised Lazarus from death."

"A lot of the things Jesus said don't make sense to me," Elise said. "First, He told His disciples that Lazarus wouldn't die. Then He told them Lazarus was only asleep. Then finally He admitted that Lazarus was dead! That makes it seem like Jesus didn't really know what was going on!"

"Oh, He knew," Bailey said. "He didn't say Lazarus wouldn't die, but that his sickness would 'not end in death.' Jesus knew He would make Lazarus's body alive again."

"Then why didn't He just say so?"

"I don't know," Bailey admitted, "but He tells us what we need to know. Remember the Bible verse we learned? 'Whoever believes in Me, though he die, yet shall he live, and everyone who lives and believes in Me shall never die' (John 11:25b–26a). That's plain enough."

The message of the cross is that Jesus died to pay for all people's sins. Because we believe in Him, death for us will be like sleep. We will rise again on the Last Day and live with God forever in glory. Those who do not believe in Jesus as their Savior often don't understand this message. But as the forgiven children of God, we trust God's Word!

_____Let's do: Look at 1 Corinthians 1:15–30. Write down some interesting opposites.

_____Let's pray: Father, thank You for sending Jesus to save me by His death. Help me to share the Good News of the cross. In Jesus' name. Amen.

G. S.

Read from God's Word

Conduct yourselves wisely toward outsiders, making the best use of the time. Let your speech always be gracious, seasoned with salt, so that you may know how you ought to answer each person.
Colossians 4:5–6 ✍

Sharing Friendship

Jim's dad grew yellow squash in his garden. One morning he picked two big buckets full. "Why don't you see if the neighbors want any, Jim?" he asked.

Jim knocked at every door, but nobody was home. The last house on the block was old Mrs. Bundy's. She was a mysterious woman who always looked angry.

Jim swallowed hard and knocked on the door. At last Mrs. Bundy dragged the door open and glared at him. Then, with the same glare, she said slowly, "Oh, squash! How nice! Are you selling them?"

"No, ma'am," Jim said, "we're giving them away."

Before Jim left he had been given cookies and milk. "I'll make squash pickles," Mrs. Bundy said. "You come back in a couple of days. I'll have some ready for you."

"Mrs. Bundy had a stroke," Jim told his dad later. "She can't help how she looks. She's really very nice!"

Jesus often showed kindness to "outsiders." He even called an outsider, the tax collector Matthew, to be His apostle. Jesus didn't just look at the outside of people. He didn't just listen to what other people said about them. He looked inside and saw each person's heart. Jesus died to earn forgiveness for all people. Young or old, pretty or ugly, rich or poor—we are all dear to Him.

_____Let's talk: What are the risks of being friendly with outsiders? What good can come of it?

_____Let's pray: Dear Jesus, help me to be a friend to those who need one. Give me courage and wisdom to talk with people I don't know well. Help me to show my faith in You. Amen.

G. S.

Check It Out!

Most computer owners use a diagnostic program to find problems in the system. Sometimes the program even offers to fix them! A small problem can often be corrected before it causes big trouble.

Sometimes we need to be checked too. We go to doctors who can diagnose our physical problems. Who can check the condition of our spiritual lives? We want to live the way God wants, yet we know we make mistakes.

Sin causes us to hate others and behave spitefully. We may quarrel with friends and family. We may throw tantrums. We may be jealous or envious. We may be selfish. We may enjoy causing problems.

Our behavior is much different if the Holy Spirit is guiding us. God helps us to love other people. We are full of joy and peace. We are kind and patient. We are faithful to God and to our duties. The Spirit gives us the ability to control ourselves when we become angry.

Read from God's Word

Now the works of the flesh are evident: sexual immorality, impurity, sensuality, idolatry, sorcery, enmity, strife, jealousy, fits of anger, rivalries, dissensions, divisions, envy, drunkenness, orgies, and things like these. I warn you, as I warned you before, that those who do such things will not inherit the kingdom of God. But the fruit of the Spirit is love, joy, peace, patience, kindness, goodness, faithfulness, gentleness, self-control; against such things there is no law. Galatians 5:19–23 ⤚

Nobody lives without sinning or without the effects of sin. But Christ willingly died to save us from the punishment we deserve for our sin. If we admit to Him that we have sinned, He will freely forgive us. He knows everything about our hearts and minds. He can fix whatever needs fixing!

_____Let's do: Write about a time when God helped you change sinful behavior.

_____Let's pray: Dear Father, help me to follow You, and forgive me when I fail. Fill me with the joy and peace of Your Spirit. In the name of Jesus. Amen.

G. S.

Read from God's Word

One generation shall commend Your works to another, and shall declare Your mighty acts. On the glorious splendor of Your majesty, and on Your wondrous works, I will meditate. They shall speak of the might of Your awesome deeds, and I will declare Your greatness. They shall pour forth the fame of Your abundant goodness and shall sing aloud of Your righteousness. Psalm 145:4–7

Great Is the Lord!

Maria and her grandfather were walking on the beach. As the waves rolled in, Maria said, "The ocean is so strong!"

"Oh, yes," Grandfather agreed. "The ocean shows some of the strength of God, who created it."

Maria pointed up. "He created the moon and all the stars!"

"And all the planets, comets, and asteroids!"

They walked in silence for a while, listening to the waves, until Maria spoke. "It's kind of scary, when you think about how powerful God is. He made everything out of nothing. All that fire, all that energy!"

"And yet He gently comes to comfort us," Grandfather replied. "He is truly our Father in heaven. He can create worlds or crush them. Yet He loves us and protects us as His own children."

The wonders of God are told from one generation to another. Grandfather was eager to tell Maria about God. We can learn from others that God daily shows us how much He loves us. He gives us all good things—home, family, food, health. But His greatest gift to us is His Son, Jesus Christ. Because Jesus took the punishment we deserve, we are forgiven. He took our sins away by dying in our place. Through Jesus, we are God's saved and blessed children, generation after generation.

_____ Let's do: Write about something someone from an older generation has told you about Jesus. Who was it? What did they tell you?

_____ Let's pray: Father, thank You for those who tell me about Your power and love. Forgive my sins and keep me close to You always. In Jesus' name. Amen.

G. S.

Plenty of Room

Michiko and her friends were planning to meet at the pool now that it was finally repaired.

When they got there, all they could see were wet, bobbing heads. "There isn't any room!" cried Michiko. "We can't get to the water."

What if we wanted to get to Jesus but people blocked the way? It happened to five men when Jesus was preaching at Capernaum.

Four of the men walked to the house where Jesus was staying. They carried the fifth man, who couldn't walk, on a mat. They wanted Jesus to heal the man on the mat. But they couldn't get close to the Lord; too many people were already there!

The men wouldn't give up. They knew Jesus could heal their friend, so they climbed up to the roof and made an opening. Then they lowered the man into the room with Jesus. Jesus healed the man's soul as well as his body (Mark 2:1–5).

Read from God's Word

"Let not your hearts be troubled. Believe in God; believe also in Me. In My Father's house are many rooms. If it were not so, would I have told you that I go to prepare a place for you? And if I go and prepare a place for you, I will come again and will take you to myself, that where I am you may be also. And you know the way to where I am going." John 14:1–4

Jesus has made it easy for us to come to Him. Jesus died on the cross and won forgiveness for all people. He comes to us in the Word of God and in the Sacraments. And when all our days have ended, this same Jesus promises to provide plenty of room for us to be with Him forever.

_____ Let's do: Jesus has given us several ways to come to Him. Write about some of them.

_____ Let's pray: Lord Jesus, what priceless gifts You have given me! Thank You that You are with me always. Amen.

G. S

No Fear

D ave's dad came home and went straight to the bedroom. He closed the door without speaking to anyone. "Mom, what's wrong?" Dave asked. "Is Dad sick?"

When the family had gathered, Dad came out and smiled a little. "I have some bad news," he said. "I lost my job. A bigger company bought the one I work for."

Nobody spoke for a while. Then Mom said, "It's all right, Don. We'll manage."

Dad hugged her, but shook his head. "We won't starve, but we'll have to sell one car right away. We have too many bills. I'll find another job soon. But for a while we'll need to be happy with less than we had before."

Dave raised his head. "We can do that," he said. "We haven't lost God. With His help, we can still be happy!"

Mom nodded. "The money does not matter. What matters is our faith in God."

God knows when things go wrong in our lives. He loves us and takes care of us every day. He loved us so much that He sent His Son, Jesus, to die for us. Because Jesus died to pay for our sins, we are rich in forgiveness. We are rich as God's own children. Knowing that, we can be content no matter what happens!

_____Let's do: Write about a problem that you or your family has. How can God help you even though the problem isn't solved yet?

_____Let's pray: Father, thank You for taking care of my family. Help me to be content. In Jesus' name. Amen.

G. S.

The Best Foundation

Read from God's Word

"Everyone then who hears these words of Mine and does them will be like a wise man who built his house on the rock. And the rain fell, and the floods came, and the winds blew and beat on that house, but it did not fall, because it had been founded on the rock. And everyone who hears these words of Mine and does not do them will be like a foolish man who built his house on the sand. And the rain fell, and the floods came, and the winds blew and beat against that house, and it fell, and great was the fall of it." Matthew 7:24–27 ᔥ

For months Matt had watched the workers on the highway near his house. The two-lane highway was being changed to four lanes.

First the workers began work on a new overpass that would carry traffic over the widened highway. "What are they doing, Dad?" Matt asked.

"They're hauling in dirt and creating a foundation for concrete that will support the new overpass," his dad explained.

"Wow," Matt said. The men were doing a lot of hard work!

Late in the spring heavy rains came, flooding some roads and low areas. Matt couldn't go to baseball practice. His backyard was full of water. Then one morning his dad came in with surprising news.

"You know that new overpass? Well, it collapsed before daylight today. There were no cars passing below, but now the highway is blocked. The foundation for the overpass was just too weak. When all the rain and wind came, it fell."

Lives, like roads, must be built on a foundation. Jesus Christ is the strongest possible foundation for our lives. Jesus makes us able to withstand the wind and rain of temptation, doubt, loss, and fear. He gave His life on the cross to earn forgiveness for the times when we aren't strong. Whoever believes in Him will have life that will never end.

_____Let's talk: Look again at Matthew 7:24. Whom does Jesus say the wise man represents? What are some ways you can be wise today?

_____Let's pray: Dear Jesus, help me put You first in my life. Amen.

G. S.

Daddy Home?

Two-year-old Nathan asks the same question almost every morning when he wakes up. He looks up at his mom and asks, "Daddy home?"

Except on weekends, the answer is usually "No, Daddy's at work. He'll be home tonight." Daddy's arrival at home is always greeted with great excitement. Nathan loves his daddy, and having him home means extra attention and fun, an extra person to talk to, and an extra sense of security.

Maybe you can understand how Nathan feels. Maybe you look forward to time you can spend with your dad. Maybe you don't get to see much of him. Perhaps your dad lives far away or just isn't home very much. Even if you've never even met your dad, you have a Father who is always around.

Your Father God never sleeps. He is never too busy for you. He is always willing to talk to you through His Word or listen to you through your prayers.

He loves you so much that He takes care of your needs. In fact, He has taken care of your greatest need by providing His own Son to be Your Savior. Now, through faith, You are blessed to call Him your Father. You are secure in His presence for He is always your Dad!

_____Let's talk: Read the First Article of the Apostles' Creed. What are some things about your heavenly Father that you appreciate?

_____Let's pray: Heavenly Father, thank You for being my perfect Father. Thank You for my earthly father as well. Amen.

M. W.

A Temporary Journey

Read from God's Word

But our citizenship is in heaven, and from it we await a Savior, the Lord Jesus Christ, who will transform our lowly body to be like His glorious body, by the power that enables Him even to subject all things to Himself. Therefore, my brothers, whom I love and long for, my joy and crown, stand firm thus in the Lord, my beloved. Philippians 3:20–4:1 ✍

Who is the oldest person you know? Living that number of years may seem like forever to you now, but compared to all of history, it really isn't very long. After all, the oldest person in the Bible, Methuselah, lived to be 969 years old (Genesis 5:27).

The length of time each person spends on earth really isn't very long at all. But don't panic about not having time to do all the things you want to do. Your life is a journey, a fascinating trip. God has great plans for you; just don't wander away from Him!

All those who trust in Jesus as their Savior from sin have forgiveness and new life. The best thing about being a Christian is that, thanks to Jesus, the destination of our journey is life forever with Him in heaven!

God encourages us to remember each day the reward He has won for us through Jesus. Through the loneliness of summer camp or the arguments with our friends, we remember we belong to God. Through Little League victories or swimming struggles we are God's children, forgiven and giving. In all the days of our journey—both good and bad—we have peace, for we have a rich inheritance.

_____Let's do: Write about some of the things you would like to do during your life. How can God use these things?

_____Let's pray: Lord, thank You for being the God of heaven and earth. Thank You for knowing what is best for me. Help me to trust You all of my life. In Jesus' name. Amen.

M. W.

Read from God's Word

But if we walk in the light, as He is in the light, we have fellowship with one another, and the blood of Jesus His Son cleanses us from all sin. 1 John 1:7 ✑

The Best Detergent

Maria sat at the kitchen table, painting a picture. She was so focused on her painting that she wasn't paying attention to the things around her. Suddenly, the pot of black paint tipped over, making a black stream across Maria's painting and a huge blotch on the front of her favorite shirt.

"They're ruined!" Maria wailed.

Maria's mom agreed that the painting was beyond hope, but perhaps the shirt could be saved. Maria watched her mom pour stain remover all over the black spot, then rub it in. "We'll just have to wait and see how it turns out," she said.

The shirt looked pretty good. There was a faint gray spot where the paint had soaked all the way through, but for the most part, it was clean.

As sinful human beings, every person is stained by sin. This stain is so bad that without a special cleaner, it would be permanent. The only thing that can clean this stain is the blood of Jesus Christ. Through Jesus' death and resurrection, the stain of sin is taken away. Unlike a lot of laundry products, Jesus' blood cleans so completely that not even a hint of a spot remains. Thanks be to God that we have been given the gift of the world's best stain remover!

_____Let's do: Sin contaminates; Jesus purifies. Write two other differences between sin and Jesus.

_____Let's pray: Lord Jesus, thank You for dying on the cross and overcoming death to remove all my sinful stains. Amen.

M. W.

Gasoline and God's Word

What is the longest road trip you have ever taken? Chicago to Orlando? Seattle to Phoenix? Toronto to Vancouver? How many times did you stop for gas? In order to keep going, the car has to be refueled regularly.

The same is true for people. Most children can go for about three hours before they need some fuel—a piece of fruit or a slice of pizza. Without that regular refueling you may feel a little helpless—too weak to push the lawn mower. You body might even have a breakdown—the kind where you end up sick.

Christians also need regular refueling. The kind of fuel we need, however, does not come from a gas pump. The kind of fuel every Christian needs comes from the Word of God and the Sacraments—Baptism and the Lord's Supper. These are the ways God connects us to His grace, refueling us by the power of the Holy Spirit. Without regular refueling, we are more likely to break down in our Christian walk and be helpless when facing the attacks of Satan.

God offers us the gift of forgiveness and salvation freely through the means of grace. These means are the best fuel around, getting us where He wants us to go!

Read from God's Word

But as for you, continue in what you have learned and have firmly believed, knowing from whom you learned it and how from childhood you have been acquainted with the sacred writings, which are able to make you wise for salvation through faith in Christ Jesus. All Scripture is breathed out by God and profitable for teaching, for reproof, for correction, and for training in righteousness. 2 Timothy 3:14–16

_____Let's talk: When have you felt a little "low on fuel" in your spiritual life? Is there anything you can do to help avoid this in the future?

_____Let's pray: Lord, thank You for being my source of spiritual fuel. Guide me to regularly "fill my tank" with Your power. In Jesus' name. Amen.

M. W.

What's in a Name?

Oh, what can be the reason to have
more than just one name?
They all refer to just one God.
Why aren't they all the same?
When reading names mysterious,
El Shaddai or Adonai,
It makes me wonder what's the point.
It makes me wonder why
God doesn't use a common name l
ike Abbey, John, or Tim.
Just maybe all these special names
reveal a special Him.
Nothing's regular in the name
Almighty God Most High,
But then, my God's an awesome God
and not a regular guy!
He's Wonderful; Jehovah; the Truth,
the Life, the Way;
The Holy One of Israel; Eternal;
and Yahweh.
He saved me from the death of sin
when nothing I could do.
He's marked me with the cross of Christ. He's named me Christian too.
It's clear from all these names for God, His love will never end,
And so I call Him Great Redeemer, Savior, and my Friend.

God is much greater than any name or any word could ever describe. Yet He loves us and gave His Son to die for our sins. Because of Jesus, someday we will be in His presence. We will no longer need words to describe His glory because we will experience it firsthand!

_____Let's do: List and find out the meanings of these names for God. A Bible dictionary is a good place to start.

_____Let's pray: Almighty God, I praise You for all of Your greatness! Help me to learn and understand as much about You as I possibly can. In Jesus' name. Amen.

M. W.

Limits That Give Freedom

Read from God's Word

But the one who looks into the perfect law, the law of liberty, and perseveres, being no hearer who forgets but a doer who acts, he will be blessed in his doing. James 1:25

Imagine a kite up in the sky. You are watching it soar and dance in the gentle wind. Does it seem restricted or penned in? Of course not. It's totally free except for one thing. A string is keeping it from going too far or into dangerous places.

Sometimes people complain about God's Law and say, "Christians just have too many rules. I don't want to obey all those strict commandments. I want to be free to do what I want." Does this sound familiar?

Let's return to that imaginary kite. As the wind carries it across the sky, the string breaks. What happens? Without its string the kite will eventually be ruined. It may crash to the ground or get blown into some trees or tangled in wires. The string that held the kite back made the kite able to fly. It also helped keep it safe.

God's Law is kind of like that kite string. It may seem to hold you back sometimes, but God doesn't give you His Law because He doesn't like you. He gives you His Law because He loves you and knows what is best for you. He loves you so much, in fact, that He gave you the ultimate freedom: freedom from sin and death through Jesus Christ!

_____Let's talk: What are some examples of situations where following God's Law would help keep you safe?

_____Let's pray: Dear Lord, thank You for the gift of Your Law. Help me to follow it willingly. Thank You for the freedom that is always found in You. Amen.

M. W.

Summer

Read from God's Word

And God said, "Let there be lights in the expanse of the heavens to separate the day from the night. And let them be for signs and for seasons, and for days and years, and let them be lights in the expanse of the heavens to give light upon the earth." And it was so. And God made the two great lights—the greater light to rule the day and the lesser light to rule the night—and the stars. And God set them in the expanse of the heavens to give light on the earth, to rule over the day and over the night, and to separate the light from the darkness. And God saw that it was good. And there was evening and there was morning, the fourth day. Genesis 1:14–19 ✐

The first day of summer has arrived in North America. How do we know when summer arrives? Astronomers study the path the earth travels around the sun, the earth's orbit.

As the earth travels in its orbit, the North Pole is either pointed away from the sun or toward the sun. Today the North Pole is pointed most nearly toward the sun.

What other things can we learn from studying the stars? Before there were compasses, sailors used the North Star to help them find their way. Now airplane pilots and astronauts can use the stars to guide them. Did you see the movie *Apollo 13?* The astronauts used the stars to direct their path when their computers failed.

God's stars are part of His marvelous creation. They can tell us many things. But they do not tell us our future, especially our future in God's plan. In Philippians Paul urges us to "shine like stars" (2:15, NIV). We can do that because God has made us His children through faith in Christ. By His power we can shine His light in a sinful world.

_____Let's do: Draw a large star. Inside it write what Jesus has done to make you "shine."

_____Let's pray: Thank You, heavenly Father, for making the sun, moon, and stars—and thanks for making me. Help me to shine for You through faith in Jesus. In His name I pray. Amen.

E. P. L.

May I Help You?

When Emma was a little girl, she liked to go to the grocery store with her mother. A clerk stood behind a counter, and the groceries were on shelves behind the clerk.

The clerk asked, "May I help you?" Emma's mother would read her grocery list. The clerk would put each item on the counter.

Today—without help—we pick out our own DVDs, shoes, or lettuce. We pump our own gas. Most of the time we think this is a good idea. We usually don't want help.

There are some things we can never do for ourselves. We can't wash away our own sins. We can't make ourselves to be perfect.

Thank God that we don't have to do these things for ourselves. God is always there to ask, "May I help you?" He wants to help and has the almighty power to do it. Because of God's help, Jesus died so our sins are forgiven. And God helps us by sending His Holy Spirit so we can have the faith and power to do things that please Him.

Read from God's Word

I lift up my eyes to the hills. From where does my help come? My help comes from the LORD, who made heaven and earth. He will not let your foot be moved; He who keeps you will not slumber. Behold, He who keeps Israel will neither slumber nor sleep. The LORD is your keeper; the LORD is your shade on your right hand. The sun shall not strike you by day, nor the moon by night. The LORD will keep you from all evil; He will keep your life. The LORD will keep your going out and your coming in from this time forth and forevermore. Psalm 121

_____Let's do: Make a list of your wants and your needs. Then ask God to give you what is best.

_____Let's pray: Thank You, dear Father, for always helping me, especially through Your Son. Help me to rely on You. In Jesus' name. Amen.

E. P. L.

Read from God's Word

"If you love Me, you will keep My commandments. And I will ask the Father, and He will give you another Helper to be with you forever, even the Spirit of truth, whom the world cannot receive, because it neither sees Him nor knows Him. You know Him, for He dwells with you and will be in you. I will not leave you as orphans; I will come to you. Yet a little while and the world will see Me no more, but you will see Me. Because I live, you also will live. In that day you will know that I am in My Father, and you in Me, and I in you. Whoever has My commandments and keeps them, he it is who loves Me. And he who loves Me will be loved by My Father, and I will love him and manifest Myself to him." John 14:15–21*

Practice, Practice, Practice!

People travel to New York City just to hear famous musicians perform in Carnegie Hall. In fact, it is the goal of many musicians to play on that stage.

One day a visitor wanted to see this famous place. She saw a man carrying a violin case, so she stopped him and asked, "How can I get to Carnegie Hall?"

The musician answered, "Practice, practice, practice!"

That didn't help the visitor find the place, but the advice was very good.

Think of the things you had to practice as a very young child—walking, talking, eating with a spoon. Add to your list all the things you learn at school—What a long list!

In addition to all that, God wants us to learn to obey Him. That will take more than just practice. No matter how hard we try, we cannot obey God's rules perfectly. Only Jesus could do that for us.

Now that Jesus has kept all the rules, we have a special kind of life. This new life we have through Christ in Baptism teaches us to practice God's ways. We haven't learned it perfectly yet. We still sin and are sinful by nature, but our forgiving God loves us and forgives us for Jesus' sake. One day we'll love perfectly with Him in heaven.

——Let's talk: Look again at the Bible reading. What are some facts about the Spirit of truth?

——Let's pray: Dear Lord Jesus, please forgive the times I don't obey Your commands. Help me to do Your will. Amen.

E. P. L.

Slippers and Sandals

Read from God's Word

Having gifts that differ according to the grace given to us, let us use them: if prophecy, in proportion to our faith; if service, in our serving; the one who teaches, in his teaching; the one who exhorts, in his exhortation; the one who contributes, in generosity; the one who leads, with zeal; the one who does acts of mercy, with cheerfulness. Romans 12:6–8

Your mom may have mules, oxfords, loafers, and sandals. Do you know what those are? Yes, they're all shoes. We wear different shoes with different clothes and for different occasions.

How do you choose a new pair of shoes? Do you choose shoes because they look nice? If they are too big or too small, that would be foolish. Would you go outside in sandals when the snow is deep? Would you wear boots at the beach?

Shoes are different for good reasons, and God has made His children different for good reasons too.

God can use His people in many different ways. When God chose Moses to lead His people, Moses couldn't speak very well. God told Moses to let his brother Aaron talk for him.

Saul was a big, strong man who wore heavy armor. He fought with a heavy sword. David was smaller. He threw stones with a leather sling. God used both of these men to lead His people.

Deborah was an Israelite. Jael was a Kenite. God used these women from different tribes to help His people. (You can read about them in Judges 4.) But all God's people are loved by Him. All are saved through faith in Jesus Christ. And all are useful in His service—including you!

_____Let's talk: What makes you different from other people? How can God use your differences to serve others?

_____Let's pray: Dear Lord Jesus, help me find ways to serve. I want to find a special way to say, "Thank You for dying for my sins." Amen.

E. P. L.

Read from God's Word

And one of the scribes came up and heard them disputing with one another, and seeing that He answered them well, asked Him, "Which commandment is the most important of all?" Jesus answered, "The most important is, 'Hear, O Israel: The Lord our God, the Lord is one. And you shall love the Lord your God with all your heart and with all your soul and with all your mind and with all your strength.' The second is this: 'You shall love your neighbor as yourself.' There is no other commandment greater than these." Mark 12:28–31

Enjoy Your Trip!

Marcie and Scott were riding in the backseat on the way to visit their grandparents. Scott, Mother, and Father were playing a game. First they looked for an object beginning with the letter A. Father said, "automobile." Then mother said, "There's a billboard for B." Scott saw a calf.

Marcie was complaining. "When will we get to Grandmother's? Why can't I sit up front?"

Who do you think was having more fun?

We know that Christians are on a trip to heaven. Jesus died so we could be there with Him forever. God wants our trip to be happy too. He doesn't make everything perfect, like it will be in heaven. But He gives us His Word and His church to guide and help us. He gives us faith and new life in Baptism. He gives us the Holy Spirit to help us grow. And He gives us Jesus, who earned forgiveness for us when we break the rules.

Jesus said the most important rules are to love the Lord, our God, and to love our neighbor. On our own we cannot do this because of sin. But through faith, Jesus is at work in us, helping us to love and leading us in God's way. And through faith, we can be happy along the way.

_____Let's talk: How can loving God and others make our life on this earth more pleasant? What are some ways you can show your love?

_____Let's pray: Dear heavenly Father, help us remember that You are always with us, always ready to help us, and always ready to forgive us. In Jesus' name we pray. Amen.

E. P. L.

Follow the Leader

I t was a lovely summer day. The school band was outdoors to practice marching. They marched away from the school and up the street, playing as they marched.

For 20 minutes they marched and played as the bandleader led them up one street and around a corner, down another street and around more corners.

The sky grew cloudy. It looked like rain.

"Who knows the shortest way back to school?" asked the lost bandleader.

One of the students said, "I do." The band followed the student uphill for 15 minutes. There was no more music; they were *really* lost.

At last they came to a place where they could see the school and a road they could follow back to it. The band members struggled down the hill in the rain.

When you follow a leader, it's best to have a leader who knows his followers and knows where he is going. Jesus is the best leader. He knows us and called us to be His own in Baptism. He will forgive us and lead us in His ways through lovely days and drizzle, now and forever.

Read from God's Word

Make me to know Your ways, O LORD; teach me Your paths. Lead me in Your truth and teach me, for You are the God of my salvation; for You I wait all the day long. Remember Your mercy, O LORD, and Your steadfast love, for they have been from of old. Remember not the sins of my youth or my transgressions; according to Your steadfast love remember me, for the sake of Your goodness, O LORD! Good and upright is the LORD; therefore He instructs sinners in the way. He leads the humble in what is right, and teaches the humble His way. All the paths of the LORD are steadfast love and faithfulness, for those who keep His covenant and His testimonies. For Your name's sake, O LORD, pardon my guilt, for it is great. Psalm 25:4–11 ✑

_____Let's do: Write about the kind of help David is asking God to give him in Psalm 25.

_____Let's pray: Lead me in Your paths, O Lord. Help me know how to please You. In Jesus' name. Amen.

E. P. L.

Read from God's Word

He who did not spare His own Son but gave Him up for us all, how will He not also with Him graciously give us all things?
Romans 8:32 ✍

You're a Winner!

[M] arcus thought about winning a million dollars. *I'd have a bigger house and a motorcycle and...*

Then he began to think about all the things he already had. *I've always had a family that loved me. There is always something to wear in my closet. There is always food in my refrigerator and on my kitchen shelves.*

There had always been a church and Sunday school where he heard about his Savior. There were always friends to meet in church. God made Marcus able to learn in school and go to college. He helped Marcus enjoy his work as a teacher.

If I tried to list everything God has given me, Marcus thought, *I would never reach the end of the list. It would take forever to tell what He has done for me.*

The best gift God gave Marcus is Jesus. Jesus came to earth for him. Jesus died on the cross to pay for his sins. Jesus rose from the dead. Jesus went back to heaven and is praying for Marcus now.

God didn't give His Son only for Marcus. Jesus did all these things for everyone in the whole world. Jesus is for you too. And since God gave us His Son, He will surely give us all we really need.

_____Let's talk: We may never have a million dollars, but we will have everything God knows we need. What gifts from God do you appreciate? Why?

_____Let's pray: Thank You, dear heavenly Father, for giving us Your Son. Thank You for giving us everything we need to live. In Jesus' name. Amen.

E. P. L.

Tools

C an you match these tasks with the proper tools?

___ 1. Nailing boards together
___ 2. Flipping pancakes
___ 3. Digging a hole
___ 4. Cutting grass
___ 5. Stirring food
___ 6. Slicing meat
___ 7. Learning God's will

a. Shovel
b. Knife
c. Lawn mower
d. Bible
e. Hammer
f. Spatula
g. Spoon

Did you wonder why the Bible is on the list? We don't usually think of the Bible as a tool. But it is.

A great thing about this tool is that we can store it in our brain. When we read or hear the Bible, we can remember what it says.

When we are alone, we can remember the Bible's promise that Jesus is near. We may be tempted to steal something, but then remember, as it says in the Bible, that Jesus lives in us and helps us resist temptation. We may become angry and want to hit someone or call him or her names, but then recall the Bible's assurance that God forgives us for Jesus' sake.

Read from God's Word

All Scripture is breathed out by God and profitable for teaching, for reproof, for correction, and for training in righteousness, that the man of God may be competent, equipped for every good work. 2 Timothy 3:16–17

Especially we can remember that the Bible tells us of our Savior, Jesus Christ, who forgives our sins and will lead us to heaven.

_____Let's talk: What do you like best about the Bible? Why?

_____Let's pray: Thank You, God, for the wonderful tool You gave us in Your Word. Guide us in Your ways. Amen.

E. P. L.

Guard My Lips

Imagine taking a can of shaving cream to the sink. You squirt a great big pile of that shaving cream into the sink. Imagine the fun! You just had to keep pushing that button and letting that creamy stuff flow out and pile up.

Now ... imagine having to put it back in. That's right. Put that fluffy pile of shaving cream back into the can. You can't do it? Once it's out, it's out!

It's the same way with the things you say. Once words come out of your mouth, you can't gather them up and shove them down your throat. You can't catch them before they reach the hearer's ear.

King David understood very well that his mouth could get him into trouble. In Psalm 141:3 he prayed, "Set a guard, O LORD, over my mouth." He knew how easy it is to let any old thing flow right out of one's mouth and how important it is *not* to do that.

Praise God! Jesus took with Him to the cross all of the unguarded words we've spoken. He paid for our sins and won new life for us, life in which, with His help, we can guard our words so they will be a blessing.

_____Let's do: Write about a time you wish you could have taken back something you said. What are some ways the words of your mouth can be guarded? Look at Psalm 119:11–16.

_____Let's pray: Dear Jesus, forgive me for the times I have said hurtful things. Help me to guard the things I say. Amen.

M. W

Good News

D o you sometimes listen to the news on television? Have you ever heard someone say, "Why do they only tell us the bad things?" What makes something get into the news?

Good things happen all the time. God sends sunshine and rain to make crops grow in all parts of the world. We don't see a long report on the news about this. One or two places may have bad storms or not enough rain; that makes the news.

There are hundreds of cities in many countries where people are living safe lives. There are a few places where there are wars and fighting. The beautiful and safe places are not shown on the news, but the others are.

How many homes are in your city? Very few of these will ever be in the news unless there is a terrible fire. Even a little fire won't be news.

Only unusual events make the news on TV or show up in the newspaper. God's goodness isn't unusual—it happens all the time. It isn't news—it's normal. God is *always* blessing us. His gift of a Savior offers forgiveness of sins and new life in Christ to all, not just a few. That's the remarkable Good News of the Gospel!

Read from God's Word

Finally, brothers, whatever is true, whatever is honorable, whatever is just, whatever is pure, whatever is lovely, whatever is commendable, if there is any excellence, if there is anything worthy of praise, think about these things. Philippians 4:8 ✍

_____Let's do: Write about something you can think about that matches the ideas found in Philippians 4:8. Share your idea with someone else.

_____Let's pray: "Whatever is true, whatever is honorable, whatever is just, whatever is pure, whatever is lovely, whatever is commendable"—Lord Jesus, help me think about these things. Amen.

E. P. L.

july

Contributors for this month:

Lisa Hahn

Phil Lang

Jessemyn Schulz

Susan M. Schulz

Susan Waterman Voss

Summer Days

Read from God's Word

No man shall be able to stand before you all the days of your life. Just as I was with Moses, so I will be with you. I will not leave you or forsake you. Joshua 1:5

Some people would call July their favorite time of the year. It's time to relax and enjoy being outside. Schedules are filled with ball games, swimming, picnics, and vacations.

We can eliminate some of the hectic parts of our routine—like lots of homework. But we wouldn't want to eliminate chances to worship and learn more about God. Vacation Bible school is a summer opportunity to learn about Jesus. Christian summer camps are open. Families may need to adjust their devotion time each day, but that can be fun too.

Schedule changes don't need to stop us from worshiping God or studying His Word. We can relax under a shade tree at the rest stop with our Bibles. We can visit a different church on summer vacation. We can invite a neighbor to vacation Bible school. Even the summer weather can help us think about God's power and care for us.

God promises never to leave us or forsake us—in summer days or school days. He did not abandon us to eternal death because of our sins. He provided an escape for us through the death of His Son. He certainly will not leave us now.

Take some time to thank God for that ever-present love. Leave lots of room for Him in your daily summer plans.

_____Let's talk: When have you been especially thankful that God will "not leave you or forsake you?"

_____Let's pray: Dear Lord, You promised to be with me always. Help me remember to make time for You in my life. In Jesus' name. Amen.

S. W. V.

Read from God's Word

"One who is faithful in a very little is also faithful in much, and one who is dishonest in a very little is also dishonest in much. If then you have not been faithful in the unrighteous wealth, who will entrust to you the true riches? And if you have not been faithful in that which is another's, who will give you that which is your own? No servant can serve two masters, for either he will hate the one and love the other, or he will be devoted to the one and despise the other. You cannot serve God and money."
Luke 16:10–13 ᴄ⋗

Serving the Master

Bo had grown up happily in a small-town backyard. But he was now a 70-pound retriever and needed more room to run and play.

Bo was given to a family who lived three miles away. Although he missed his first owners, he grew to love his new farm family.

Often in the evening Bo would take a romp through the countryside. One night he somehow happened upon a familiar scent. He managed to travel three miles back to town, to the doorstep of his original family.

The family was glad to see Bo and allowed him to spend the night. The next morning Bo's new owners came to retrieve him. He was overjoyed to see them as well. But Bo cannot have two masters.

The masters in our Bible reading are God and money. God doesn't want to share the number one spot in our lives with an itching desire for money or the things it can buy. God wants us to see money as it truly is—His gift. God wants to have first place in our lives.

This generous God gives us faith and forgives all our sins because of Jesus' sacrifice on the cross. Moved by God's great mercy, we are thankful that He is our only master—the only One who deserves our total love and loyalty.

_____Let's talk: How could earthly wealth be wisely used for an eternal benefit?

_____Let's pray: Dear God, help us always to serve only You. Thank You for Your countless blessings. In Your Son's holy name. Amen.

S. W. V.

Don't Give Up

Read from God's Word

Then Moses and the people of Israel sang this song to the LORD, saying, "I will sing to the LORD, for He has triumphed gloriously; the horse and his rider, He has thrown into the sea. The LORD is my strength and my song, and He has become my salvation; this is my God, and I will praise Him, my father's God, and I will exalt Him." Exodus 15:1–2 ⸏

avid Graham lined up with hundreds of other runners. Although he was just seven years old, David had trained to run in the Independence Day two-mile run.

The two-mile run seemed extra long to David. He finally realized he had missed the turnaround for his race and was now in the middle of a different, longer race.

David could stop and wait to be driven back to the finish line, or he could keep going. His mom had seen him miss the turn. She ran alongside him and encouraged him to keep going. David kept running. What a surprise—he won the gold medal!

In today's Bible reading Moses wanted to quit before he had even begun. God didn't accept Moses' excuses. Instead, He gave Moses the help and strength he needed to go on and do the job.

Sometimes we feel like David and Moses. The job may seem too hard or unpleasant. We want to quit. But God will give us strength for the tasks that are pleasing to Him. He showed us that strong love when He won salvation for us, sending His Son to suffer in our place. Surely that strong Lord will help us through the tasks of our lives here on earth.

———Let's talk: Read Exodus 4:10–16. Give some examples of times when God has given you strength.

———Let's pray: Dear Lord God, give us the strength to do all that is pleasing to You. In our Savior's name we pray. Amen.

S. W. V.

Read from God's Word

"And when you pray, do not heap up empty phrases as the Gentiles do, for they think that they will be heard for their many words. Do not be like them, for your Father knows what you need before you ask Him. Pray then like this: 'Our Father in heaven, hallowed be Your name. Your kingdom come, Your will be done, on earth as it is in heaven. Give us this day our daily bread, and forgive us our debts, as we also have forgiven our debtors. And lead us not into temptation, but deliver us from evil.'" Matthew 6:7–13 ✑

Cotton-Candy Prayers

Leah did not want to be late. Today was carnival day—the best day of the summer.

At the top of Leah's list was sampling cotton candy. She had seen that dazzling pink puff, but she had never eaten it. She went straight to the cotton candy when she arrived at the park. She was determined to finally get her first taste.

Leah waited and finally reached the front of the line. The huge mound was in her hand. She took a bite. What? There must be some mistake, she thought. Cotton candy was nothing but sugar. It really wasn't much of anything.

"Empty phrases," like cotton candy, lack substance. Jesus tells us not to use empty phrases when we pray. God is not impressed with "cotton-candy" prayers. Those kinds of prayers sound impressive, but they lack meaning. God wants us to talk to Him with words from our hearts. The Lord's Prayer is that kind of prayer, simple and to the point. Jesus gave it to us as an example to guide us in speaking to our heavenly Father.

Thank God that He allows us to talk to Him about anything. Thank God that we have forgiveness through Jesus and faith from the Holy Spirit so we can come confidently to Him in prayer.

_____Let's do: Read Matthew 6:1–4. Write about the right and wrong way to give to the needy. Do you see any connections to Jesus' directions for prayer?

_____Let's pray: Today pray the Lord's Prayer or make up a simple prayer of your own.

S. W. V.

Jesus Makes Us New

There was one slight mishap at vacation Bible school this year. One staff member was trying to coax some purple paint out of a clogged plastic pump. Suddenly the entire bottle seemed to erupt. Paint was everywhere—on faces and clothing and even on the carpet. What a relief that hair, skin, and clothes could be rinsed clean. Everything looked normal again except the carpet.

Purple tempera paint simply does not come out of gold carpet. We tried everything! We spent hours blotting and scrubbing, but the stains remained. It was no use. Professional cleaners were called in, but they failed as well. Only a miracle could remove the stains.

Our sins are like those purple paint stains. There is nothing on earth that can remove the consequences of our sinful acts or sinful condition. Try as we may, we simply cannot erase the damage done by even one little, teensy-weensy sin. It takes a miracle to make us new.

Jesus Christ is that miracle. He came to earth to blot out the stain of sin. He suffered and died in our place. He rose from the dead to take away the sin of the world, leaving us clean and pure. By His grace we are spotless. By His grace we are new.

Read from God's Word

From now on, therefore, we regard no one according to the flesh. Even though we once regarded Christ according to the flesh, we regard Him thus no longer. Therefore, if anyone is in Christ, he is a new creation. The old has passed away; behold, the new has come. All this is from God, who through Christ reconciled us to Himself and gave us the ministry of reconciliation; that is, in Christ God was reconciling the world to Himself, not counting their trespasses against them, and entrusting to us the message of reconciliation. 2 Corinthians 5:16–19 ✐

————Let's do: What does *reconciliation* mean? Write out verse 18 using that new meaning.

————Let's pray: Dear Lord God, thank You for sending Jesus to remove the damage of sin in our lives and giving us His perfection. In Jesus' name we pray. Amen.

S. W. V.

Read from God's Word

"Let not your hearts be troubled. Believe in God; believe also in Me. In my Father's house are many rooms. If it were not so, would I have told you that I go to prepare a place for you? And if I go and prepare a place for you, I will come again and will take you to Myself, that where I am you may be also." John 14:1–3 ⌇

My Father's Home

For two months Annie had looked forward to her family's vacation. She wasn't disappointed. Annie and her family swam, fished, and hiked. They visited tourist attractions, snapped photos, and bought souvenirs. Annie even rode the double-loop roller coaster at the amusement park.

As the family drove home, Annie gazed out the window. After a while she noticed that the scenery was familiar. She began to feel excited again, but this time she was excited about going home. Even after her fantastic vacation, nothing sounded better to her right now than sleeping in her own bed, seeing her friends, and playing with her dog. Getting away for a while is nice, but coming home often feels even more special.

Jesus spoke about longing for heaven that way. Although we have never been there, heaven is our final home. The Bible tells us that it will be better than anything here on earth. With God our Father there, it will truly be our home—more comfortable, safe, and secure than any place we could imagine.

We did not earn heaven. It is God's salvation gift. He planned it for His children. Jesus Himself earned it for us when He gave up His life and rose again. What a wonderful homecoming it will be to join our Savior in eternal glory!

_____Let's talk: What problem did the disciples have in verse 1 of today's reading? What was God's direction/solution in that same verse? How can that message help you?

_____Let's pray: Thank You, God, for the wonderful promise of heaven. Help me to trust in You. In Jesus' name. Amen.

S. W. V.

One Thing Is Needful

Susan received a picnic basket as a gift. It was large enough to hold what was necessary and small enough to carry easily. Inside were some special things—a plastic tablecloth to spread on not-so-clean tables, two plates and cups, two sets of silverware, and a package of paper napkins. Sounds perfect, right?

One very important thing was missing. You can't have a picnic without food! The basket was packed with all the "extras." The things left for Susan to provide were the most essential—food and drink.

Our lives on this earth are somewhat like that picnic basket. Many people are without things necessary for daily life. However, most of us reading this probably have the basics—food, water, clothing, a place to call home, and people who care for us.

Those are wonderful things to have. Even so, one very important item is missing. To make our lives worthwhile, we need to have Christ living in us.

Read from God's Word

Now as they went on their way, Jesus entered a village. And a woman named Martha welcomed Him into her house. And she had a sister called Mary, who sat at the Lord's feet and listened to His teaching. But Martha was distracted with much serving. And she went up to Him and said, "Lord, do You not care that my sister has left me to serve alone? Tell her then to help me." But the Lord answered her, "Martha, Martha, you are anxious and troubled about many things, but one thing is necessary. Mary has chosen the good portion, which will not be taken away from her." Luke 10:38–42* ☙

God gives us that new life in Baptism. Through faith in our Savior, God gives us salvation from sin and eternal life with Him in heaven. God gives us everything needed.

In our reading Mary knew what was really important—Jesus Christ. Ask God to help you keep Jesus as the most important part of your life.

_____Let's do: Write about or draw a picture of one of the places where you, like Mary, can learn of Jesus.

_____Let's pray: Dear Father in heaven, we often forget how important You are in our lives and how much You love us. Help us by Your Spirit to keep You always on our minds and in our hearts. For Jesus' sake. Amen.

S. W. V.

Chosen

Paul and Tyrone chose to be friends. Tyrone would load up his red wagon with toys and pull it over to Paul's house. They played at Paul's house in the morning and at Tyrone's house in the afternoon. The good memories of Paul have remained with Tyrone long after his family moved away.

Good friends show respect for one another, accept differences, and delight in one another. They acknowl-edge one another's interests and strengths. Good friends share feelings.

Jesus is a good friend. In fact, Jesus is the best kind of friend. He is with us wherever we go. He accepts us and delights in us. He is interested in our ideas. He is always around so we can talk to Him in prayer. His Word tells us about His love. It keeps us close to Him. Our friend Jesus chose us and named us to be His own in Baptism. He chose us to be part of the holy Christian church, giving us lots of Christian friends.

Jesus loves sinners. He loved them so much that He laid down His life for them all—every single one. He took the eternal punishment for sin when He died on the cross. And now, victorious, He makes us friends with God again and chooses us to share His love with others.

——Let's do: How are obedience and love connected in today's reading? Write about that idea.

——Let's pray: Dear Jesus, thank You for choosing me and for being my best friend! Amen.

P. L.

The Question Is

L isten to the question of the day," announced Mr. Goodbar. "What kinds of things do the following words have in common—MOUNDS, HEATH, SKOR, YORK, 5TH AVENUE, MILK DUDS, and WHOPPERS?"

Javier raised his hand, "They're all proper nouns."

Monique blurted out, "No, they are all things made with chocolate."

"I get it!" interrupted Xiang. "They are all candy."

"Yes," responded Mr. Goodbar. "They are all names of candy that have chocolate in them. However, there is another surprising way that they are all alike. They are all made by the same company! How are people like these candies?"

The class came up with lots of ideas—we look different, talk and act differently. And they said that we all have the same Maker—God! God made His children with lots of variety, and that's good. God also declared us perfect in Baptism.

Read from God's Word

Then God said, "Let us make man in our image, after our likeness. And let them have dominion over the fish of the sea and over the birds of the heavens and over the livestock and over all the earth and over every creeping thing that creeps on the earth." So God created man in His own image, in the image of God He created him; male and female He created them. And God blessed them. And God said to them, "Be fruitful and multiply and fill the earth and subdue it and have dominion over the fish of the sea and over the birds of the heavens and over every living thing that moves on the earth." Genesis 1:26–28 ✑

Mr. Goodbar reminded the class that when Adam and Eve sinned, the perfect relationship between God and man was broken. God sent His own Son to restore that broken relationship, to make the way for a perfect salvation. Jesus did that restoration. He lived perfectly, died painfully, and rose triumphantly. Our victorious Jesus redeemed, restored, and renamed us as His. That's good news for every day.

_____Let's talk: What are some of the "sweet" benefits of being made by God and then reclaimed by God?

_____Let's pray: Thank You, God, for making and loving all people. Help me to love everyone like You do. In Jesus' name. Amen.

P. L.

Read from God's Word

Have this mind among yourselves, which is yours in Christ Jesus, who, though He was in the form of God, did not count equality with God a thing to be grasped, but made Himself nothing, taking the form of a servant, being born in the likeness of men. And being found in human form, He humbled Himself by becoming obedient to the point of death, even death on a cross. Therefore God has highly exalted Him and bestowed on Him the name that is above every name, so that at the name of Jesus every knee should bow, in heaven and on earth and under the earth, and every tongue confess that Jesus Christ is Lord, to the glory of God the Father. Philippians 2:5–11 ✍

Name That Name

 Name the Bible character described by each clue:

1. He spent three days in the belly of a great fish.
2. She became queen and saved the Jews from being killed.
3. He had long hair and was really strong.
4. David had him killed in order to marry his wife, Bathsheba.
5. He was known as the wisest man in the world.

1. _____
2. _____
3. _____
4. _____
5. _____

Scan down the first letter of each name that you filled in. Do you see another name? You probably found the name *Jesus!*

God put Jesus in first place—a name above every other name. Why did God do that? Philippians 2:6–7 says that *Jesus* gave up His divine throne in heaven so He could come to earth as one of us. *Jesus* humbled Himself to suffer and die for all our mistakes and disobedience. Because Jesus did so much out of love for us, God made *Jesus* the name that every tongue must confess to be saved. All of this is done by God's grace and for God's glory. Praise the name of *Jesus!*

_____Let's do: Write the letters of the name *Jesus* in a scattered fashion. Decorate each letter as you praise the name of Jesus.

_____Let's pray: Dear Jesus, Your name is wonderful. Thank You for loving me and saving me from eternal death. Amen.

P. L.

Three Surprises

P eter, come here. I have a surprise for you!" said Dad.

"What is it?" asked Peter curiously.

"It's a gift. I even wrapped it."

"But it isn't my birthday or Christmas. Why are you giving me a present?"

"Why?" responded Dad. "Just because you are my son. I love you. I want to give you a gift that will help you remember something."

Peter had the gift unwrapped in seconds. The things inside puzzled him, so he asked his dad, "Why did you give me a cross and a chalkboard eraser?"

"I want you to use the cross and the eraser to remind yourself every day that Jesus gives you the best gift of all," explained Dad.

"What's that?"

"Forgiveness for all your sins. Jesus died on the cross and then rose from the grave. He erased all the punishment for your sin. I want you to know, Son, that I could never give you a gift as valuable as the one Jesus gave you on the cross."

"Thanks, Dad."

"I'm glad you love Jesus. Let's celebrate with ice cream. See if there is a coupon in the bottom of the box."

"Wow! What a sweet idea!"

Now Peter has three special ways to remember God's love.

Read from God's Word

For by grace you have been saved through faith. And this is not your own doing: it is the gift of God, not a result of works, so that no one may boast. For we are His workmanship, created in Christ Jesus for good works, which God prepared beforehand, that we should walk in them. Ephesians 2:8–10

_____Let's talk: What item could you combine with a cross as a gift to help someone understand more about Jesus' love?

_____Let's pray: Dear God, thank You for the gift of forgiveness. Help me share that gift with others. In Jesus' name. Amen.

P. L.

Bars and Belts

Read from God's Word

God is our refuge and strength, a very present help in trouble. Therefore we will not fear though the earth gives way, though the mountains be moved into the heart of the sea, though its waters roar and foam, though the mountains tremble at its swelling. Psalm 46:1–3 ✍

Madison's favorite roller coaster starts out like a lightning bolt. Before she can count to 10, the coaster is roaring, twisting, and doubling back. To the screams and delight of the riders it climbs then plunges down a hundred feet.

Day-to-day situations in life are like an exciting-but-scary roller-coaster ride. The twists in our friendships and the turns of our achievements can shift us from feeling secure to feeling insecure. Sometimes it is exciting, but sometimes it is intimidating. It is not enough that we try to "hang on" for dear life even on the good days. We simply don't have the strength.

Psalm 46 reminds us that God is our refuge and strength. God keeps us safe even when life is screaming along and tilting our security. God knows the permanent damage and danger of sin. God provided Jesus as our belt of refuge—a Savior for all. Jesus won that belt of forgiveness and life everlasting for all believers by being the perfect sacrifice for our sin.

_____Let's talk: What God-given attitude is found in Psalm 46:2? When might this attitude help you or your family?

_____Let's pray: Dear Lord Jesus, thank You for keeping me safe through all the twists and turns of life. Lead me each day. Amen.

P. L.

Frank's Fiasco

Frank planted lettuce, peas, squash, and turnip seeds. But he didn't plant his "seeds" in the ground; he planted them in the lives of his family. He would expect a harvest of good behavior because he had told his children how to act.

Frank would say to his children, "Lettuce (let us) be kind." He would say, "We should strive for peas (peace) of mind and of heart. Squash the grumbling, squash the gossip and lies, and squash the meanness." With all that squashing, Frank expected great things to turnip (turn up)—like a cheerful and happy family.

Frank's style of gardening flopped. Frank forgot about sin. On their own, Frank's family couldn't do any of the good things in a way that God accepts. They all needed God's help.

We need God, the expert gardener. God tells us that He is the vine and we are the branches. We are connected to Him through Jesus, our Savior. We are connected to Him through baptismal waters and God's Word. We are connected to Him through His Spirit, who helps us produce all kinds of fruit—the fruit of righteousness.

We can thank Jesus. He "lettuce" be His by "squashing" the devil and the power of sin and giving us "peas" with God. With God, good things can "turnip"!

Read from God's Word

"I am the true vine, and My Father is the vinedresser. ... Abide in Me, and I in you. As the branch cannot bear fruit by itself, unless it abides in the vine, neither can you, unless you abide in Me. I am the vine; you are the branches. Whoever abides in Me and I in him, he it is that bears much fruit, for apart from Me you can do nothing. If anyone does not abide in Me he is thrown away like a branch and withers; and the branches are gathered, thrown into the fire, and burned. If you abide in Me, and my words abide in you, ask whatever you wish, and it will be done for you. By this My Father is glorified, that you bear much fruit and so prove to be My disciples." John 15:1–8 ✐

_____Let's do: Read Galatians 5:22–23. Write about some of the fruit listed.

_____Let's pray: Dear Jesus, may my life be fruitful for You and in You. Amen.

P. L.

Dog Days

What are the dog days of summer? They are not days when it is so hot that dogs lie around, tongues hanging out, panting for water.

The dog days of summer are actually named after the star Sirius (Sir-ee-us), due to its proximity to the sun during the summer. Sirius is in the Canis Major (the big dog) constellation and the brightest star in the night sky. It rises and sets with the sun during certain days of July and August.

Abram (God changed his name to Abraham in Genesis 17) was a stargazer. The word of the Lord came to Abram as a promise. Abram's children, grandchildren, great-grandchildren, and all his descendants would be greater in number than the stars in the sky. What a vision! Not only that, but one of those stars represented the brightest birth of all. That was a descendant of Abram born in Bethlehem—Jesus, born to be the Savior of all.

The dog days of summer are days when you can look into the night sky, search out Sirius, and think about the Wise Men who watched the sky and saw the star that announced the birth of the Messiah: Jesus, our Savior. Think about Jesus—God's brightest and best gift for the dog days and every day.

_____Let's talk: How is Galatians 3:29 connected to today's reading? How are you connected to today's reading?

_____Let's pray: Dear Jesus, thank You for shining the light of Your love in my life. Thank You for calling me to be Your child. Amen.

P. L.

Home Away from Home

ngela's grandfather loves to sit in his own chair and sleep in his own bed. He goes to sleep when he wants, and if he wakes at 5 a.m. and wants breakfast, he can eat it without bothering anyone. Yes, home is the best place for Grandfather.

God is preparing another home for us. It is our home in heaven—a city of pure gold, decorated with jewels, brilliantly lit with the glory of God. In this place "death shall be no more, neither shall there be mourning nor crying nor pain anymore" (Revelation 21:4).

The Bible says we cannot even imagine how wonderful and beautiful it is. The most amazing part, however, is not the beauty of it. The amazing part is that God lets us in at all.

God absolutely hates sin and will not allow sin in His presence. Yet we sin every day. Ever since the fall of Adam and Eve, all people are born sinful. Thankfully, God loves us enough to prepare heaven for us and to send Jesus.

Jesus lived a perfect life in our place and died on the cross to cover us with His righteousness. Our sins are washed away with the blood of Jesus. Now God welcomes us in His presence and, one day, He will welcome us in heaven, our home.

Read from God's Word

But, as it is written, "What no eye has seen, nor ear heard, nor the heart of man imagined, what God has prepared for those who love Him." 1 Corinthians 2:9 ⮿

_____Let's talk: Read more about heaven in Revelation 21. What information did you find interesting?

_____Let's pray: Dear Lord God, thank You for preparing a wonderful home for me in heaven. Thank You for taking away my sins and for giving me Your righteousness. In Jesus' name. Amen.

S. M. S.

Read from God's Word

So that Christ may dwell in your hearts through faith—that you, being rooted and grounded in love, may have strength to comprehend with all the saints what is the breadth and length and height and depth. Ephesians 3:17–18 ✍

Measures for Love

A sia is wide. It is more than 5,000 miles wide and takes about 8 months to walk across. Do you know what is wider than Asia? God's love, which covers all people across the world.

The Nile River is over 4,000 miles long. Do you know what is longer than the Nile River? God's love. God has loved His people from before the beginning of time and will continue to love us forever.

Mount Everest is over 29,000 feet high. That's like walking up more than 3,600 flights of stairs. Do you know what is higher than Mount Everest? God's love, which is high enough to cover the mountain of our sin.

The Pacific Ocean is deep. Its deepest point is more than 36,000 feet deep. That is about 7 miles. Do you know what is even deeper than the Pacific Ocean? God's love. God's love is so deep that Jesus came down from His throne in heaven to be born as a baby on this earth. He lived among sinners and died on the cross to pay for our deep-down sin.

Now that's love—a love that's so wide and long and high and deep that we can enjoy its blessings today, tomorrow, the rest of our lives, and forever in heaven!

_____Let's do: Make some comparisons of your own. Write "I know God's love is wider (longer, higher, etc.) than because. . . ." Fill in the blanks and then write a prayer thanking God for His wonderful gifts.

_____Let's pray: Dear God, thank You for Your great love in sending Jesus as our Savior. Please help us grasp how wide and long and high and deep that love of Christ really is. In His name. Amen.

S. M. S.

Ugly or Beautiful

Have you heard ugly words? You might overhear them on the soccer field or while riding bikes. You hear boys or girls saying sarcastic remarks to one another about the way they look or a mistake they just made. That talk is ugly because it is a cruel way to talk. That talk's not humor, even when it's meant to be funny. Why do people think that put-downs are jokes? Why do we think that it's funny and okay to hurt someone's feelings?

The answer is simple. We are sinners, and sin often twists our words into pain-inflicting weapons. We may pretend these weapons can't hurt us, but they do. And they hurt others too.

God says to His children, "Let no corrupting talk come out of your mouths, but only such as is good for building up, as fits the occasion, that it may give grace to those who hear." God wants our words to be beautiful and He gives us His help.

God sent Jesus to die on the cross to pay for our ugly words and all our sins. Forgiven in Christ, we have power for a new attitude. Forgiven in Christ, we can bring to others what we have received in Christ. Forgiven in Christ, we can share the message of His love. Those are beautiful words.

_____Let's do: Reread Ephesians 4:32. Write out descriptions of the positive Christlike qualities listed.

_____Let's pray: Dear Jesus, we are sorry for the many times we hurt You and others with our sinful jokes. Help us to use our words to be kind, compassionate, and forgiving. Amen.

S. M. S.

A Secret to Share

Read from God's Word

Not that I am speaking of being in need, for I have learned in whatever situation I am to be content. I know how to be brought low, and I know how to abound. In any and every circumstance, I have learned the secret of facing plenty and hunger, abundance and need. I can do all things through Him who strengthens me. Philippians 4:11–13

Here is a secret you can share: The apostle Paul learned the secret of contentment. He learned to be satisfied whether he was rich or poor, comfortable or miserable. Paul's contentment came from God's relationship with him.

The secret of contentment is hard to have and hard to keep. Computer pop-up ads, television commercials, and sometimes our own friends cause us to believe that happiness depends on having the latest, the best, the newest, the fastest, the smallest, the most expensive shoes, shirts, talents, toys, height, and on and on.

That message is a lie many people believe because they haven't learned the secret. We belong to Jesus and therefore are filled with His love. We trust God to provide all our needs.

You probably don't have all the things you want. You may even have lots of problems you don't want. The apostle Paul had been without food and sleep, poorly clothed, falsely imprisoned, beaten, and shipwrecked. But even after all that, he could say he was content. Why? He had the love of God in Christ Jesus so He knew he had everything he really needed. He had a Savior who forgave his sin and gave him a heavenly home.

You have that secret too, and you can share it!

_____Let's talk: What other secret blessings does God give?

_____Let's pray: Forgive us our sins of jealousy and want, Lord. Fill us with Your powerful love so we are content. In Jesus' name. Amen.

S. M. S.

Great Ideas

U mberto, would you help Yesenia get the knot out of her shoe?"

"Why should I?" Umberto whined. "She got it in there!"

Does that conversation sound familiar? Serving someone else, especially when we think they don't deserve it, doesn't seem like much fun.

Jesus' attitude about greatness is different from Umberto's or yours or mine. He came to this earth not to live as the mighty God-King He is, but to live as a humble servant. He willingly touched and healed people with ugly skin diseases. He lovingly welcomed sinners. He washed His disciples' dirty feet. And best of all He hung on a cross—a punishment meant for the very worst of criminals.

He did all this because of love. In love, God created men and women in His own image. In love, God planned and promised to send a Savior from sin. In love, God forsook His own Son,

Read from God's Word

And Jesus called them to Him and said to them, "You know that those who are considered rulers of the Gentiles lord it over them, and their great ones exercise authority over them. But it shall not be so among you. But whoever would be great among you must be your servant, and whoever would be first among you must be slave of all. For even the Son of Man came not to be served but to serve, and to give His life as a ransom for many." Mark 10:42–45 ✑

who died on the cross for the sins of the world. In love, God sends His Holy Spirit to change our hearts and minds through His Word and Sacraments.

Our sinful hearts want special seating assignments, gifts, and awards, but Jesus stoops down and gladly ties shoestrings. May God give us that kind of love.

_____Let's do: Look up the word *humble*. What are some synonyms? What are some antonyms?

_____Let's pray: Dear Jesus, thank You for dying on the cross to pay for our sins of pride and selfishness. Work humble attitudes in our hearts that we may joyfully serve others. Amen.

S. M. S.

Fixed to Win

Read from God's Word

Looking to Jesus, the founder and perfecter of our faith, who for the joy that was set before Him endured the cross, despising the shame, and is seated at the right hand of the throne of God. Hebrews 12:2 ✑

Lois was the best bread-cutter in the county. In fact, she won a blue ribbon at the fair. Every slice she cut was as uniform as the slice before it. Lois kept her eyes on the goal—the bottom of the loaf. She didn't blink, she didn't look at the judges, and she didn't daydream about salami sandwiches.

God has a goal for us too. He wants to bring us to be with Him in heaven. His Word tells us where to focus. "[Look] to Jesus, the founder and perfecter of our faith."

Our sinful nature, the sins we do, and the sinful world all tempt us to take our eyes off Jesus. We worry about grades and are tempted to cheat. We doubt God's love and think that Jesus doesn't love us anymore. We covet computer games and CDs.

When we focus on our problems or wants, we turn from God's path and end up with trouble and temptation. God shows us the cross, where we see the cost of Christ's great love and forgiveness. He brings our eyes back into focus. He fixes them, just as He fixed our broken relationship with the Father. He gives us life with Jesus, and that's better than any blue ribbon.

_____Let's do: Draw a set of eyes fixed on a cross. Write descriptions of problems or sins that might tempt you to take your eyes off Jesus.

_____Let's pray: Dear Jesus, forgive us when we take our eyes off You and focus on our problems. Strengthen us with Your Word. Amen.

S. M. S.

God's Description

Go ahead. Describe God in the space below. List some of the adjectives you would use.

Did you use the word *powerful*? Or *awesome*? Or *full of glory*? Although God is all of these things, in our Bible reading He doesn't use any of these words to describe Himself. God's description may surprise you. Read Exodus 34:4–7a and fill in the blanks below.

God describes Himself as "_____ and _____, slow to _____, and abounding in steadfast _____ and _____, keeping steadfast _____ for thousands, _____ iniquity and transgression and sin."

What a great God we have! It's scary to consider what our lives would be like if God were only powerful without being compassionate and gracious. And what if God weren't slow to anger? He would have punished us long ago for our many sins. And scariest of all—what if God didn't love us? What if He would not have used His power to rescue us from sin? What if He had not sent Jesus to save us?

Our God is indeed an awesome God. His description of Himself assures us that He will use all that He is and all that He has to bless us every day.

_____Let's do: Write a prayer praising God for all that He is and all that He does for you.

_____Let's pray: Dear God, You are a great God in every way! Thank You. In Jesus' name I pray. Amen.

S. M. S.

Read from God's Word

But let all who take refuge in You rejoice; let them ever sing for joy, and spread Your protection over them, that those who love Your name may exult in You. For You bless the righteous, O LORD; You cover him with favor as with a shield. Psalm 5:11–12

Surrounded

Ty liked to build forts. His favorite time for fort-building happened each week when his mom scrubbed the kitchen and dining-room floors. She would put all the chairs in the living room. Ty and his sister stretched blankets over the chairs to make walls. There were no holes or openings anywhere (except for the door flap). They were completely surrounded.

Some of their fort creations seemed to end up crooked or with big spaces between the uneven walls. Sometimes there wasn't enough room to sit up without getting a sore neck. But their dining room fort was always just right—cozy, comfortable, and safe.

God's love is like that. Our psalm for today says that God's protection and favor surround us. That means that no matter which way we turn, God is there to watch over us. He protects us from danger and evil. He gives us His commandments so we know what is best for us.

There's nothing like being in God's "fort." Nothing can come in and harm our faith. The walls are like a shield. We have all the treasures and blessings we will ever need as His children. Best of all, we have the promise of eternal life through Jesus.

_____Let's talk: What are some things from which God protects you? How has He protected you already this week?

_____Let's pray: Jesus, thank You for surrounding me with Your love. Thank You for keeping me safe. Amen.

L. H.

Perfect Vision

Read from God's Word

Trust in the LORD with all your heart, and do not lean on your own understanding. In all your ways acknowledge Him, and He will make straight your paths.
Proverbs 3:5–6

Have you ever come in from playing outside on a bright, sunny day and been unable to see? Your eyes take a while to get used to the dim light indoors. If the room is dark enough, you may not be able to see at all for a moment.

Sometimes your future can look dark or dim. You may strain your mental "eyes" to see what's coming tomorrow, next week, or next year. But to God's eyes, your future is clear and bright. He has a perfect plan for you, and He gives you the power to trust Him as He leads you.

Rejoice that you have a heavenly Father who has perfect vision. He can see when it's light, when it's dark, and anything in between. God can also see everything about you, including your sins. That's why He sent Jesus to pay for all of your sins on the cross. Because you are His own child, God not only has a plan for your life on earth, but is also making a place for you with Him in heaven.

So when life is looking a little dim and uncertain to you, remember that God can see everything. He gives you faith to trust Him and follow Him, and He will lead you every day.

_____Let's do: Which parts of your future do you worry about? Which parts seem dim or even a little scary? Read Proverbs 3:5–6 again. See if, by the end of the day, you can say it from memory. Then say it to yourself whenever you feel uncertain.

_____Let's pray: Lord Jesus, sometimes I worry. Forgive me, and strengthen me through Bible verses like this. Thank You for having a plan for me. Amen.

L. H.

And those twelve stones, which they took out of the Jordan, Joshua set up at Gilgal. And he said to the people of Israel, "When your children ask their fathers in times to come, 'What do these stones mean?' then you shall let your children know, 'Israel passed over this Jordan on dry ground.' For the LORD your God dried up the waters of the Jordan for you until you passed over, as the LORD your God did to the Red Sea, which He dried up for us until we passed over, so that all the peoples of the earth may know that the hand of the LORD is mighty, that you may fear the LORD your God forever." Joshua 4:20–24

Memory Stones

In today's Bible reading the Israelite families had just witnessed a great miracle. In order to reach the border of Jericho and prepare to conquer the city, they had to cross the Jordan River. God parted the waters and the people safely crossed to the other side.

God told Joshua, their leader, to set up a monument made of stones from the Jordan to remember God's power and His care for them. Each time one of the Israelite families came near the river, they probably pointed out the stones and told the story of God's power. After they retold the story enough times, just the sight of the "memory stones" may have been a reminder of their mighty God.

Your words and actions can remind people that there is a mighty God who cares for you—and for them. God put you in a special place and time on this earth. When people see you, they will see Jesus' kindness as they watch you helping someone. They will see His patience as they watch you wait for your turn. They will see His forgiveness as they see you forgiving others.

You are God's child. He has forgiven your sins because of the suffering and death of His Son, Jesus. God has made you a "memory stone" for Him today.

_____Let's do: Draw several stones in a pile. On each stone write something God has done for you.

_____Let's pray: Dear Jesus, thank You for forgiving me when I fail to be a good witness for You. Help me show others Your love. Amen.

L. H.

Learn and Grow

Did your family have a reunion this summer? Maybe you grilled hot dogs, roasted marshmallows, or made ice cream.

In our family, my Aunt Judy makes the world's best cranberry marshmallow salad. And I finally have the recipe! Now I don't have to wait for special family gatherings to enjoy it. I can make the salad anytime, right in my own kitchen. I have other favorite recipes that I never want to lose or forget—Grandma Rydlund's molasses cookies, Aunt Hazel's fudge, and my mom's barbecued hamburgers.

God has a recipe for our spiritual nutrition. At least three writers in the Bible—Ezekiel, David, and the apostle John—speak of *eating* God's Word. By this God means that we should take His Word in—learn it so well that it becomes a part of the way we talk, think, and act. Learning and memorizing God's Word helps us grow in our faith in Jesus, just like eating food makes our bodies grow.

Eating a variety of healthy foods gives us the nutrients we need, and reading and learning God's Word feeds us with the ability to endure problems or with the words to encourage others. God's Word is true. God's Word is inspired. God's Word is without error. God's Word is nutritious—it produces results. It's great food every day.

Read from God's Word

For whatever was written in former days was written for our instruction, that through endurance and through the encouragement of the Scriptures we might have hope. Romans 15:4 ✑

———Let's do: Draw a rebus to help you memorize Hebrews 13:8 or Psalm 119:105.

———Let's pray: Lord God, teach me to love and learn Your Word so I might endure hardships and encourage others with the hope You give. In Jesus' name. Amen.

L. H.

Read from God's Word

Therefore, if anyone is in Christ, he is a new creation. The old has passed away; behold, the new has come.
2 Corinthians 5:17

Perfect Repairs

"Sarah, would you please hand me the hammer?" called Dad. "Oh, and a couple more nails too," he added. Sarah and her dad were fixing their dock. After a couple of new boards and some large nails were added, it would be as good as new. Just hours later, Sarah was doing cannonballs off of the dock into the shimmering lake.

Do you like to help fix things? Maybe you have even tried hammering nails or using other tools. It's fun to help make things better than they used to be. Jesus probably helped His earthly father fix things too. He and Joseph may have done lots of hammering and fixing in Joseph's carpenter shop.

But the biggest repairs Jesus made were done with His heavenly Father. The world was broken and filled with sin. God sent Jesus to fix it. Two wooden boards and some iron nails were used to hang Jesus on the cross to die for each one of us. When Jesus paid for our sins and rose from the dead, we weren't just repaired—we were made brand new!

God's repair shop is always open. Call on Him often. He created you and chose you through Baptism to be His. Each time you come to Him, broken by sin, He forgives you.

_____Let's talk: Are there some repairs you can think of that your heart needs right now? God will forgive every sin you bring to Him.

_____Let's pray: God, thanks for repairing me through Jesus. Thank You for making me new and for making me Your child. Amen.

L. H.

Prepare and Share

"H APPY BIRTHD" read the sidewalk in front of Minh's house. Today was her brother's 16th birthday. But just as she finished the D in "BIRTH-DAY," she realized she had used up her last piece of chalk.

Minh choked back tears. She had wanted to surprise her brother. How she wished she had planned her special message more carefully! If she had only made the letters a little smaller or kept track of how much chalk she was using, she would have been able to complete her message. If only she had been prepared!

Minh was glad her mom helped her make a paper "AY" to put on the sidewalk. Her brother still enjoyed his birthday surprise.

Today's Bible reading says to always be prepared to tell others why you trust Jesus to care for you and why you know He will take you to heaven someday. God will help you give others a clear message about who saved you so others can know His saving love.

Read from God's Word

But in your hearts regard Christ the Lord as holy, always being prepared to make a defense to anyone who asks you for a reason for the hope that is in you. 1 Peter 3:15 ✍

_____Let's do: Draw a rebus to help you memorize John 6:47. The rebus will help you learn a verse that is a terrific, complete message to anyone who might ask you about your faith in Jesus.

_____Let's pray: Jesus, help me joyfully share Your promises with others. Amen.

L. H.

Read from God's Word

I will greatly rejoice in the LORD; my soul shall exult in my God, for He has clothed me with the garments of salvation; He has covered me with the robe of righteousness, as a bridegroom decks himself like a priest with a beautiful headdress, and as a bride adorns herself with her jewels. ... The nations shall see your righteousness, and all the kings your glory, and you shall be called by a new name that the mouth of the LORD will give. Isaiah 61:10; 62:2 ↩

Get Noticed!

Have you ever forgotten your swimsuit for swimming lessons? Have you ever gotten to gym class only to realize you had left your gym clothes sitting by the backdoor?

When something like this happens, it is pretty hard to hide. You may feel embarrassed and wish you could just disappear.

What do you think would happen if you went to camp this summer dressed like a bride or a priest? Or back to school this fall wearing a white robe? You surely would draw some attention! Isaiah 61:10 tells us that God has clothed us with a robe of righteousness, a special hat of some sort, and the jewels of a bride! By this the Bible means that we have been forgiven and made fit for heaven through Jesus, our Savior.

You still should stand out in a crowd, not because of your clothes or jewelry, but because of who you are in Christ—a forgiven child of God. People you meet will see Jesus' love reflected through you as easily as they would see a white robe if you were actually wearing one. When they hear you speak and see how you act, it will be clear to them that you are different. Let everyone you meet today see clearly that you are God's own.

_____Let's do: Design a robe to wear that would show others you have been forgiven in Christ.

_____Let's pray: Dear Father, help me to stand out in a crowd as Your child. Give me strength to show my faith in You and to share it with joy. In Jesus' name. Amen.

L. H.

Bleeding Hands

The other day Jason's friend asked why he goes to church. Jason wasn't exactly sure what to say. Then in church the next Sunday, he heard this story:

There once was a young girl who lived in a faraway country, where it was against the law to be a Christian. One day soldiers came to her house and found her reading her Bible, and they tried to steal it. That little girl held on to her Bible tightly! Then they hit her fingers until they bled, but she still would not let go. Finally the soldiers gave up and went away. Today that girl has scars on her hands, but she smiles because she still has a Bible to cling to.

Then Jason knew what to tell his friend. It's not always easy to be a Christian and to stand up for what's right. We are not always able to resist temptation to sin. We sometimes fail to do God's will. But we have a Savior, Jesus Christ, who endured beatings, mocking, and death on the cross so we might have forgiveness for all our sin. Through Him we have new life now and in eternity. Even when we cannot cling to Him, He clings to us.

And that's exactly what Jason said to his friend.

Read from God's Word

"And then many will fall away and betray one another and hate one another. And many false prophets will arise and lead many astray. And because lawlessness will be increased, the love of many will grow cold. But the one who endures to the end will be saved. And this gospel of the kingdom will be proclaimed throughout the whole world as a testimony to all nations, and then the end will come." Matthew 24:10–14 ✍

_____Let's talk: Why do you go to church?

_____Let's pray: God, thank You that it's not against the law where I live to go to church, to read my Bible, or to believe in Jesus. Help me want to do those things. For Jesus' sake. Amen.

J. S.

Read from God's Word

"In My Father's house are many rooms. If it were not so, would I have told you that I go to prepare a place for you? And if I go and prepare a place for you, I will come again and will take you to Myself, that where I am you may be also. And you know the way to where I am going." John 14:2–4 ⌒

Waiting

Jana loves summer—swimming in the pool, eating ice-cream cones, catching caterpillars. She loves staying up late because there's no school the next day and having all the neighborhood kids over to play baseball in her yard. Summer's just awesome!

Sometimes it gets really hard to wait for summer, especially on gray rainy March days. Waiting for Jesus to come back is a lot like waiting for summer. Heaven is an incredible place. The Bible, trying to teach us about a place unlike any we've ever seen, describes heaven as having streets made of gold and walls made of jewels—a place of great beauty. Every person who ever believed in Jesus will be there together!

But even better, God lives there. Because Jesus died for our sins and through faith in Him, which the Holy Spirit has given us, we will be with Him forever. It's easy to get so excited thinking about it that sometimes it's hard to wait. But the Bible says that Jesus will come—at just the right time.

———Let's do: What do you think heaven will be like? Draw a picture of the best place you can imagine. Heaven will be far better than even that!

———Let's pray: Dear God, thanks for wanting me to be in heaven and giving me faith in Your Son. Please come soon, Jesus. Amen.

J. S.

Railroad Tracks

icole's braces were as big and noticeable as railroad tracks across her teeth. Or so she thought. She was sure that every time she smiled, someone was secretly laughing at her "tin grin." How she hated those stupid braces! *I want normal, straight teeth like everyone else,* she thought. *It's just not fair!*

It's hard when you feel like you don't fit in with other people. Jesus felt that way too. In fact, one time when He returned home from a trip, the people in His hometown of Nazareth told Him to leave! He was always doing things that set Him apart—healing the sick, raising the dead, and feeding thousands of people with a few fish and loaves of bread. Not everyday stuff.

Jesus knows what it's like to feel different. And He wants you to know that He loves you just as you are, braces or no braces. He loves you so much that He paid the death penalty for your sins through His own death on the cross. When you feel lonely or like you just don't fit in, remember that God knows what you're going through and He'll always be with you.

Read from God's Word

For we do not have a high priest who is unable to sympathize with our weaknesses, but one who in every respect has been tempted as we are, yet without sin. Let us then with confidence draw near to the throne of grace, that we may receive mercy and find grace to help in time of need. Hebrews 4:15–16 ✍

_____Let's talk: When might Jesus have felt lonely, sad, or different from others? He knows our every human experience and loves us through them all.

_____Let's pray: God, sometimes I feel like I don't fit in. Thanks for understanding and for loving me exactly as I am. In Jesus' name. Amen.

J. S.

august

Contributors for this month:

Carla Fast

Joan Gerber

Elaine Hoffmann

Craig Otto

Eileen Ritter

Jessemyn Schulz

Perfection

Danny wasn't very good at base-ball. It's not that he didn't try hard. He just never got the bat around fast enough to hit the ball. He couldn't hold the glove tight enough to catch a pop fly. Every day at recess the kids in his class rushed out to the field and chose teams. Danny was always picked last.

There's probably something you're not very good at yet, either. Maybe division is hard, or spelling. You might not get straight A's. You're just not perfect.

You know what? The Bible says that there is not one perfect person in the whole world. We all have a hard time doing the right thing sometimes. Maybe you don't always tell the truth. Or maybe you aren't always kind. You're not alone. No one is perfect. Except for Jesus.

That's right! Jesus had no sin. He led a perfect life. He suffered, died, and rose again to take away our sins. Now God no longer sees our sins and imperfections. He sees us as His perfect children.

God doesn't promise to make everyone a great ballplayer or straight-A student. But He promises to forgive our sins. And through His Spirit, He is at work in our lives, making us new and perfect in God's sight each day.

Read from God's Word

For all have sinned and fall short of the glory of God, and are justified by His grace as a gift, through the redemption that is in Christ Jesus. Romans 3:23–24

_____Let's talk: God makes us new and perfect in His sight every day—how is He at work in your life?

_____Let's pray: Dear Father, thanks for loving me just as I am. Thanks for sending Jesus to bring forgiveness and new life. Continue to guide me with Your Holy Spirit. In Jesus' name. Amen.

J. S.

Read from God's Word

For if while we were enemies we were reconciled to God by the death of His Son, much more, now that we are reconciled, shall we be saved by His life. Romans 5:10 ✍

Paid Up

Carla just finished a game of Monopoly. She lost because she owed so much money to everyone else that she couldn't pay her debt. In Monopoly you either pay up or you're gone. Carla was a goner.

A long time ago people who couldn't pay what they owed were put in jail. They were told they would stay in prison until they could pay their debts. As you can imagine, not many of them ever got out of jail. They were goners!

At one time we were all goners. We were in an eternal jail because we could not pay for our sins. As a result we were condemned to eternal death.

Yet God loved us so much that He placed the sentence of death upon His only Son, not on us. Jesus suffered and died to pay our debt and free us from prison.

Our sins are forgiven—they have been paid off. We are now free because of Christ's love for us, shown most clearly on the cross. Although we are still sinful, we are not condemned. Jesus paid the price of our debt, saving us from eternal death. He offers us love, forgiveness, and eternal life! What an amazing God we have!

_____Let's do: Because Jesus paid the debt of our sin, we are able to joyfully respond to others with Jesus' forgiveness. Write about a time when Jesus' love helped you forgive someone.

_____Let's pray: Dear Jesus, You paid our debt in full. Thank You for restoring us. Help us share this love and forgiveness with others. In Your name we pray. Amen.

C. F.

The Mediator

Read from God's Word

For there is one God, and there is one mediator between God and men, the man Christ Jesus.
1 Timothy 2:5*

"Y ou're the one who broke it!" Aaron yelled.

"Yeah, but you're the one who said to throw the ball as hard as I could," countered Al.

"Boys!" Their mom appeared in the doorway of the house. "What is all the shouting about out here?"

After hearing her sons explain, Mom said, "Okay, boys, I'll be your mediator with Dad."

"What's a mediator?" they asked.

"Well, let's read about it." Mom brought out a Bible and read 1 Timothy 2:5. "A mediator," she explained, "is someone who helps to solve the problems between people so they can make peace with one another again.

"Jesus is the Mediator between us and God. We were separated from God because our sins were in the way. But our sins aren't in the way anymore. Jesus' death and resurrection took away our sins, solving the problem between God and us.

"Now God sees Christ in us, instead of our sin. Through Jesus, we can approach God the Father. Because of Jesus' death, we are restored to a peaceful relationship with God—we are His children and can call Him Father once again. And speaking of *fathers*, let's go talk to your dad now."

"Okay, Mom!" the boys said.

_____Let's do: List three ways your life would be different if Jesus had not come to be your Mediator.

_____Let's pray: Dear heavenly Father, thank You for forgiving us through Your Son. In Jesus' name we pray. Amen.

C. F.

From Death to Life

Read from God's Word

But in fact Christ has been raised from the dead, the first-fruits of those who have fallen asleep. For as by a man came death, by a man has come also the resurrection of the dead. For as in Adam all die, so also in Christ shall all be made alive.
1 Corinthians 15:20–22 ✍

Cancer is a terrible disease. While some types of cancer are curable, many are not. Some people with cancer go from being healthy to dying in just two months.

It is hard to see someone slowly die from sickness. We love that person and will miss him or her. It's also painful to watch because God made us for life, not death. He intended for us to live forever.

But since the first sin of Adam and Eve, all humans have been dying. You could say we have a cancer called "sin." It will affect each part of us, and eventually we will die. But 1 Corinthians 15:20–22 reveals that death is not the end of the story.

It's true that we will experience an earthly death, but we will not stay dead! We will be made alive again, thanks to Christ. Christ's death and resurrection are the cure for sin. He paid the penalty for sin and guarantees us eternal life. Through Him we know that all those friends and relatives who have died in Christ will be alive with us one day. They will be healthy and vibrant, praising the Lord who loved us enough to save us from eternal death.

_____Let's talk: Do you know anyone who has died and is with Jesus? How do you know you will see that person again?

_____Let's pray: Dear Father in heaven, thank You for giving us life. We know You have given us eternal life through Jesus Christ, Your Son, because the Bible tells us so. In His name we pray. Amen.

C. F.

What Do You Need?

S uppose we are taking one last camping trip before the summer is over. What are some things we will need to take along? A tent, pegs, ground cloth, sleeping bag, pillow, food, plates and utensils, boots, shorts, sweatshirt, and socks.

There are other things we'll need, but this list is a good start. There are a lot of things we need out in the wilderness. We want to be fully prepared!

No matter how long our list is, there is one need only God can fill. It is recorded in Psalm 116:1–6.

This psalm was written as a word of thanks to God for saving someone from death. This person needed help—and God gave it to him. This psalm is one that we can pray too. Because of our sins, we are cast away from God. We deserve death as the penalty for sin, and we cannot free ourselves from our sins.

But God knew exactly what we needed. He had mercy upon us and sent Jesus, who willingly gave His life for us. Through Jesus' death and resurrection, He gave us what we so desperately needed—*forgiveness*. Now we have salvation, life in heaven with Him forever! We join the psalmist in giving thanks to our God, who lovingly gives us, His children, what we need.

Read from God's Word

I love the LORD, because He has heard my voice and my pleas for mercy. Because He inclined His ear to me, therefore I will call on Him as long as I live. The snares of death encompassed me; the pangs of Sheol laid hold on me; I suffered distress and anguish. Then I called on the name of the LORD: "O LORD, I pray, deliver my soul!" Gracious is the LORD, and righteous; our God is merciful. The LORD preserves the simple; when I was brought low, He saved me. Psalm 116:1–6 ∽

_____Let's talk: What could you pack if you were going on a camping trip? How can these things help you remember all the blessings God gives you?

_____Let's pray: Dear Lord, thank You for meeting all my needs, especially my need for salvation in Jesus. In His name I pray. Amen.

C. F.

Read from God's Word

For whatever was written in former days was written for our instruction, that through endurance and through the encouragement of the Scriptures we might have hope. Romans 15:4 ∽

What's It For?

Math," Alicia groaned. "I just don't get it. My teacher gave me these problems to work on over the summer. She said they'd help me with next year's stuff."

Her brother Jon sat down. "Well, first let's look at the book."

"Book?"

"Your math book! Always study the examples and directions! It's a lot better than trying to figure this out on your own!"

Textbooks are made to instruct and guide. That is their purpose. For help in math, a math book is a good place to start.

The Bible is also a book with a purpose. Romans 15:4 says the Bible was written to teach us. God tells us in His Word how He wants us to live. The Bible also gives examples of sinful people—like us—in need of a Savior. The Bible helps and encourages us, teaching us that Jesus saves us from our sins and gives us new life. Salvation through Jesus is Scripture's most important message.

By reading and studying the Bible, we face our days with encouragement and hope. We know that whatever problems we have here on earth, our future is certain in Christ. God gave us His Word as a gift to be used. And how comforting to know that we can turn to the Word for hope, encouragement, and life!

_____Let's talk: How many Bibles do you have in your house? Which one do you prefer to read from? Why?

_____Let's pray: Lord, thank You for the gift of Your Word. Through the Bible I learn about the new life and salvation You give me through Jesus. Help me share Your Word with others. In Jesus' name I pray. Amen.

C. F.

Blueberry Picking

Read from God's Word

The eyes of all look to You, and You give them their food in due season. You open Your hand; You satisfy the desire of every living thing. Psalm 145:15–16 ✎

What is your favorite month? December for Christmas? June for summer vacation?

My favorite is August—for blueberry season. I live in Ottawa County, Michigan, where the most important crop is blueberries. Throughout the summer blueberry farmers prune, weed, spray, and fertilize their bushes. In mid-July the earliest bushes ripen. By August, the bushes are covered with clumps of large, sweet berries ready to be picked.

On many August mornings I dress in jeans and my oldest shoes. Hooking a pail to my belt, I go out to pick blueberries. As I reach into a bush and find thick bunches of dark, ripe berries, I think about God's goodness in providing abundant food for His people.

The ker-plunk of berries on the bottom of my metal pail is soon replaced by the quiet thud of berries falling on layers of other berries. My pail runs over with berries before I have finished picking the second bush—like God's mercy overflows to me as He forgives me again and again for the sake of Jesus. I eat a handful of berries as I leave the field, their sweet taste reminding me once more of God's great love for me.

_____Let's talk: Which gifts of God in nature remind you of God's love for you?

_____Let's pray: Thank You, God, for providing me with Your goodness. Thanks for sending Jesus to be my Savior from sin. I pray this for Jesus' sake. Amen.

E. R.

Read from God's Word

Incline Your ear to me; rescue me speedily! Be a rock of refuge for me, a strong fortress to save me! For You are my rock and my fortress; and for Your name's sake You lead me and guide me. Psalm 31:2–3

A Hard Day

After work Mrs. Mueller picked up her son, Brett, from Grandma and Grandpa's house. She didn't say much on the way home, but Brett could tell she was unhappy.

"Mom, what's wrong?"

"Nothing," she told him. "I'm sorry I'm this way. Don't worry about it."

But Brett was worried, especially when his mother closed her bedroom door and made a phone call. It upset him to hear her angry voice. "What's happening?" he wondered.

Sometimes adults have hard days. As a result, they might yell, cry, slam a door, or become very quiet. Have you ever done that?

You will have hard days. Someone may hurt your feelings, you may be in a bad mood, or you may not get along with your brother or sister. Thankfully, Jesus loves you so much that He died and rose for you. He promises to be with you, and the Holy Spirit gives you strength to believe that and rely on Him, even on hard days.

_____Let's do: Make a list of Bible verses that encourage you. Now make a copy to share with someone else.

_____Let's pray: Dear God, thank You for loving me even on hard days. In Jesus' name I pray. Amen.

C. O.

Waiting for the Lord

B eth Ann, Hayden, and Alex were excited about staying in a motel on vacation. While their father paid for the room, Hayden called out, "Look! A pool!"

Alex begged, "Mom, can we get our swimsuits out of the car?"

The motel lobby got very loud as the kids talked about their plans. But after a few minutes, Hayden lost his patience. "Hurry up, Dad!" he whined. "This is taking *too long!*"

Long ago the Israelites were restless as they waited for happier days. God had promised a time when they would come together and celebrate. But some people grew impatient and stopped believing God's promise.

That's when God's prophet Micah reminded them of the Lord's plan. He said they would break through the gate and go out: "Their king passes on before them, the LORD at their head."

Read from God's Word

I will surely assemble all of you, O Jacob; I will gather the remnant of Israel; I will set them together like sheep in a fold, like a flock in its pasture, a noisy multitude of men. He who opens the breach goes up before them; they break through and pass the gate, going out by it. Their king passes on before them, the LORD at their head. Micah 2:12–13 ✎

Jesus was the King Micah spoke about. When God promised eternal life, many people in Israel followed Him and found the happiness that only He could give them.

In God's time, He sent forth His Son to be the Savior of the world. Through Jesus' death and resurrection He won the victory over sin. He sends us the Holy Spirit to help us look to Jesus, who delivers us through our troubles in His time.

_____Let's talk: At times, we all become impatient with our families. How do we know that God remains patient with us?

_____Let's pray: Heavenly Father, help me to trust that Your plans are best for me. In Jesus' name I pray. Amen.

C. O.

Read from God's Word

And the waters prevailed on the earth 150 days. But God remembered Noah and all the beasts and all the livestock that were with him in the ark. And God made a wind blow over the earth, and the waters subsided. The fountains of the deep and the windows of the heavens were closed, the rain from the heavens was restrained, and the waters receded from the earth continually. At the end of 150 days the waters had abated, and in the seventh month, on the seventeenth day of the month, the ark came to rest on the mountains of Ararat. And the waters continued to abate until the tenth month; in the tenth month, on the first day of the month, the tops of the mountains were seen. Genesis 7:24–8:5 ⤶

God Remembers Us

Craig was invited to go on a camping trip with the church youth group. The kids wished the all-day drive didn't have to take so long. Crowded in the van with sleeping bags and backpacks, they hoped for a sign that their drive was over.

Soon Craig saw dark clouds ahead on the horizon. But as they drew closer, he realized it wasn't clouds—it was a huge mountain range. "We're here! Hooray!"

You have probably been on a long road trip. But think about Noah's family inside the ark for more than 150 days! Do you think they were crowded, tired of the animals, and hoping their trip was over?

The Bible says, "God remembered Noah" and made the waters go down. Soon Noah could look out the ark's window and see the tops of the mountains. He must have thought, "Land! Hooray!"

Think about the mountains near Jerusalem where Jesus was crucified. Jesus died there to pay for our sins and then rose from a nearby tomb to promise everlasting life.

Just as God remembered Noah and showed him the mountains, God remembers you and shows you Mount Calvary. Your journey isn't to another place where God might be—your journey is with God as you thank Him for providing a Savior. "I see the mountain! Hooray!"

_____Let's talk: What are some trips you have taken? How is your journey with God the most important one you will take?

_____Let's pray: Dear Lord Jesus, continue to guide me. Give me faith to endure my journey with joy. Amen.

C. O.

People Are Hurting

Read from God's Word

Tyson had gone to school with the same classmates through eighth grade. As he looked at each face in his yearbook, he remembered what they had gone through together.

And Jesus went throughout all the cities and villages, teaching in their synagogues and proclaiming the gospel of the kingdom and healing every disease and every affliction. When He saw the crowds, He had compassion for them, because they were harassed and helpless, like sheep without a shepherd. Then He said to His disciples, "The harvest is plentiful, but the laborers are few; therefore pray earnestly to the Lord of the harvest to send out laborers into His harvest." Matthew 9:35–38

Lindsey missed lots of school when she had a liver transplant. Joshua's dad lived in a different city. Eddie had sleepovers at his house until his father lost his job; then they had to move. Amy's parents were divorced. Natalie's brother was in jail for selling drugs.

Tyson began to realize they weren't "just friends." They were people going through hard times; they were people who needed acceptance and encouragement. He prayed, "God, this world is kind of scary. Health problems, divorce, crime ... what if these things happened in my family?"

When Jesus walked upon the earth, He went from town to town to talk to people. Jesus knew they needed His acceptance, the faith He offered, and forgiveness for their sins. So He healed them and preached the Good News of the kingdom of heaven.

Jesus knows people need encouragement, so He invites us to bring love to those we know. Think about the people around you. What do they need? More than anything, they need the forgiveness Jesus gives. Share the Good News of Jesus!

_____Let's talk: What are some things you can do to encourage others with Jesus' love?

_____Let's pray: Dear Jesus, help my family and friends through their problems, assuring them of Your love. Amen.

C. O.

Read from God's Word

The crowd that had been with Him when He called Lazarus out of the tomb and raised him from the dead continued to bear witness. The reason why the crowd went to meet Him was that they heard He had done this sign. So the Pharisees said to one another, "You see that you are gaining nothing. Look, the world has gone after Him." John 12:17–19*

We Can Live Forever!

How would you react if you had seen Jesus raise Lazarus from the dead? Maybe you would have gone home and said, "Mom! Lazarus is alive! It was so cool—he came out of the tomb when Jesus called him. Jesus is incredible. I've never seen anyone like Him!"

The Jewish people had never seen anyone like Jesus either. It scared them to know that Jesus could make a dead man alive. What would He use His powers to do?

In the two thousand years since His ministry on earth, we have never seen another person in history who compares to Jesus. He amazed everyone who saw His miracles.

Today Jesus' power is still at work within the church, washing away sin in Baptism and pouring out forgiveness through the Sacrament of the Altar. There is power in the Word of God as it is read and preached. His miracles still inspire us!

When Lazarus died, Jesus explained to Lazarus's sister Martha that Lazarus had eternal life by knowing and trusting in Him. "I am the resurrection and the life," He told her. "Whoever believes in Me, though he die, yet shall he live" (John 11:25).

Because of Jesus' life, death, and resurrection, we can live in heaven with Him forever. Praise the Lord!

_____Let's talk: Read John 5:24. What is God's promise to you? Why is it important?

_____Let's pray: Dear Lord, come soon and gather us to be with You! In Jesus' name I pray. Amen.

C. O.

Just Getting Along

Read from God's Word

Finally, all of you, have unity of mind, sympathy, brotherly love, a tender heart, and a humble mind. Do not repay evil for evil or reviling for reviling, but on the contrary, bless, for to this you were called, that you may obtain a blessing. 1 Peter 3:8–9

Renee and Cheyenne shared a room while growing up. Renee was five years older so she was very busy with school, friends, and hobbies.

Cheyenne wanted her older sister to include her. "Can I go with you?" she asked while Renee was getting ready to meet friends. But Renee didn't want her little sister getting in the way.

The two sisters argued with each other a lot. Cheyenne complained that Renee never had time for her, and Renee complained that Cheyenne was always getting in the way.

They forgot that Jesus invites us to "love your neighbor" even in our own families (Matthew 22:39). One day Renee met a new friend and spent two hours with him. She thought, *If I'm so friendly to this person I just met, why can't I be nicer to Cheyenne?* She said a silent prayer and asked God's forgiveness for ignoring her sister.

The next day Renee brought a soda to Cheyenne. "I'm sorry I've been too busy," said Renee. "I want to be a better sister. Forgive me?"

Cheyenne's big smile was her answer.

Christ died for all sin, including sins like not caring for others, being too busy to pray, and arguing with family members. The Holy Spirit empowers us to share forgiveness and peace in our families.

_____Let's talk: Name a family member with whom you have recently argued. Through the power of the Holy Spirit working in your life, how can you get along with him or her?

_____Let's pray: Dear God, help me be kind and loving to my family. I pray this in Jesus' name. Amen.

C. O.

Read from God's Word

"You are the salt of the earth, but if salt has lost its taste, how shall its saltiness be restored? It is no longer good for anything except to be thrown out and trampled under people's feet. You are the light of the world. A city set on a hill cannot be hidden. Nor do people light a lamp and put it under a basket, but on a stand, and it gives light to all in the house. In the same way, let your light shine before others, so that they may see your good works and give glory to your Father who is in heaven." Matthew 5:13–16

Pictures of Love

Peter, can I use the red marker when you're done with it?" Kim asked.

"Okay. Just a second, I'm almost finished." Peter finished the house he was drawing and handed the marker to his sister.

"I think Dad will really like these pictures, don't you?" Kim asked as she finished her drawing.

Peter nodded yes. "He always does."

Kim and Peter love to draw pictures for their father. They use bright colors and draw many happy scenes with rainbows, green grass, flowers, and sunshine. Every line Kim and Peter draw is made with love. The light of Christ shines in their hearts. And Kim and Peter share the light with their father when they freely give their pictures to him.

Kim and Peter mailed their pictures to their dad, who was serving in the military in Afghanistan. Dad thanked them when he called. "Your pictures are light for my day," he said. "They are good reminders that the light of Christ shines in your hearts."

Kim and Peter beamed with delight at their father's words. They knew Jesus had paid for their sins on the cross. And as holy, baptized children of God, their love for Jesus was shown in their actions.

Thanks be to God who gives us the strength to be lights for Him!

_____ Let's do: As Christians, we want to share our love for Jesus with others. Draw a picture for someone you love.

_____ Let's pray: Dear Jesus, shine down Your love in my life today. In Your holy name I pray. Amen.

C. O.

It's Not Easy

I t's not easy to always be in-between—not a little kid anymore, but not an adult either. You still have to go to bed when your mom or dad says. You still have to sit with the little kids when company comes over. Can't anyone see that you're growing up?

Young pastor Timothy must have felt like that sometimes. He loved Jesus very much and was chosen by the apostle Paul to bring God's Word to people in some of the churches Paul had started. But often, some people who were older than Timothy ignored him just because he was young. The apostle Paul sent him a letter to encourage him. Read 1 Timothy 4:12 to see what he wrote.

No, you're not the pastor of a church, but there is encouragement in Paul's words for you too. God wants all His children of all ages to share His message of love in Jesus with others. God can use people of any age to serve others and to share His Word. We can all be examples of His forgiving love.

Watch for ways you can reflect God's love to others through the things you say and do. No matter how little people may think you are, God can do BIG things through you!

Read from God's Word

Let no one despise you for your youth, but set the believers an example in speech, in conduct, in love, in faith, in purity. 1 Timothy 4:12

_____Let's talk: What are some ways you can be an example for others "in speech, in conduct, in love, in faith, in purity"?

_____Let's pray: God, it's hard to be in-between, but You know just who I am. Please help me to share Your love with others. In Jesus' name. Amen.

E. H.

Yahoo!

Read from God's Word

Make a joyful noise to the LORD, all the earth! Serve the LORD with gladness! Come into His presence with singing! Know that the LORD, He is God! It is He who made us, and we are His; we are His people, and the sheep of His pasture. Enter His gates with thanksgiving, and His courts with praise! Give thanks to Him; bless His name! For the LORD is good; His steadfast love endures forever, and His faithfulness to all generations. Psalm 100*

amie's favorite expression was "yahoo!" Jamie's friends heard it so often they started to say it too.

You might say "yahoo!" when you make your bed right the first time. You might be thinking it as you round first base and head for second. Or maybe you just finished a B-flat scale on your clarinet with absolutely no squeaks.

Jamie doesn't limit his "yahoo!" to events. It came out as he saw the sunset slicing the clouds into pieces of blue, gold, and orange. It sounded almost like a song when he saw a litter of newborn black labs. Jamie even said it in a singsong way when his cousins were coming for the weekend.

In Psalm 100 the writer is excited about what God has done for His people and he can't help but be thankful.

Saying or singing "yahoo!" is a great way to shout for joy. It's a great way to show gladness and thanks for what God did in sending Jesus to earth. Jesus spoke His love for us when He said, "It is finished" (John 19:30), and died on the cross for the sins of all. His resurrection victory gives us daily a reason to say or sing, "Yah who!"

_____Let's talk: Psalm 100 lists some ways we worship God. What are they?

_____Let's pray: Dear Lord God, thank You for all the wonders of this life and for Your enduring love. Help me worship You with joy and gladness. In Jesus' name I pray. Amen.

E. H.

True or False?

(O) ne day at Javier's house, Richard hit a ball into the neighbor's garden. Richard tried to be careful, but he squashed several tomatoes when he rescued the ball. He quickly ran back to Javier's yard, hoping no one saw what he did.

"If you don't tell, it's the same as a lie," replied Javier. "And if you lie, God won't let you into heaven."

Richard felt sick. He didn't want to play anymore so he went home. His dad noticed him sitting by himself on the porch and sat next to him. "Dad," Richard said, "is it true that I won't go to heaven if I'm not honest?"

Dad put an arm around his son's shoulders, "Believers go to heaven because Jesus died for their sin. You have been given God's grace through faith at your Baptism. But that doesn't mean you should be dishonest. God's Word tells us that one way to love God and each other is to tell the truth. When we don't, we sin. When that happens God invites us to repent and confess our sin. He forgives our sin for Jesus' sake."

Richard nodded. "I get it. Thanks, Dad. I'll be back in a minute." And with that, he ran to apologize to Javier's neighbor.

Read from God's Word

For by grace you have been saved through faith. And this is not your own doing: it is the gift of God, not a result of works, so that no one may boast. For we are His workmanship, created in Christ Jesus for good works, which God prepared beforehand, that we should walk in them. Ephesians 2:8–10 〜

_____Let's do: List two people who have shared the true message of Jesus' love with you. Thank God for them.

_____Let's pray: Dear Jesus, I believe that You died for me. Thank You for taking my sins away. Help me to share this Good News. Amen.

E. H.

The Missing Lepidopteran

Read from God's Word

"Or what woman, having ten silver coins, if she loses one coin, does not light a lamp and sweep the house and seek diligently until she finds it? And when she has found it, she calls together her friends and neighbors, saying, 'Rejoice with me, for I have found the coin that I had lost.' Just so, I tell you, there is joy before the angels of God over one sinner who repents." Luke 15:8–10

Alex loves lepidoptera, better known as butterflies. Alex has butterfly wallpaper, butterfly mobiles, and even a butterfly tie. The favorite item in his collection is seven trays of real butterflies. The trays are mounted on the wall across from his bed.

One morning Alex noticed that the blue morpho was missing. He scoured the area with his mom, trying to find it, but he couldn't. After an hour Mom was ready to give up, but Alex spotted something on the windowsill. The breeze from the fan must have blown the missing lepidopteran up there. "Yeah!" Alex shouted. After they put the butterfly back in its place, Alex and Mom had a celebration snack.

Mom told Alex about the woman from today's Bible reading who says, "Rejoice with me, for I have found the coin that I had lost." Jesus goes on to say, "I tell you, there is joy before the angels of God over one sinner who repents."

We were lost because of sin. But God loves us sinners so much that He sent Jesus to die for us to give us eternal life with Him. When the Holy Spirit brought us to repentance and faith in Jesus, there was rejoicing in heaven!

_____Let's talk: How can you celebrate that you are a child of God?

_____Let's pray: Dear Jesus, thank You for saving me, finding me, and naming me Yours forever. Amen.

E. H.

A Secret Place

Read from God's Word

"Am I a God at hand, declares the LORD, and not a God afar off? Can a man hide himself in secret places so that I cannot see him? declares the LORD. Do I not fill heaven and earth?" declares the LORD." Jeremiah 23:23–24 ✍

It was the last day of vacation. Darcy and her family had been camping in a park with interesting caves to explore. In the morning Darcy found a secret place. It had beautiful rocks and a little hole in the top where light gleamed through. She walked back to the secret place after lunch and saw the light make patterns on the rocks. No one knew she was there.

That night as Darcy said her prayers, she said, "Dear Lord, I had such a good time in the secret place today. I wish You could have been there!"

Darcy didn't remember that the Lord *was* with her in the secret place. The Bible reading says, "'Can a man hide himself in secret places so that I cannot see him? declares the LORD. Do I not fill heaven and earth?'"

Some people don't want God to be everywhere. They don't want God to know what they are thinking or doing. But He knows—He's there. Our loving God, who sacrificed His own Son to pay for our sins, is everywhere. We are God's people; He made us and He is with us wherever we go, even in the secret places no one else knows about!

_____Let's talk: How is the message of Psalm 139 like that of Jeremiah 23:23–24?

_____Let's pray: Dear God, thank You for loving me and taking care of me. Help me remember that You are with me even in secret places. In Jesus' name. Amen.

E. H.

The Dilemma

Shelby had $2.57. She thought it should be enough money to buy the cookie dough she needed for the vacation Bible school snacks. But when Shelby got to the checkout line, she found out she was wrong. The cashier asked for $3.39—more money than she had. Shelby was stunned. What a dilemma (problem)!

Shelby meant well, but that wasn't enough when it came to paying for the cookie dough. Many children mean well when they do nice things. Maybe you are one of them. You might wash your parents' car or take out the trash without being asked. You might clean all the mirrors or empty the wastebaskets. Maybe you set the table as a surprise.

Now these are good things to do, but they aren't good enough in one important way—you could never do enough good things to "check out" of earthly life and "pay" for heaven.

Jesus did it all for us. He paid the price of sin. He suffered and died to earn salvation for us. We are now free to wash cars and take out trash and empty wastebaskets in response to His love. We are now free to walk with joy through this life with Jesus into the next.

_____Let's do: Draw a gift-wrapped box. Add a tag made out to you from God. What's inside? Reread Romans 6:23.

_____Let's pray: Dear Lord, thank You for giving me all I need. In Jesus' name. Amen.

E. H.

Lost and Found

School will begin soon. What do you like about school? Reading? Math? Lunch? What about field trips?

In preparation for field trips, teachers spend time going over rules and giving instructions. They also ask parents to come on the trip. Adults supervise groups of children for one reason: safety.

On field trips, adults constantly watch students to make sure they are safe. If a student goes missing, the entire trip comes to a halt. Every place is searched until the lost student is found and returned to safety. Cheers and laughter erupt when that child is returned to the group.

In today's Bible reading Jesus talks about sheep and a shepherd. The shepherd's job is to keep the sheep safe. If one is lost, the shepherd does not rest until he finds the lost sheep.

And that's how God deals with us. He does not leave us lost in our sins. Jesus, our Good Shepherd, found us in Baptism and gave us life with Him through the life He gave up for us on the cross.

It's amazing how much God loves us. No matter how we may have sinned, He still comes to us with love and forgiveness. He gathers us and keeps us safe with Him.

Read from God's Word

"See that you do not despise one of these little ones. For I tell you that in heaven their angels always see the face of my Father who is in heaven. What do you think? If a man has a hundred sheep and one of them has gone astray, does he not leave the ninety-nine on the mountains and go in search of the one that went astray? And if he finds it, truly, I say to you, he rejoices over it more than over the ninety-nine that never went astray. So it is not the will of my? Father who is in heaven that one of these little ones should perish." Matthew 18:10–14

_____Let's talk: How does knowing that God forgives even your worst sins make you feel?

_____Let's pray: Dear Jesus, You are my Good Shepherd. Thank You for searching for me and finding me. Keep me safe in Your fold. Amen.

C. F.

Brothers and Sisters

Do you have a brother or sister? Have teasing and fighting turned the past weeks into a long, hot summer?

Fighting among brothers and sisters has gone on since Adam and Eve's children were growing up. Can you identify these Bible siblings?

Who killed his brother because he was jealous? (Genesis 4:2–8)

Who used tricks to receive his brother's inheritance and blessing? (Genesis 27:1–30)

Who complained because her sister wouldn't help her prepare a meal for Jesus? (Luke 10:38–42)

Acting jealously, wanting the best for yourself, making sure no one is treated better than you—sounds familiar, doesn't it?

Sin leads to fighting in our families, just as it did among people in the Bible. But God sent His Son, Jesus, into our world. He became our Brother, to live and grow up in a family like ours. He obeyed God perfectly and did not sin. Jesus died on the cross, and through Him all our sins have been forgiven.

Through Jesus we have the power to love our brothers and sisters. As Aaron helped Moses (Exodus 17:10–13), you can help them in their work or play. As Joseph forgave his brothers (Genesis 45:1–15), you can forgive others when they are unkind to you.

_____Let's talk: What are three ways to show Jesus' love to your brothers and sisters?

_____Let's pray: Thank You, Jesus, for loving me enough to die for me. Forgive me for fighting with my brothers and sisters. Help me love them as You have loved me. Amen.

E. R.

Someone to Watch over Me

After giving the secretary his mom's letter, Cameron left the office. Approaching the stairs, he saw the elevator. His mom had said to take the stairs, but Cameron didn't think one ride would hurt.

Just before reaching the first floor, the elevator came to a stop. There was silence. Cameron waited a few moments and then began pushing buttons. Still nothing happened. He realized he was in trouble and began crying.

Cameron decided to yell for help. Just then, the doors opened. A man's smiling face appeared level with the elevator floor. Mr. Hartman, his mother's boss, had come to his rescue.

As he helped Cameron climb out of the elevator, Mr. Hartman said, "I saw you go into the elevator. I wondered why you didn't read the out-of-order sign. Then I knew you were going to need help."

God watches over us even better than Mr. Hartman. He is with us, guarding and protecting us. God loves us so much that He rescued us from our worst problem—sin. Jesus' death and resurrection provided that rescue about two thousand years ago—before you were born, before you could even be aware that you were in danger from sin!

Read from God's Word

The LORD will keep you from all evil; He will keep your life. The LORD will keep your going out and your coming in from this time forth and forevermore. Psalm 121:7–8

_____Let's talk: Whom has God sent to help watch over you?

_____Let's pray: Dear Lord, thank You for always watching over me. I know that You are with me and will never leave me. In Jesus' name I pray. Amen.

C. F.

Summer Squabbles

"I will be so glad when school starts again!" said Ed's mother. "All you kids have done this summer is fight!"

"It's not my fault," complained Ed. "Andrew was cheating, and Peter threw all the money on the floor. Ben said he and I were the automatic winners because Peter and Andrew were cheating. Andrew called Ben a cheater, so Ben got really mad and swore at him. Then I packed up my game and came inside."

Mom sat quietly for a few minutes. "And now you have nothing to do and no friends to play with, right?" she asked.

"Right, and Peter and Andrew won't talk to me," Ed answered.

"Then why don't you finish those posters you were making for the closing service at vacation Bible school? You know, you could even invite your friends to the closing service," suggested Mom.

Ed thought for a moment. He knew that Peter and Andrew's family never went to church. They didn't know Jesus and the forgiveness He won on the cross for them. Ed knew that Jesus loved and died for everyone. And he wanted Peter and Andrew to know that too. "Good idea, Mom. I want Peter and Andrew to be at the closing service. I'm going over to their house to apologize and invite them. Okay?"

_____Let's talk: Because Jesus loves us, we can show His love to others. What can you do to share Jesus' love with a friend?

_____Let's pray: Heavenly Father, thank You for loving us so much. Help us to love each other. I pray in Jesus' name. Amen.

E. R.

The Palm of God's Hand

Read from God's Word

"My sheep hear My voice, and I know them, and they follow Me. I give them eternal life, and they will never perish, and no one will snatch them out of My hand. My Father, who has given them to Me, is greater than all, and no one is able to snatch them out of the Father's hand. I and the Father are one."
John 10:27–30

Rachel and Mary were snuggled into sleeping bags on the bedroom floor.

"You won't believe my big sister," Rachel said. "She turns music on real loud and doesn't turn it off until late. I can hardly concentrate on my prayers."

Mary asked, "You say prayers every night? What do you say?"

"I say the Lord's Prayer and a bed-time prayer," said Rachel.

"I do too," Mary said. "My dad says in the Lord's Prayer, Jesus reminds us to forgive and be forgiven. If I hurt others or myself, I ask God to forgive me. Then if I am mad at other people, I pray for them too."

"How can you pray for people who make you angry?" wondered Rachel.

"Well," said Mary, "my dad told me to close my eyes and picture the people I'm angry with sitting in the palm of God's hand. Then I remember that God loves those people just as much as He loves me. Jesus died and rose for them too. If they said or did mean things to me, I ask God to be with them. Then I'm not upset anymore because God takes the problem."

Rachel thought about that for a minute. "I'm going to try that tonight and every night!"

_____Let's talk: Think of someone who bothers you. What do you usually do when it happens? How can Matthew 6:12 help?

_____Let's pray: Dear Jesus, thank You for showing me how to pray. Help me remember that I am in Your hands. Give me a love big enough to forgive others. Amen.

J. G.

Read from God's Word

But now the righteousness of God has been manifested apart from the law, although the Law and the Prophets bear witness to it—the righteousness of God through faith in Jesus Christ for all who believe. For there is no distinction: for all have sinned and fall short of the glory of God, and are justified by His grace as a gift, through the redemption that is in Christ Jesus, whom God put forward as a propitiation by His blood, to be received by faith. This was to show God's righteousness, because in His divine forbearance He had passed over former sins. It was to show His righteousness at the present time, so that He might be just and the justifier of the one who has faith in Jesus. Romans 3:21–26 ✍

Mistakes or Sins?

The Garcias have a four-slice toaster with a problem. One side pops up automatically, but the other side doesn't. Often, Mr. Garcia gets so busy with other kitchen chores that he doesn't notice when one side pops up.

When he smells something burning, he rushes to the toaster. He tosses the burned toast in the trash, opens windows to air out the room, and sighs as his children tease him about being forgetful.

Have you ever made the same mistake twice? If it's something like burned toast, we may learn to laugh at ourselves after a while.

Some mistakes are not so funny. If our misdeed hurts others or ourselves and goes against God's will, it's called sin. Romans 3:23 says, "All have sinned and fall short of the glory of God." When we sin, we move away from God. Then we need to get close to Him again.

God knows we can't do this by ourselves. Romans 3:24–25 tells us the solution to our problem. We are justified through faith in Jesus. The dictionary tells us the word *justify* means "to pronounce free from guilt or blame." Jesus freed us from the guilt and blame of our sins. He shed His blood on the cross and rose from the dead so we can live with Him forever!

_____Let's talk: Read Romans 3:20. Give an example of how God's Law helps Christians.

_____Let's pray: Thank You, Father, for giving me a sense of humor so I can laugh at my silly mistakes. Thanks for sending Jesus, who justifies me. Guide me by the Holy Spirit in all I do. In Jesus' name I pray. Amen.

J. G.

Coming Home

id you go to camp this summer? Did your family take a vacation?

If you spent even a short time away, you've experienced it—the feeling you get when you come back to the place you call home. A few blocks from home, your heart starts beating a little faster. Inside, you run from room to room, making sure nothing has changed. Then the welcome begins—a parent's hug, your pet's greeting, the eager questions of brothers and sisters who have missed you. You're home!

The cot at camp was all right, but you sleep better in your own bed. You enjoyed eating fast food along the road, but Mom's cooking tastes better than ever. But the best part of coming home is being with the people who love you most of all.

We Christians look forward to a special homecoming at the end of our earthly lives. We enjoy many things here on earth. But we know that heaven will be much better because there will be no sin. And the best part of heaven will be being with Jesus, the One who loves us most of all—who loved us enough to die for us so we could live with Him forever.

Read from God's Word

One of the criminals who were hanged railed at him, saying, "Are you not the Christ? Save yourself and us!" But the other rebuked him, saying, "Do you not fear God, since you are under the same sentence of condemnation? And we indeed justly, for we are receiving the due reward of our deeds; but this man has done nothing wrong." And he said, "Jesus, remember me when You come into Your kingdom." And He said to him, "Truly, I say to you, today you will be with Me in Paradise." Luke 23:39–43 ☙

_____Let's talk: Look at the Bible reading again. Compare the comments of the criminals who hung beside Jesus.

_____Let's pray: Dear Lord Jesus, I know that I am sinful and do not deserve to go to heaven. But You died to make me holy, and You have promised to welcome me home. Thanks, Jesus. Amen.

E. R.

Shopping for New Clothes

Read from God's Word

You are all sons of God through faith in Christ Jesus, for all of you who were baptized into Christ have clothed yourselves with Christ. There is neither Jew nor Greek, slave nor free, male nor female, for you are all one in Christ Jesus. Galatians 3:26–28, NIV

Think how you would feel if, on the first day of school, everyone else came dressed in crisp, fresh, clean new clothes, but you showed up in outgrown shorts and a mustard-stained tee shirt. Or what if you came in your swim trunks and fishing hat? Your classmates would think you didn't know how to dress for school, and your teacher might ask for a good explanation.

So we shop for new school clothes—clothes that fit, covering scrapes, scars, and bug bites from summer. School clothes help us look and act like students.

St. Paul wrote about new clothes—new clothes that belong to every baptized Christian. "All of you who were baptized into Christ have clothed yourselves with Christ." These "Christ clothes" can't be bought at a store. As sinful humans, we can't earn Christ clothes with good behavior. These clothes are God's gift to us, bought with Jesus' blood on the cross, given to us in Baptism.

When God looks at us, He sees our Christ clothes, which cover the scrapes and scars of our sins with Jesus' perfect righteousness. Christ clothes help us look and act like followers of Jesus. They are the perfect clothes for every occasion, even for school.

_____Let's do: Draw or write about the Christ clothes God has given you.

_____Let's pray: Dear Lord Jesus, You cover my sins with Your righteousness. Thank You. Be with me today and in the new school year too. Amen.

E. R.

School Supplies

L ay your school supplies on your bed or the kitchen table. Think about how you will arrange them in your desk or locker. Then mentally add the books your teacher will give you the first day of school. Include a dictionary, a couple of library books for good measure, and several folders for your homework and completed assignments.

We need all these supplies—or tools—for school, but did you know there is one all-purpose tool for learning about Jesus?

Paul described such a tool to young Timothy. Paul said that the Bible has many purposes: to correct us when we disobey God; to teach us about Jesus' death, which saves us from sin; and to train us to live according to God's will. We know the Bible is true because God breathed His own words into the minds of the Bible's writers.

Read from God's Word

All Scripture is breathed out by God and profitable for teaching, for reproof, for correction, and for training in righteousness, that the man of God may be competent, equipped for every good work. 2 Timothy 3:16–17 ∽

The Bible shows us the way of salvation. It teaches us the depth of God's love—that He sent His Son to die for us. It teaches us about the Holy Spirit, who enables us to believe in Jesus and live as children of God. It's better than any school supply. It supplies nourishment for our life of faith.

_____Let's talk: Which school supplies are most important? What is the most important truth you have learned from the Bible?

_____Let's pray: Heavenly Father, help me as I study Your Word to learn more about Jesus, my Savior from sin. Amen.

E. R.

Read from God's Word

Therefore let everyone who is godly offer prayer to You at a time when You may be found; surely in the rush of great waters, they shall not reach him. You are a hiding place for me; You preserve me from trouble; You surround me with shouts of deliverance. Psalm 32:6–7

Immunizations

Terry couldn't wait to start kindergarten. His new clothes were neatly folded in his dresser drawers, and he had packed his new backpack with crayons, scissors, and glue. Every morning he marked off another day on the calendar and counted the number of days until school started.

One morning Terry's mother said, "This afternoon we're going to the doctor's office, Terry. Dr. Baker will give you a checkup. Then she'll give you some shots so you'll be ready for kindergarten."

"Shots!" screamed Terry. "I don't want any shots!"

"You can't go to kindergarten without shots, Terry. The shots immunize you against disease. They'll protect you from getting sick and missing lots of school," Mom explained.

The person who wrote Psalm 32 speaks of a different kind of protection. He says that God will protect him from trouble. And he urges people to pray to the Lord.

Like the psalmist, we pray to God for protection. We know He can keep us safe from any danger. To save us from the danger of sin and death, He sent His Son, Jesus, to die on the cross in our place. He forgives our sins, protecting us from eternal death so we may live as His children. Through Christ we have been immunized against eternal death and the disease of sin.

_____Let's talk: Think about a time God protected you from danger. Why is sin a greater danger than disease, fire, hurricane, tornado, or flood?

_____Let's pray: Thank You, Father, for keeping me safe in You. Forgive my sins and protect me from sin and danger, for Jesus' sake. Amen.

E. R.

Father Knows Best

For a three-year-old, Ahmad communicates pretty well. He knows quite a few words and lets his parents know his needs. But there are times when Ahmad can't say what he needs. He may not know the correct words, or he may be too upset to think correctly. So what does Ahmad do when he can't say what he wants? He cries and reaches out his arms, trusting that his parents will help him.

According to Romans 8:26–27, God knows all our wants and needs. The Holy Spirit intercedes for us when we don't know what to pray. Have you ever been so troubled that you don't know what to say in prayer? Sometimes our troubles hurt so badly that we just moan in pain.

God hears our cries. Jesus understands all our pain. He sends the Holy Spirit to be with us. The Spirit makes sure our Father hears our prayers—even when we don't know the words to say!

Read from God's Word

Likewise the Spirit helps us in our weakness. For we do not know what to pray for as we ought, but the Spirit Himself intercedes for us with groanings too deep for words. And He who searches hearts knows what is the mind of the Spirit, because the Spirit intercedes for the saints according to the will of God. Romans 8:26–27

Our heavenly Father listens to us because we are His children. Through Jesus' death and resurrection, we became His own. He grants us eternal life in heaven, and He cares for us here on earth. When there are troubles, God knows what our cries mean. As our perfect Father, He understands our pain and sends help.

_____Let's do: Make a list of people to pray for. Remember, even when you don't know what to say, the Holy Spirit is right there with you!

_____Let's pray: Dear Father, thank You for sending Your Spirit to intercede for us when we don't know what to pray. Thank You for being our true Father. I pray this in Jesus' name. Amen.

C. F.

september

Contributors for this month:

James Hahn

Heather Ketron

Phil Lang

Eleanor Schlegl

Julie Stiegemeyer

Work?

I t's Labor Day—a day off for many workers. What kind of worker do you want to be when you grow up? A teacher, a farmer, a salesperson, a mechanic, a doctor, a pastor, or a _____? There are many kinds of work for Christians.

Someday your work will earn you a paycheck. What will that work be? It is okay if you don't know yet. Still you might think ...

What would I really like to do?

What am I good at doing?

Do I want to be helpful and serve others?

Do I want to please God in all I do?

What does God want me to do?

What a comfort to know that the Bible, God's Word, has some help for you. In 1 Corinthians 10:31 we read, "So, whether you eat or drink, or whatever you do, do all to the glory of God."

Read from God's Word

Whatever you do, work heartily, as for the Lord and not for men, knowing that from the Lord you will receive the inheritance as your reward. You are serving the Lord Christ. Colossians 3:23–24 ∽

Going to school is probably your work right now. Are you doing it to God's glory? We all mess up in our work, even our schoolwork. God loves us so much that He gave to Jesus the work of saving us from danger, death, and the devil. Jesus did His work perfectly to cover all the times we mess up. Praise God for His wonderful work through Jesus!

_____Let's talk: List some of the work you like to do and don't like to do. How does Colossians 3:23–24 encourage you to look at all your work?

_____Let's pray: Dear God, help me to do all my work for Your glory and the good of others. In Jesus' name I pray. Amen.

P. L.

Read from God's Word

Then I saw a new heaven and a new earth, for the first heaven and the first earth had passed away, and the sea was no more. And I saw the holy city, new Jerusalem, coming down out of heaven from God, prepared as a bride adorned for her husband. And I heard a loud voice from the throne saying, "Behold, the dwelling place of God is with man. He will dwell with them, and they will be His people, and God Himself will be with them as their God. He will wipe away every tear from their eyes, and death shall be no more, neither shall there be mourning nor crying nor pain anymore, for the former things have passed away."
Revelation 21:1–4 ✍

Perfect Circles

"Mom, my school supply list says I need a compass. Do they think I'm going to get lost at school?"

"I think they mean a compass for drawing circles."

"How does a compass help?" wondered Laura.

"The compass has two legs. You put the pointed leg in the center, set the distance between the legs, and use the leg with the pencil to draw a circle around the center point. If you work carefully, you draw a circle that is so perfect you can't tell where it begins or ends. Does that remind you of anything?"

"No beginning or end? No."

"Well, a circle reminds me that God has no beginning or end. He was before time because He created time. When time comes to an end, He will still be forever. And those who have faith in Jesus Christ will live forever with Him in the new heaven and earth He creates, just as He promises in the Bible.

"Since Adam and Eve, all people have disobeyed God. We deserve death because of our sin. But God created a salvation plan. Jesus stretched out His arms on the cross so we can be embraced in God's loving arms. Those who have faith in Christ are promised eternal life in heaven with Him."

_____Let's talk: Name some circles in your home or classroom. Tell how they remind you of God's many gifts to you. (For example, your plate may remind you of God's gift of food.) What gift will never end?

_____Let's pray: Dear God, I don't understand how You can be forever, but I'm glad You love me and have prepared a home in heaven for me. In Jesus' name. Amen.

P. L.

ABC

C ynthia, what was fun in third grade today?" Dad asked.

"Well, we played a game with our ABCs and fruit! Each person had to name a fruit using the next letter of the alphabet: *A* is for apple, *B* is for banana, *C* is for cherry, and so on."

"That's great! Can you think of animals using A, B, and C?"

"Sure! *A* is for aardvark, *B* is for buffalo, and *C* is for chimpanzee!"

"How about cities?"

"Okay. *A* is for Atlanta, *B* is for Baltimore, and *C* is for Chicago."

"I'm impressed," responded Dad. "I'll bet you did well in the game. Can you do some ABCs from the Bible?"

"You mean like *A* is for angels, *B* is for Bethlehem, and *C* is for Christ?" Cynthia asked.

"Wonderful! I can tell you God's story in ABCs. *A*—All have sinned and fall short of the glory of God. *B*—But we are justified freely by His grace in *C*—Christ Jesus, our Redeemer, who came into the world to save us from sin, death, and the devil."

"Hey, Dad. That's an easy way to remember the Gospel."

"I have one last ABC for you, Cynthia," added Dad. "May God help you always to believe in Christ. He loves you and lives in your heart."

Read from God's Word

But now the righteousness of God has been manifested apart from the law, although the Law and the Prophets bear witness to it—the righteousness of God through faith in Jesus Christ for all who believe. For there is no distinction: for all have sinned and fall short of the glory of God, and are justified by his grace as a gift, through the redemption that is in Christ Jesus. Romans 3:21–24 ✍

_____Let's do: Create your own Bible alphabet: *A* is for _____, *B* is for _____, *C* is for _____, and so on through the letter Z. Romans 3:21–24 can give you some good ideas.

_____Let's pray: Dear God, thank You for everything—from *A* to *Z*. Thank You that by Your grace I can read Your Word and trust in Jesus to rescue me from sin. In Your Son's holy name. Amen.

P. L.

New Clothes

H i, girls! What did you do this sum- mer?" asked Annie.

"I went camping with my family," said Katie.

"We went to Disney World," responded Rebecca.

"I got to go to the Mall of America. It's the biggest and best place to shop. That's where I got this awe- some outfit. Isn't it sweet?" bragged Madison.

"It's nice," answered Annie, "but I have a much more expensive outfit that I got for my birthday."

"Well, I'm getting a brand-new outfit after school today," replied Rebecca.

Katie felt a little left out. She did- n't get new clothes very often. When she did, they were more practical than beautiful.

It might cheer Katie up to remem- ber that she, and everyone else with faith in Jesus Christ, has something better than all the new clothes in the world. The Bible says that all believ- ers have a beautiful spotless robe that we received in our Baptism. No amount of money can buy it. Jesus purchased this robe of righteousness for us with His death on the cross.

Our earthly clothing, no matter how expensive or stylish, will wear out or fade. God's promise of eternal life will never wear out or fade. It's a promise Katie (and you) can share with friends.

_____Let's talk: What does it mean to "clothe" yourself with the Lord Jesus Christ? See 2 Corinthians 5:21 for a clue.

_____Let's pray: Dear Jesus, thanks for purchasing a robe of righteousness for me through Your death and resurrection. Keep me close to You in faith. Amen.

P. L.

Not Good Enough?

Mrs. Monday asked her fourth graders to line up along the wall of the classroom. She challenged them to jump all the way across the room in one leap.

"Wow, I jumped twice as far as Maria did," Carlo bragged.

"But, Carlo, I asked you to jump across the whole room. Did you make it? Were you even close?"

"No, I guess not."

"So you see, you're in the same situation as Maria. You failed! I asked you to do this to illustrate a Bible lesson. God's Law commands us to be perfect."

"That would be impossible, just like jumping across this room in one jump is impossible!" exclaimed Maria.

"So it would seem," said Mrs. Monday. "Maria, try your jump one more time. Go ahead and jump."

When Maria jumped, Mrs. Monday caught her and carried her across the room. Her feet never even touched the floor. She made it in one jump.

"I get it," said Carlo. "We can't do it ourselves. Someone else has to take over."

"That's a *perfect* answer," said Mrs. Monday. "God sent Jesus to be perfect for us. Through His death and resurrection, Jesus lifts the burden of sin from us and carries us all the way to heaven. Through our Baptism God sees Jesus' perfection in us."

Read from God's Word

Therefore, if anyone is in Christ, he is a new creation. The old has passed away; behold, the new has come. All this is from God, who through Christ reconciled us to Himself and gave us the ministry of reconciliation; that is, in Christ God was reconciling the world to Himself, not counting their trespasses against them, and entrusting to us the message of reconciliation. Therefore, we are ambassadors for Christ, God making His appeal through us. We implore you on behalf of Christ, be reconciled to God. For our sake He made Him to be sin who knew no sin, so that in Him we might become the righteousness of God. 2 Corinthians 5:17–21

_____Let's do: Write about a time when you needed someone's help. In what way is Jesus much more than just a helper?

_____Let's pray: Dear Jesus, You died and rose again to make me perfect in God's eyes. Thanks. Be with me so I can live for You. Amen.

P. L.

Read from God's Word

This is the message we have heard from Him and proclaim to you, that God is light, and in Him is no darkness at all. If we say we have fellowship with Him while we walk in darkness, we lie and do not practice the truth. But if we walk in the light, as He is in the light, we have fellowship with one another, and the blood of Jesus His Son cleanses us from all sin. If we say we have no sin, we deceive ourselves, and the truth is not in us. If we confess our sins, He is faithful and just to forgive us our sins and to cleanse us from all unrighteousness. If we say we have not sinned, we make Him a liar, and His word is not in us. 1 John 1:5–10 ✎

Did You Use Soap?

Juan had just come in from playing baseball. He turned the faucet on and ran his hands through the water. As he was wiping his hands dry, he heard, "Did you use soap?"

"Aw, Mom, my hands weren't *that* dirty!"

"No soap, no supper!" Mom instructed.

After washing again, Juan came to the kitchen. "Okay, Mom, I'm ready. What's for supper?"

"Food for your body and food for your soul," Mom replied. "Look up 1 John 1:7 in your Bible. The last part will tell you about being really clean."

Juan said, "'And the blood of Jesus His [God's] Son cleanses us from all sin.' Does that mean I should wash my hands in blood?"

Mom explained, "No, it means the dirt in our lives, sin, is washed away by Jesus' blood, not by soap and water. Jesus, God's Son, came to wash away our sins and make us perfectly clean—holy. He lived a perfect life for us. He took all our punishment on Himself when He suffered and died on the cross. That's why in Psalm 51:2 we pray, "Wash me thoroughly from my iniquity, and cleanse me from my sin!"

Juan replied, "So I am really clean because of what Jesus did for me."

"That's right," replied Mom. "Now I think it's time for pizza."

_____Let's do: Name a brand of cleaning product and see if you can use the word in a sentence about Jesus. (For example, Jesus brings me *Joy*.)

_____Let's pray: Dear God, You have made me clean from sin through Jesus. Help me to show others Your love. In Jesus' name. Amen.

P. L.

Who Am I?

ere's a riddle: *I love you. I spoil you with treats. I'm not your parent. Who am I?* I'm your grandma!

Daniel loved his grandma. She baked him cookies every time he came over to her house. She played games with him whenever he asked. She praised him for his report card even when it had more B's than A's. *Why can't parents be more like grandmas?* Daniel wondered.

"Why do you love me so much, Grandma?" Daniel asked one day.

"Daniel, I accept you just the way you are because God accepts me the way I am. God knows all my faults and failures. Yet He loved me enough to send Jesus to be my rescuer, my Savior from sin."

"You mean God doesn't care what we do?"

"I didn't say that. God tells us in the Bible how He wants us to live. However, He knows we can't follow His commandments perfectly. He forgives us and sends His Holy Spirit to us so we can love others the way He loves us."

"So that's why you like me the way I am. It's because of Jesus."

"Yes. And because I'm your grandma."

Read from God's Word

And Zacchaeus stood and said to the Lord, "Behold, Lord, the half of my goods I give to the poor. And if I have defrauded anyone of anything, I restore it fourfold." And Jesus said to him, "Today salvation has come to this house, since he also is a son of Abraham. For the Son of Man came to seek and to save the lost." Luke 19:8–10

_____Let's do: Read Luke 19:1–10 in your Bible. Make a list of the special things a grandparent does for you. Make a list of the special things Jesus does for you.

_____Let's pray: Dear God, thank You for accepting me as I am and making me perfect in Jesus. Help me to share Your love with others. For Jesus' sake. Amen.

P. L.

Read from God's Word

Have this mind among yourselves, which is yours in Christ Jesus, who, though He was in the form of God, did not count equality with God a thing to be grasped, but made Himself nothing, taking the form of a servant, being born in the likeness of men. And being found in human form, He humbled Himself by becoming obedient to the point of death, even death on a cross. Therefore God has highly exalted Him and bestowed on Him the name that is above every name, so that at the name of Jesus every knee should bow, in heaven and on earth and under the earth, and every tongue confess that Jesus Christ is Lord, to the glory of God the Father. Philippians 2:5–11 ✑

Bible Name Game

See if you can use the clues to fill in the Bible names. (*Hint:* First and last letters overlap and have been filled in for you.)

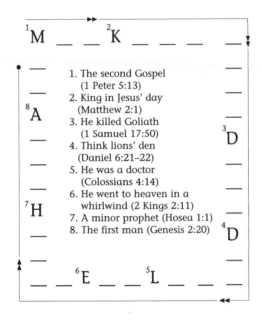

1. The second Gospel (1 Peter 5:13)
2. King in Jesus' day (Matthew 2:1)
3. He killed Goliath (1 Samuel 17:50)
4. Think lions' den (Daniel 6:21–22)
5. He was a doctor (Colossians 4:14)
6. He went to heaven in a whirlwind (2 Kings 2:11)
7. A minor prophet (Hosea 1:1)
8. The first man (Genesis 2:20)

Did you figure out the puzzle? The Bible is full of names, but some names in the Bible are more important than others. Our Bible reading emphasizes the importance of Jesus' name. There is no other name by which we can be saved (see Acts 4:12). Jesus, and no one else, lived, died, and rose to save us. God sends us His Holy Spirit, who enables us to confess our sins, trust in Jesus for forgiveness, and live lives that are holy and pleasing to Him.

_____Let's do: How many different names or titles for Jesus do you know? Make your own Bible name game using these names and titles.

_____Let's pray: Dear Jesus, help me honor Your name above all other names. Help me trust in You always. Amen.

P. L.

Relief Pitcher

U ncle Pete, I'm sorry you saw me pitch such a lousy game." Jason had invited Uncle Pete to come to his game, but then he pitched the worst game of his life.

"Jason, it's okay. Remember, your team still won the game. The relief pitcher came in when you were behind 4 to 1. He didn't let anyone else score."

"Yeah, and on top of that he hit a grand slam in the ninth inning to win the game, 5 to 4. That part was great," said Jason.

"Do you know who the all-time greatest relief pitcher is?" asked Uncle Pete.

"No, who?"

"Jesus of Nazareth. Think about it, Jason. When we try to win the game of life by ourselves, we end up losing every time to the team of Satan and his evil teammates. They're just stronger and smarter than we are. Jesus is kind of like a relief pitcher.

Read from God's Word

"O death, where is your victory? O death, where is your sting?" The sting of death is sin, and the power of sin is the law. But thanks be to God, who gives us the victory through our Lord Jesus Christ. 1 Corinthians 15:55–57

He'll strike out the evil ones. He'll throw Satan out. Best of all, He hit the grand-slam to win all games when He rose from the grave on Easter morning. That's our victory too!"

"Yeah, it does feel good to be on the winning team."

"With Jesus as your relief pitcher, you're on the winning team every day!"

_____Let's talk: Why do we need a relief pitcher to win the victory over sin, death, and the devil for us? When we gain the victory over these foes, who should have all the credit? See 1 Corinthians 15:57.

_____Let's pray: Dear Jesus, thank You for saving me from sin, from death, and from the power of the devil. Amen.

P. L.

Read from God's Word

But as for you, continue in what you have learned and have firmly believed, knowing from whom you learned it and how from childhood you have been acquainted with the sacred writings, which are able to make you wise for salvation through faith in Christ Jesus. All Scripture is breathed out by God and profitable for teaching, for reproof, for correction, and for training in righteousness, that the man of God may be competent, equipped for every good work. 2 Timothy 3:14–17 ✍

Animal Training

Can you "retrain" these letters to spell trainable animals?

PAHELNET:

_____ carries a trunk

RAPROT:

_____ talks a lot

WAKH:

_____ flies high

"Let's go see the elephant show!" yelled Natalie as her family entered the zoo.

"How do they get elephants to wave like that?" asked Dan.

"Watch what the trainer does," replied Dad.

"Look! He gives the elephant food when he does the trick well," exclaimed Natalie.

At the birdhouse Dan watched closely. "The parrot got food every time it talked, and the hawk was fed after the diving trick."

"That's the secret," said Dad. "It's called positive reinforcement. The trainer rewards the animal for doing the desired actions."

"I'm glad God isn't like an animal trainer," mused Dan.

"What makes you say that?" asked Dad.

"Because God doesn't reward us for what *we* do—He rewards us for what *Jesus* did! He sent Jesus *because* we are sinful and unable to do His will. Jesus earned our heavenly reward. He gives us the Holy Spirit in our hearts through faith, teaching and empowering us through the Word of God."

"That's a great way to explain it, Dan," said Dad. "Thanks for the training."

_____Let's talk: Name some of the rewards that God has given you. Why has He given them to you?

_____Let's pray: Dear Jesus, thank You for earning the reward of heaven for me. Guide me in following Your directions for my life. Amen.

P. L.

Disinfects and Lubricates

Read from God's Word

This is the message we have heard from Him and proclaim to you, that God is light, and in Him is no darkness at all. If we say we have fellowship with Him while we walk in darkness, we lie and do not practice the truth. But if we walk in the light, as He is in the light, we have fellowship with one another, and the blood of Jesus His Son cleanses us from all sin. If we say we have no sin, we deceive ourselves, and the truth is not in us. If we confess our sins, He is faithful and just to forgive us our sins and to cleanse us from all unrighteousness. If we say we have not sinned, we make Him a liar, and His word is not in us. 1 John 1:5–10 ✐

Sarah stared at the tall orange spray can on the hairstylist's counter. "What in the world is that stuff?" she asked Chloe, the stylist.

"Oh, that's Clippercide™," said Chloe as she continued to trim Sarah's hair. "It's a special spray to clean our clippers and scissors so we don't spread germs from one customer to another."

"What are those other words— *fungicide* and *tuberculocide?*" Sarah asked.

"Those are some of the specific germs the spray will get rid of. That can of spray will kill any germ that finds its way onto my clippers," answered Chloe.

On the way home, Sarah told her mom how the Clippercide™ gets rid of germs. "You know," said Sarah, "wouldn't it be great if there were a spray can to get rid of sin?"

"Well," said Mom, "sin is like a germ. It spread from Adam and Eve to all other people. But we don't need a special can of spray to get rid of our sin, do we?"

"No, I guess you're right," said Sarah. "God has already taken away our sin for us. He gave us His Son, Jesus, who died for our sins. Through Jesus' death and resurrection, we are 'germ-free,' making our spirits clean and healthy."

_____Let's talk: What is something that reminds *you* of how your sins are forgiven?

_____Let's pray: Dear God, thank You for giving me faith in Your Son, Jesus, who has taken away the "germ" of sin. In Jesus' name I pray. Amen.

H. K.

Heavenly Thoughts

Ben was riding in the car with his mother. They were going to the store. As he was looking out the car window, he noticed that the sky was so clear and blue.

"Mom," said Ben, "the sky is so clear and bright. It seems like I should be able to see all the way into heaven. If I could, I would like to reach up and pull Grandma back to earth so she wouldn't be dead anymore."

"You know, Ben," said Mom, "it would be great to see Grandma on this beautiful day. But she is not coming back to earth. When she died, she went to be with Jesus forever."

"I know," said Ben. "She's not sick anymore. It's just that I miss her."

"I do too. But Jesus died for us so we can live with Him in heaven. We will see Grandma again when we get to heaven," said Mom as they pulled into the store's parking lot.

"Could we buy something to remind ourselves that we will be with Grandma and Jesus in heaven someday?" asked Ben.

Mom gave Ben a hug. "Sure," she said.

_____Let's talk: Do you know of someone who is already in heaven with Jesus? What is something you can do to remember your loved one and your special place in heaven?

_____Let's pray: Father, You love me so much that You give me forgiveness of sins and eternal life. Thank You for the gift of faith in Jesus. Help me remember Your promise of eternal life in heaven. In Jesus' name I pray. Amen.

H. K.

Pressing On

"I want to stop," moaned Alexis. "I can't make it." Alexis and her parents had entered a local one-mile race.

"Press on, Alexis," said her dad. "You can make it!"

Although it would have been easier to quit, Alexis kept on running. Finally she looked up and saw the finish line.

That's it, Alexis thought. *My goal is to cross it running.* When she crossed the finish line, Alexis felt great!

"I did it, Dad. I pressed on and finished the race. I'm so glad I kept running instead of giving up," said Alexis as she drank a cup of water.

"Just think how great it is to press on to win the greatest prize ever," said Mom.

"Huh?" asked Alexis.

Dad explained, "Mom isn't talking about a prize for running. She is talking about the prize God has given you through faith in Jesus."

Read from God's Word

That I may know Him and the power of His resurrection, and may share His sufferings, becoming like Him in His death, that by any means possible I may attain the resurrection from the dead. Not that I have already obtained this or am already perfect, but I press on to make it my own, because Christ Jesus has made me His own. Brothers, I do not consider that I have made it my own. But one thing I do: forgetting what lies behind and straining forward to what lies ahead, I press on toward the goal for the prize of the upward call of God in Christ Jesus. Philippians 3:10–14 ✎

"Oh, you mean going to heaven?" asked Alexis.

"Yes," said Mom. "Because of what Jesus did for us on the cross, we are winners! Through Jesus' power we can press on during both good and bad times toward what awaits us: the crown of eternal life. The Holy Spirit will guide us in all we do."

_____Let's do: When is it hardest for you to press on, to keep going? How does faith in Jesus motivate you?

_____Let's pray: Dear Jesus, thank You for pressing on to die on the cross for my sins. Guide me in all I do. In Your name I pray. Amen.

H. K.

Read from God's Word

For while we were still weak, at the right time Christ died for the ungodly. For one will scarcely die for a righteous person—though perhaps for a good person one would dare even to die—but God shows His love for us in that while we were still sinners, Christ died for us. Romans 5:6–8 ᗡ

Friends

In the blanks next to each number, write the name of a close friend.

1. _____
2. _____
3. _____

Now answer the following questions for each of your friends. Write the answer for each question next to your friend's name.

Does this friend help you live as Jesus wants you to?

Does this friend stand up for you and help you?

Would this friend be willing to die for you?

If you answered yes to those questions, you have some pretty good friends! It is important to have good friends, especially friends who build you up in faith. God warns us to choose friends wisely. Do you know why? Some friends may trick you into sin, lead you away from God, and even do mean things to you.

Jesus is the ultimate friend, loving you enough to lay down His life for you. And you can share this message with your friends!

_____Let's do: Using each letter of the word friend, write one way you can share your faith in Jesus with a friend.

F_____ R_____ I_____ E_____ N_____ D_____

_____Let's pray: Dear Jesus, You are my best Friend! Thank You for giving Your life for me. Amen.

H. K.

Following the Rules

"Attention, please!" shouted Mr. Mitchell. "I know everyone is excited about our camping retreat, but I must tell you some special rules."

"Oh, no," groaned Dave. "More rules. I thought we came to have some fun."

"We must be safe in order to have fun. That is why we have two special rules," explained Mr. Mitchell. "First, do not swim or hike alone. Second, do not leave your tent at night. You might get lost. Raise your hand if you promise to follow the rules."

All the campers and counselors raised their hands.

"That's it?" asked Dave. "Those are the rules? I thought you would have at least 10 rules!"

"You mean as in the Ten Commandments?" said Mr. Mitchell. "God gave us His Law to reveal our sin and guide us in daily living. All people who have faith in Jesus Christ strive to keep the commandments, but because of our sinful nature, we cannot keep God's commandments perfectly. Because of Jesus' death and resurrection, we have forgiveness for those times we break God's rules. He frees us from sin's guilt, punishment, and power."

"Now therefore, if you will indeed obey My voice and keep My covenant, you shall be My treasured possession among all peoples, for all the earth is Mine; and you shall be to Me a kingdom of priests and a holy nation. These are the words that you shall speak to the people of Israel." So Moses came and called the elders of the people and set before them all these words that the LORD had commanded him. All the people answered together and said, "All that the LORD has spoken we will do." And Moses reported the words of the people to the LORD. Exodus 19:5–8

Mr. Mitchell turned and faced all the campers. Then he asked, "With God's help, will you follow the camp rules and God's rules too?"

Every hand was raised.

_____Let's talk: Can you list all 10 of God's commandments? (Look in Exodus 20:1–17 for help.) How do these commands help you to live as God's child?

_____Let's pray: Dear God, I know I have broken Your commandments. Please forgive me. Thank You for sending Your Son, Jesus, who kept Your commands perfectly. Guide me with Your Holy Spirit. For Jesus' sake. Amen.

H. K.

Brotherly Love

Read from God's Word

John was standing with two of his disciples, and he looked at Jesus as He walked by and said, "Behold, the Lamb of God!" The two disciples heard him say this, and they followed Jesus. Jesus turned and saw them following and said to them, "What are you seeking?" And they said to Him, "Rabbi" (which means Teacher), "where are You staying?" He said to them, "Come and you will see." So they came and saw where He was staying, and they stayed with Him that day. ... One of the two who heard John speak and followed Jesus was Andrew, Simon Peter's brother. He first found his own brother Simon and said to him, "We have found the Messiah" (which means Christ). He brought him to Jesus. John 1:35–42

Rex and Rover were born in the same litter and looked like twins. Rover lived in an upstairs apartment, and Rex lived in the apartment directly below Rover. Just as human brothers get into squabbles, the two German shepherd dogs didn't get along very well. In fact, they had to be kept completely apart or chaos would break out in the apartment building.

One day, Rover's gate was accidentally left open. He angrily charged down the stairs toward Rex. Soon, the owners came running to break up the fight. They shook their heads and commented, "That's no way for brothers to behave!"

The Bible reading tells us about two brothers. Andrew and another man saw Jesus and followed Him. They spent the day talking to Him. The first thing Andrew did was to go out and look for his brother, Simon Peter. He told Peter, "We have found the Messiah."

Andrew gives us a good example of brotherly love. His brother was the first person he brought to Jesus. Peter and Andrew shared their faith in God. This made a difference in the way they treated each other.

Jesus' love moved Him to die for our sins of lovelessness. His love and grace enable us to love our brothers and sisters.

_____Let's talk: How has a brother, sister, or friend been kind to you lately? What difference does this make in the way you treat them?

_____Let's pray: Dear Father in heaven, fill us with love for all our brothers and sisters in Christ so we live together in peace, honoring Your name. In Jesus' name. Amen.

E. S.

Witnesses

Rosa and Rico were walking home from their grandmother's apartment. Suddenly they heard a shout. When they turned around, they saw a man push a woman down. He grabbed her purse and started to run. But before the man could get away, a neighbor, Mr. Sanchez, jumped on his back. Mr. Sanchez yelled to the children to call 911 from their grandmother's apartment.

After the police arrived, one of the officers said, "Children, we need to take your statements about what happened. You are witnesses."

At home, Rosa and Rico told their parents about what they witnessed. "Did you know that you are witnesses all the time?" asked their mother. "Every day your words and actions testify about your faith in Jesus."

"That's right," said their father. "You might not be asked to go to court to tell what happened today. But each day you have the opportunity to tell others that Jesus loves you and died for you—and for them too."

"I get it," said Rosa. "A witness tells the truth of what happened."

"And," said Rico, "because Jesus truly has saved us from our sins, His Spirit helps us to be witnesses for Jesus!"

Read from God's Word

The disciples of John reported all these things to him. And John, calling two of his disciples to him, sent them to the Lord, saying, "Are You the one who is to come, or shall we look for another?" And when the men had come to Him, they said, "John the Baptist has sent us to You, saying, 'Are You the one who is to come, or shall we look for another?'" In that hour He healed many people of diseases and plagues and evil spirits, and on many who were blind He bestowed sight. And He answered them, "Go and tell John what you have seen and heard: the blind receive their sight, the lame walk, lepers are cleansed, and the deaf hear, the dead are raised up, the poor have good news preached to them. And blessed is the one who is not offended by Me." Luke 7:18–23

———Let's talk: Name two things you know that Jesus said or did. Now name one way He makes a difference in your life. Share this message with someone!

———Let's pray: Dear Jesus, thank You for all that You have done for me. Make me Your joyful witness. Amen.

H. K.

The Bad Day

Today's Bible reading doesn't seem to fit the mood of a bad day. "Rejoice?" "Sing to the Lord?" On bad days it seems like it would be better to hide under the blankets and cry.

Read the verses again. "But I have trusted in Your steadfast love; my heart shall rejoice in Your salvation. I will sing to the LORD, because He has dealt bountifully with me."

And truly the Lord is good. He loves us with a love that never stops. He saves us from sin and hell. He makes us His children in Baptism. Because Jesus died on the cross for our sins, we can rejoice and sing to the Lord on days full of happiness—and also on days that aren't so great.

Sometimes, bad days help us to rely on Him. We are led to pray or to read our Bible. God loves us even in the hard times, and He wants us to let Him bear our burdens.

So when you have great days, rejoice in the Lord. He loves you. He saves you. He's good to you. And also when you have bad days, rejoice in the Lord. He still loves you. He still saves you. He's still good to you. You can count on that!

_____Let's talk: How can you rejoice in God, even in difficulties? What has Jesus done for you that makes you rejoice?

_____Let's pray: Lord God, help me to trust You even when it's difficult, rejoice in You even when I'm sad, and sing to You even when I feel like crying. Thank You for the love You show me in Your Son, Jesus. Amen.

J. S.

By Faith

Today we're going to think about the beginning of the universe," Mrs. Healy said.

George had heard the creation story in the Book of Genesis so many times he knew it by heart.

"At the very beginning of the universe, there was a big bang," Mrs. Healy began.

Uh-oh, George thought. *This isn't the creation story.*

While we trust teachers to instruct and guide us, sometimes they may teach things that go against God's Word. For example, we may hear that evolution is a fact, that the Bible is not really true, or that other religions are the same as Christianity.

While it is always be helpful to learn about all sorts of viewpoints, it can also be difficult to hold strong to our faith when we come against different teachings. "Now faith is the assurance of things hoped for, the conviction of things not seen," begins Hebrews 11. It continues by naming many Old Testament believers who had faith in God when others believed differently.

In times when our faith is challenged, we need God's strength, which we receive in His Word and Sacraments. The truth of God's Word overcomes the world's falsehoods and our doubts. Our faith is made stronger. Then, with God's help, we can share His love with others.

Read from God's Word

Now faith is the assurance of things hoped for, the conviction of things not seen. For by it the people of old received their commendation. By faith we understand that the universe was created by the word of God, so that what is seen was not made out of things that are visible. Hebrews 11:1–3 ✎

_____Let's talk: What is challenging your faith today? How can God's Word help you to have strong faith?

_____Let's pray: Lord God, Maker of heaven and earth, sometimes I get confused when I hear about teachings that are different from what I've learned in Your Word. Please help me to understand the truth and to trust in You always. I pray this in Jesus' name. Amen.

J. S.

An Understanding Father

Read from God's Word

Continue steadfastly in prayer, being watchful in it with thanksgiving. Colossians 4:2 ✍

"Dónde está mi mamá?" 4-year-old José asked the librarian.

"What, honey?" asked the librarian.

"¿Dónde está mi mamá?" repeated José, his voice growing louder and panicked. The librarian looked confused. "Mama!"

A woman came around the corner. "José?" José ran into his mother's arms and cried.

José was lost. He was separated from his mom and couldn't communicate with the librarian to get help. Have you ever felt like José? Did you have a frightening experience similar to this when you were a young child?

For little children, life can be scary. But it can also be confusing as we grow up. You're not scared of losing your mom at the library anymore, but maybe there are changes in your life. Maybe you even brought trouble on yourself by your own mistakes and sins.

Our Father in heaven is ready to hear us and help us in all changes and difficulties. God always understands us, unlike the librarian who couldn't understand José. He knows what we need even before we can ask it. God our Father, who loved us enough to send His Son to die for our sins, listens to our prayers.

We pray, expecting God to listen and help us. We pray with gratefulness since God has already given us so much—even His own Son as our Savior.

———Let's do: Talk to the Lord in your journal today. What is on your mind? What are you thankful for?

———Let's pray: Lord God, thank You for hearing me when I pray. Please help me to trust You even when I'm confused. In Jesus' name. Amen.

J. S.

The Flood

Read from God's Word

For Christ also suffered once for sins, the righteous for the unrighteous, that He might bring us to God, being put to death in the flesh but made alive in the spirit, in which He went and proclaimed to the spirits in prison, because they formerly did not obey, when God's patience waited in the days of Noah, while the ark was being prepared, in which a few, that is, eight persons, were brought safely through water. Baptism, which corresponds to this, now saves you, not as a removal of dirt from the body but as an appeal to God for a good conscience, through the resurrection of Jesus Christ, who has gone into heaven and is at the right hand of God, with angels, authorities, and powers having been subjected to him. 1 Peter 3:18–22 ✍

Missy watched the water pour over the wiggling baby. It looked like every other Baptism. But this time, Missy didn't just watch. She questioned what was so great about water.

That night in her room Missy saw a Sunday school craft she had made. She jiggled the rainbow of beads and ribbons and remembered the lesson about Noah's ark. Missy had more questions.

Why did God flood the earth? she wondered. She read some verses from Genesis and then found the answer: "The LORD saw that the wickedness of man was great in the earth, and that every intention of the thoughts of his heart was only evil continually" (Genesis 6:5). *God decided to wash away the sin.*

I wonder if Baptism is supposed to remind us of Noah's ark, Missy thought. She asked her mom to help her understand.

"That's right, Missy." Mom read from 1 Peter 3, "In Noah's ark, 'a few, that is, eight persons, were brought safely through water. Baptism, which corresponds to this, now saves you.' In Baptism," Mom continued, "our sins are washed away because Jesus died to forgive us."

Missy finally had her answers. "God keeps us safe in the arms of Jesus through Baptism, and that's a good flood."

_____Let's talk: What questions do you have about Baptism?

_____Let's pray: Dear Father, thank You for sending Jesus to die for me so I could become Your child in Baptism. In Jesus' name. Amen.

J. S

Just a Stage Manager

Read from God's Word

Rendering service with a good will as to the Lord and not to man. Ephesians 6:7 ✐

Mom expected to see Jia's smiling face. Instead, her daughter was almost in tears. "Oh, no, you didn't get a part, did you?" Mom asked.

"No!" Jia cried. "I'm just a lousy stage manager!"

"I know how disappointed you must be, but you might find that you like being stage manager. It's a very important job," Mom said. She read Ephesians 6:7, and then said, "Jia, Jesus served us by becoming a man and dying on the cross for our sins. You can serve others out of love and gratefulness to your Savior."

Although Jia was disappointed, she still went to play practice every day and tried to do her best as stage manager.

On the night of the performance, Jia got all the props and costumes ready. The play started well enough, but then, one by one the actors needed Jia's help for something. She ran to find bobby pins. She uncrushed a hat. She found an extra chair for a prop.

Jia then realized how important her job was. If not for her help, there would have been lots of mistakes during the performance. She thought back to the Bible verse her mom had shown her and realized that serving others sometimes can be done even in simple ways—like being a stage manager.

_____Let's talk: Whom could you serve today?

_____Let's pray: Dear Father in heaven, thank You for sending Jesus to serve me and die for my sins. Please help me to live a life of thankfulness to You by serving others. I pray in Jesus' name. Amen.

J. S.

Trusting in God

Many years ago Irene was headed to the beach with a group of friends when tragedy struck. The car careened into a tree, and everyone in it was injured. In a split second, her spine was broken, and Irene became a quadriplegic, unable to move from the neck down.

Irene lived the rest of her life in a wheelchair. Although she had to depend on others to help her in nearly every aspect of her life, she could awkwardly move her arms to feed herself if a fork was secured in the metal brace that aided her hands and arms. She could move around in her wheelchair through her one-story house.

But she had to hire helpers to dress her, bathe her, clean up after her, cook her meals, clean her house. Everything that comes easily to us was impossible for Irene. She was dependent on others.

It is the same in our life of faith. We depend on God for everything—life, health, safety, and most of all, our salvation in Christ. We can be certain of God's love for us, since He loved us enough to send His Son to die for us. In Jesus, our sins are forgiven, our salvation is sure, and we can trust that God will take us to heaven one day.

Read from God's Word

But I am like a green olive tree in the house of God. I trust in the steadfast love of God forever and ever. I will thank You forever, because You have done it. I will wait for Your name, for it is good, in the presence of the godly. Psalm 52:8–9 ✍

_____Let's talk: What adjustments do you think Irene had to make in her life? What things didn't change?

_____Let's pray: My dear Savior, Jesus, thank You for dying on the cross to save me. Thank You that I can depend on You for everything. Amen.

J. S.

Read from God's Word

*Oh, taste and see that the
Lord is good! Blessed is the
man who takes refuge in Him!
Psalm 34:8*

In the Small Stuff of Life

The day was perfect for a trip to the amusement park. The Simon family packed a cooler and headed out.

About a mile from home, the car died. The Simons were stranded in the middle of heavy traffic on the way to a fun-filled day. They were stuck—miles from home, miles from the amusement park.

Disappointed, the children sat on the curb, waiting for the tow truck to come. "At least we have drinks," Mom said, patting the cooler.

Then, slowly, they noticed little things. Missy noticed the kindness of the convenience store clerk when she let Dad use the phone. Mike noticed the friendliness of the tow-truck driver, who gave them a ride to the repair shop. Dad noticed the generosity of the mechanic, who offered to let them borrow his car to go to the amusement park.

These small things added up to something big. God was with the Simon family, helping them even when bad things were happening.

Sometimes when we feel most helpless and needy, we realize how much we truly need God's care. God is with you too—even on days that don't turn out like you expect. He takes care of you in unexpected ways—in a manger, on a cross, from a heavenly throne, and even within you.

———Let's talk: Think back to a time when life was not perfect. Now, looking back, can you see that God was helping you and taking care of you?

———Let's pray: Dear heavenly Father, thank You for taking care of me by sending Jesus to die for me. In Jesus' name I pray. Amen.

J. S.

Sycamore Christians

Read from God's Word

"Blessed is the man who trusts in the LORD, whose trust is the LORD. He is like a tree planted by water, that sends out its roots by the stream, and does not fear when heat comes, for its leaves remain green, and is not anxious in the year of drought, for it does not cease to bear fruit." Jeremiah 17:7–8

What do a tree and a believer in Jesus as Savior of the world have in common?

A sycamore tree has white bark and a woody fruit ball in the fall. Hikers use the distinctive bark of the sycamore to locate riverbanks, where these trees like to grow. Along the Mississippi and Ohio River valleys, these trees may grow 175 feet tall. The sycamore survives hot, dry summers on the prairies because its water source is near. The long roots drink from the water in the ground.

Christians are planted near different kinds of water sources. Strength for living as God's children comes from the Word of God and the Sacraments, especially the Sacrament of Holy Baptism. When anger or unkind words lead us to be anxious, we have the gift of faith. When our sinful thoughts and actions nag us, we have the power of God's Spirit to confess them and receive forgiveness. When fears about our future haunt us, we have God's peace.

The words from Jeremiah say we become like trees planted by a never-ending source of water. We stand tall and strong, and we continue to grow because of God. We are like sycamores, growing at the water's edge.

_____Let's do: Draw a tree. On the branches of that tree write ways that God strengthens you.

_____Let's pray: Dear God, thank You for refreshing me with Your Word, strengthening my faith, and using me for Your purposes. In Jesus' name. Amen.

J. H.

Read from God's Word

And we know that for those who love God all things work together for good, for those who are called according to his purpose. For those whom He foreknew He also predestined to be conformed to the image of His Son, in order that He might be the firstborn among many brothers. And those whom He predestined He also called, and those whom He called He also justified, and those whom He justified He also glorified. Romans 8:28–30 ✎

Safe and Secure

Jasmine thought it seemed like such a long trip to their grandparents' place. They packed the car in the early morning darkness, checking off a list of family assignments—adjust the thermostat, lock the doors, grab the pillows, and bring books to read.

As the hours went by, Mom helped the family pass the time by singing songs and playing games. Before long Jasmine and her sisters would be lulled to sleep by the humming of the car engine.

They never worried about how they would get to Grandma and Grandpa's home. They never worried about their safety. Dad was at the wheel. Everyone was in his safe hands.

With God our heavenly Father in control of our lives, we never have to worry about where we are going. We don't have to fear the events that come our way—the move to a new neighborhood, the death of a grandparent, the exam that reveals that braces are needed. All things are known by God and are held in His hands, the best hands.

God's love in Jesus makes our ride through life secure. Jesus was victorious over all the dangers of this day and all our days to come. At the end of our earthly days, we will arrive safely to be with Him forever.

_____Let's talk: What changes have you experienced in the last year? How was God with you?

_____Let's pray: God, You are all-powerful and have everything in Your hands. Thank You for holding me close to You always. In Jesus' name. Amen.

J. H.

No-See-Ums

Read from God's Word

Be clear-minded and alert. Your opponent the devil is prowling around like a roaring lion, looking for someone to devour. 1 Peter 5:8 ✍

Find one-eighth of an inch on a ruler. That is the length of a no-see-um, a pesky biting fly. Those little critters are at beach parties and campouts and go unnoticed until you get bitten—a painful bite. The only way to escape is to leave the area.

"No-see-um" might be a good name for the devil. He seems to go unnoticed, tempting here and there. He sneaks into our thinking and suggests that wrong is right and right is wrong.

The devil tempted Adam and Eve centuries ago. When these two people ate the fruit that God had forbidden, they sinned. All people since then have been born with a condition called original sin.

Christians have this condition of sin. Sin disconnects us from God. But God promises to help us withstand temptation. With His help, we can walk away from a fight. We can ask an adult for guidance. We can close our eyes in prayer. We can spend quiet time in our room reading God's Word.

But no one can live without sinning. Because of this, God, in His mercy, sent His Son, Jesus, to save us. Jesus was tempted too, but He was able to resist all of Satan's temptations, every single one. Jesus died to conquer sin, death, and the devil for us.

_____Let's do: Read the Sixth Petition of the Lord's Prayer in your catechism and the meaning that follows. Write about all that tries to deceive or mislead you.

_____Let's pray: Our Father, give us strength to resist and overcome temptation. Forgive our sins for Jesus' sake. Amen.

J. H.

Bitten

The camping trip had finally arrived. Church families gathered around the lake to enjoy one another, hike in the autumn wonder, and study the Bible. Tents were set up. Lights were strung from campers' awnings. Coolers were set out. Lawn chairs were gathered.

And now that the setup was done, the children were off squealing with delight. That delight ended when Heidi screamed, "I've been bitten by a snake!" People rushed to help. Heidi's dad checked her ankle and found the puncture marks. Other parents grabbed flashlights, searched, and found the poisonous copperhead.

Heidi was taken to a nearby hospital and examined by a doctor. There she received the snakebite antivenom and was delivered from the poisonous bite.

God rescues us from "poisonous bites" that are designed to hurt us in body and soul, possessions and property. The Lord helps us overcome the venom of the poisonous bites that the devil and our own sin bring into our lives. The Lord helps us endure the loss of friends, the disappointment of failures, and the painful results of sinful choices we make.

God's grace forgives our sinful choices. His grace is the antivenom that delivers us from the poisonous bite of sin, death, and the devil.

_____Let's talk: When are you most tempted by the devil? What do you need to do to resist his temptations?

_____Let's pray: Dear God, deliver me from every evil through Jesus Christ, my Lord and Savior. In His name. Amen.

J. H.

Lessons to Help

Philip recited the golf tips he learned at his lessons. Keep your head down. Bend your knees. Swing easily.

He stood at the first tee, lifted the club, swung, and missed the ball completely. How embarrassing! It was as though he had forgotten everything he had been taught.

From an early age, Christians have many lessons in learning right from wrong. We memorize the Ten Commandments, the Apostles' Creed, and the Lord's Prayer. We even memorize lots of Bible passages. We *know* what God desires, but no matter how hard we try, we can't *keep* the laws of God. At times we fail completely. Paul confessed this fact in today's Bible reading. We confess it too. We don't do what we know we should, and we often do what we shouldn't. That is the struggle we face every day as a follower of Jesus.

God helps us to confess our sins and ask for God's forgiveness. God grants us forgiveness for Jesus' sake. Through His Word and Sacraments, He gives us power to follow Him. How thankful we can be that He doesn't remember our sins or hold them against us. Having been saved, we, too, can say, "Thanks be to God through Jesus Christ our Lord!" (Romans 7:25).

Read from God's Word

I do not understand my own actions. For I do not do what I want, but I do the very thing I hate. ... For I have the desire to do what is right, but not the ability to carry it out. For I do not do the good I want, but the evil I do not want is what I keep on doing. Now if I do what I do not want, it is no longer I who do it, but sin that dwells within me. So I find it to be a law that when I want to do right, evil lies close at hand. For I delight in the Law of God, in my inner being, but I see in my members another law waging war against the law of my mind and making me captive to the law of sin that dwells in my members. Wretched man that I am! Who will deliver me from this body of death? Thanks be to God through Jesus Christ our Lord! So then, I myself serve the Law of God with my mind, but with my flesh I serve the law of sin. Romans 7:15–25

_____Let's talk: What do you sometimes have trouble doing although you know you should? Describe how it feels to be forgiven.

_____Let's pray: Loving God, forgive me for times I fail to follow Your commands and choose my own way. Help me to seek Your will. In Jesus' name I pray. Amen.

J. H.

Read from God's Word

I will make with them a covenant of peace and banish wild beasts from the land, so that they may dwell securely in the wilderness and sleep in the woods. And I will make them and the places all around my hill a blessing, and I will send down the showers in their season; they shall be showers of blessing. And the trees of the field shall yield their fruit, and the earth shall yield its increase, and they shall be secure in their land. And they shall know that I am the LORD, when I break the bars of their yoke, and deliver them from the hand of those who enslaved them. Ezekiel 34:25–27

Showers of Candy

Emilee's friends had arrived at the birthday fiesta. The house was decorated with banners, flags, and pictures. There were games to play, cake and ice cream to eat. After all the presents were opened, it was time for the piñata.

One by one the birthday guests were blindfolded and given a stick to swing at the piñata. Each person tried, but couldn't break the piñata. The guests were restless until Ashlee had a turn. She kept swinging and swinging until she finally broke open the piñata. Candy showered down like rain.

God showers blessings on us that are sweeter than candy. Jesus opens the piñata of His grace to give us His peace and joy every day. We don't do anything to make His blessings happen. God did it. His love sent Jesus to die for the sins of all. His peace is better than a shower of candy at a birthday fiesta. It's perfect!

Jesus poured out His love for us on the cross, suffering and dying for our sin. His victory means we have a full life as friends with God. This peace showers down on us like life-giving rain. His victory means we have a full life with God forever.

_____Let's talk: What areas of your life don't seem peaceful? Where are places you can find God's peace?

_____Let's pray: Dear God, help me to remember the showers of Your blessing when I feel unhappy. Thank You for Your love for us in Christ Jesus. Amen.

J. H.

october

Contributors for this month:

Kim Bejot

Jacqueline Loontjer

Kristine Moulds

Judy Williams

Read from God's Word

Since then we have a great high priest who has passed through the heavens, Jesus, the Son of God, let us hold fast our confession. For we do not have a high priest who is unable to sympathize with our weaknesses, but one who in every respect has been tempted as we are, yet without sin. Let us then with confidence draw near to the throne of grace, that we may receive mercy and find grace to help in time of need. Hebrews 4:14–16 ✑

Temptation

Leah walked into the girls' bathroom to wash her hands. Next to the sink was Marguerite's new ring. The turquoise stone was set in silver. It was beautiful! Leah looked around to make sure no one else was in the bathroom. She slipped it into her pocket, washed her hands, and returned to the classroom.

Later Mrs. Shank announced, "Students, Marguerite can't find a ring she wore to school today. Has anyone seen it?"

Leah was sure no one knew she had the ring. But Leah felt guilty. She remembered the Seventh Commandment, "You shall not steal." Leah had given in to the temptation to steal. Her conscience bothered her a lot, so she walked over to Marguerite and handed her the ring.

"Here, Marguerite! I took your ring from the bathroom. You left it there when you washed your hands. I'm sorry I took it."

"Thanks for returning it," said her friend. "That ring belonged to my grandmother when she was a little girl in Paraguay."

When Leah returned to her seat, she silently asked Jesus to forgive her for giving in to temptation.

Even Jesus was tempted. But unlike us, Jesus resisted temptation perfectly and led a perfect life. He defeated sin and death so we can have forgiveness and eternal life.

_____Let's do: Write about a time when you were tempted to sin.
How does Jesus' death on the cross give us victory over sin?

_____Let's pray: Dear Lord God, help me to remember to love others.
Forgive me for Jesus' sake when I sin. Amen.

J. W.

A Special Celebration

When Rob woke up, he knew it was a special day. His parents always remembered his Baptism birthday.

Right away he noticed two things in the kitchen. His Baptism candle stood in the middle of the table with a note: "Happy Baptism Birthday, Rob!" And there was a package next to his plate. When he took off the white bow and wrapping paper, he found a special plaque with his name on it.

At dinner that evening, Rob's Baptism candle was burning. After dinner, Rob's dad led the family in their special Baptism birthday prayer:

"Dear God, thank You for washing each of us clean in Baptism. Remind us that You have forgiven all our sins because of what Your Son, Jesus, did for us on the cross. Let us wake up each day to live the new life You have given us in our Baptism. Amen."

Then, as Dad gave the blessing, each member of the family made the sign of the cross. "The grace of the Lord Jesus Christ and the love of God and the fellowship of the Holy Spirit be with [us] all. [Amen]" (2 Corinthians 13:14).

That night as Rob went to bed, he thought again how special it is to be a child of God.

Read from God's Word

He saved us, not because of works done by us in righteousness, but according to His own mercy, by the washing of regeneration and renewal of the Holy Spirit, whom He poured out on us richly through Jesus Christ our Savior, so that being justified by His grace we might become heirs according to the hope of eternal life. Titus 3:5–7 ✑

_____Let's talk: Do you know when your Baptism birthday is? What can your family do to celebrate this special day?

_____Let's pray: Baptism gives new power to live our lives. For today's prayer, use the prayer Rob and his family prayed.

J. W.

Good Food

Read from God's Word

So put away all malice and all deceit and hypocrisy and envy and all slander. Like newborn infants, long for the pure spiritual milk, that by it you may grow up to salvation—if indeed you have tasted that the Lord is good. 1 Peter 2:1–3

On the bus ride home, Sierra was planning a big surprise. Earlier at school, Sierra's teacher taught the class to make pizza—that would be her supper surprise.

As soon as Sierra got home, she checked to see if they had the ingredients: English muffins, pepperoni, cheese, and pizza sauce. Yes! Everything she needed was there. Sierra separated the muffin halves and placed them on a cookie sheet. She spread pizza sauce on each half. Then she added cheese and pepperoni. Mmm! It smelled good! She set the table and waited for Mom.

When Mom arrived home, Sierra told her that supper was nearly ready. Mom was surprised, and she sat down to wait.

When the oven timer rang, Sierra said, "Dinner's ready."

There wasn't much talk at dinner, just a lot of "mmmm, good." Afterward, Mom said, "That was delicious, Sierra. Thank you! You know, God provides food for the body. But He also provides food for the soul. God's Word shows us Jesus' victory over sin. God's Word nourishes our souls and strengthens our faith."

"I get it," replied Sierra. "It's time for our soul food!" The plates were pushed aside. The family Bible and devotion book were opened. God was now feeding their souls as Sierra had fed their bodies.

_____Let's talk: What is your favorite food? How does God's spiritual food, His Word, take care of your most important needs?

_____Let's pray: Thanks, God, for my favorite food, and also for the spiritual food I receive in Your Word. Thanks for giving me faith in Your Son. In His name I pray. Amen.

J. W.

The Paint Job

Read from God's Word

Whatever you do, work heartily, as for the Lord and not for men, knowing that from the Lord you will receive the inheritance as your reward. You are serving the Lord Christ. Colossians 3:23–24 ⌇

Imagine 17 people, ages 79 years to 6 months, all in the same house for two days. Now add paint, rollers, brushes, and drop cloths to your picture. Does it sound wild? It was!

The large Logan family came together to paint Grandma's house. Each painter had an assigned task. Each did his job and allowed the others space to do theirs. By the end of the second day, they had totally transformed 10 rooms!

Why did the Logans do all that work? Because they love Grandma and wanted to show her that they do. It's that simple!

Teamwork—a group working toward the same goal—is necessary. Whether we're on a sports team, working at a job, or doing chores, teamwork makes it easier. We cooperate.

Working together on Jesus' team is important too. He has given us the task of telling others about Him. Jesus gives us guidance and direction through His Word. But our teamwork breaks down when sin interferes. Our petty problems may make us lose sight of our goal. That goal is the salvation of all people. When our group falls apart, repentance and forgiveness through Jesus are the glues that reunite us.

Why do we do it? Jesus' love for us moves us to love and help others. It's that simple!

_____Let's do: Write about a large task you could do with others. Thank God that you have each other's help.

_____Let's pray: Lord Jesus, our team leader, unite us in our purpose for You. Keep Your goals always fresh in our minds, and give us Your guidance. In Your name we pray. Amen.

J. L.

Nails!

Sam was thinking about the devotion they had in Sunday school that morning. His teacher talked about nails.

"Nails," said Mr. Ji, "are used to build all sorts of things—furniture, buildings, and even crosses. But God didn't use nails to make a building. He used nails to build up His people, the church."

Mr. Ji showed them a wooden cross. "Jesus was nailed to a cross at Calvary. He took the punishment for our sins upon Himself. Jesus' death and resurrection is the head building block of the church."

Mr. Ji continued, "God also used nails to build up His church through Martin Luther. In the sixteenth century, Luther nailed his statements, the Ninety-five Theses, to the church door for everyone to see. Luther proclaimed what the Bible says—that Jesus' death, and not our good works, saves us. This event was the beginning of the Reformation, which helped spread the Gospel throughout the world."

Sam came up with an idea. He got a piece of wood, a hammer, and some small nails. He made a cross and hammered the nails into the four arms. Then he wrapped yarn back and forth among the nails to make a beautiful design. He hung it in his room as a reminder that Jesus had saved him.

_____Let's do: Jesus died for you too. What can you make to remind yourself of Jesus? Write down your ideas.

_____Let's pray: Dear God, thank You that Jesus was nailed to the cross for us. Thank You for using nails to build up the church. In Jesus' name we pray. Amen.

J. W.

Speaking Kind Words

As Mom listened to LeRoy and Kyle play, she was saddened by what she heard. She wrote down some of the cutting remarks she heard them say to each other.

After supper she asked them to stay at the table for a little while. She told them that she wanted their home to be a place where each person showed love to the others. Then she read the words she had written down.

The boys looked at each other. "But we didn't mean them," they said.

Mom said, "Some people talk to one another this way all the time. Saying mean things to others is wrong—it's a sin. We don't want to sin. But because of our sinful nature, we still do it, although we know it displeases God."

"We're sorry," said LeRoy and Kyle, their faces downcast.

Mom held the boys' hands. She reminded them of the forgiveness God gives them. Mom led them in prayer. "Dear God, we know it saddens You when we sin. Please forgive us. Thank You for loving us enough to send Your Son, Jesus, to die on the cross for our sins. Guide us with Your Holy Spirit so we speak kind words to one another. In Jesus' name we pray. Amen."

Read from God's Word

If we put bits into the mouths of horses so that they obey us, we guide their whole bodies as well. Look at the ships also: though they are so large and are driven by strong winds, they are guided by a very small rudder wherever the will of the pilot directs. So also the tongue is a small member, yet it ... is a restless evil, full of deadly poison. With it we bless our Lord and Father, and with it we curse people who are made in the likeness of God. From the same mouth come blessing and cursing. My brothers, these things ought not to be so. James 3:3–10

———Let's do: Read James 3:3–10 in your Bible. Make a list of kind words you can say to others. Make another list of kind words God says to us in the Bible.

———Let's pray: Pray the prayer that LeRoy, Kyle, and their mom prayed.

J. W.

Better Than a Role Model

Therefore, if anyone is in Christ, he is a new creation. The old has passed away; behold, the new has come. All this is from God, who through Christ reconciled us to Himself and gave us the ministry of reconciliation; that is, in Christ God was reconciling the world to Himself, not counting their trespasses against them, and entrusting to us the message of reconciliation. Therefore, we are ambassadors for Christ, God making His appeal through us. We implore you on behalf of Christ, be reconciled to God. For our sake He made Him to be sin who knew no sin, so that in Him we might become the righteousness of God. 2 Corinthians 5:17–21

Keil laid out his unique trading cards. He proudly looked over his pictured collection of basketball players on his brother's high school team. Keil was the only one in his class who had all the cards.

Keil's family thought the trading card program was a good one. Students in high school who qualified for the program had to take part in school activities, maintain a B or higher grade average, and promise to be drug-, tobacco-, and alcohol-free. The program gave young students role models. It also gave the older students a sense of responsibility and commitment.

Christians have something even better than a role model. Jesus, God's Son, came to earth on our behalf and lived a perfect life. He kept the Law perfectly for us—because in our sinfulness we never could. But Jesus did not do it to be a role model. He did it to be our Savior. He paid the penalty for our sins on the cross and won for us forgiveness and eternal life. He lives in our hearts, helping us through His Spirit to live according to God's will.

This world needs good role models. More important, this world needs the forgiveness of sin and eternal life that God graciously gives through Jesus.

_____Let's talk: Explain this statement: Jesus is better than a role model.

_____Let's pray: Dear Jesus, thank You for living and dying for us. Now live in us so we can live for You. In Your name we pray. Amen.

J. W.

A History Surprise

I 've got everything memorized for tomorrow's history test," Allison said proudly. "I know everything important about America in the 1830s. Jackson and Van Buren were presidents, Morse code was invented, and the Underground Railroad was developed."

"Is that so?" said Grandpa with a grin. "Then tell me about the Saxons and Franconians."

"The who?" asked Allison. "My textbook doesn't say anything about them!"

"So, Allison, everything important for you to learn is not in your history book after all. Not many history books include much about Jesus Christ and the spreading of God's Word."

"I certainly want you to do well on your history test, Allison. But the Bible is a book of accurate history and true religion. In it God tells us all that Jesus died to save us from our sins and how important it is to keep learning about Him.

"I see your point, Grandpa," said Allison. "Sometime will you tell me more about those Saxons and ... what did you call them?"

"The Saxons and Franconians were German Lutheran immigrants to North America who brought the Christian faith to many people. I'd be happy to tell you about them," Grandpa said. And so Grandpa's history lessons began.

Read from God's Word

Remember the former things of old; for I am God, and there is no other; I am God, and there is none like Me, declaring the end from the beginning and from ancient times things not yet done, saying, 'My counsel shall stand, and I will accomplish all My purpose,' calling a bird of prey from the east, the man of My counsel from a far country. I have spoken, and I will bring it to pass; I have purposed, and I will do it. Isaiah 46:9–11

———Let's talk: What book *does* contain "everything important"? What is the most important thing in the Bible?

———Let's pray: Dear God, thank You for those who brought Your Word to others. Help me to share Your Word too. I pray in Jesus' name. Amen.

K. M.

Read from God's Word

Only be strong and very courageous, being careful to do according to all the Law that Moses My servant commanded you. Do not turn from it to the right hand or to the left, that you may have good success wherever you go. This book of the Law shall not depart from your mouth, but you shall meditate on it day and night, so that you may be careful to do according to all that is written in it. For then you will make your way prosperous, and then you will have good success. Have I not commanded you? Be strong and courageous. Do not be frightened, and do not be dismayed, for the LORD your God is with you wherever you go. Joshua 1:7–9 ✍

An Ocean Crossing

This was the first of Grandpa's history lessons: Justina stood on the wooden deck. The year was 1838. She was 14 years old, and now she was aboard the ship *Copernicus* on her way to the New World. Staring at the horizon, Justina could no longer see land.

"Hello, Justina," said her new friend Wilhelm, "Aren't you excited? In eight weeks our families will be in America!"

"But we're leaving Germany, Wilhelm. We're leaving so much behind!" Justina sighed. She didn't expect a *boy* to understand.

"Yes, but we're headed for a new life, like Moses and Joshua headed for the Promised Land!"

"I suppose," agreed Justina, snuggling into her quilt. "Papa says we Lutherans will have great freedom in America. We will be able to preach and teach the truth of the Gospel. But I already miss home."

Wilhelm comforted Justina by saying, "Don't be afraid. God loves us. After all Jesus did to pay for our sins and bring us new life, He won't desert us now."

Like Justina and Wilhelm, we need a guide. The Bible says, "That this is God, our God forever and ever. He will guide us forever" (Psalm 48:14). God promises to guide us to a new land—the promised land of heaven.

_____Let's talk: If you could travel anywhere in the world, where would you go? How do you know God is with you?

_____Let's pray: Lord, thank You for being with me and loving me in all circumstances. In Jesus' name I pray. Amen.

K. M.

1842

Wilhelm stared from his bedroom window at the oak sapling. He'd planted an acorn he had brought from Germany.

It will grow well here, Wilhelm thought. Through the churches and schools we build, God's Word will grow here too. With that conviction, Wilhelm returned to his Bible to read a chapter.

Meanwhile, in her own home not far away, Justina lay in bed under Mama's patchwork quilt. Wilhelm had been right. Life in America wasn't so bad! Their new house was fast becoming home. Best of all, the government didn't control their churches. The preaching and teaching were faithful to God's Word.

In one corner of Mama's quilt, through a tiny hole between the stitches, Justina had hidden a paper from Wilhelm on which he had written a Bible verse. "[God says,] 'My word ... shall not return to Me empty, but it shall accomplish that which I purpose, and shall succeed in the thing for which I sent it'" (Isaiah 55:11).

Remembering this verse made Justina feel safe and secure. God had kept the promises of His Word in many ways, especially in sending His Son, Jesus, to rescue them from sin.

———Let's talk: In America, we can study God's Word freely. When do you take the time to study His gracious Word?

———Let's pray: Heavenly Father, thank You for Your Word and my opportunities to study it freely. I pray this in the name of Your Son, my Savior, Jesus Christ. Amen.

K. M.

And Peter said to them, "Repent and be baptized every one of you in the name of Jesus Christ for the forgiveness of your sins, and you will receive the gift of the Holy Spirit. For the promise is for you and for your children and for all who are far off, everyone whom the Lord our God calls to Himself." ... So those who received his word were baptized, and there were added that day about three thousand souls. And they devoted themselves to the apostles' teaching and fellowship, to the breaking of bread and the prayers. And awe came upon every soul, and many wonders and signs were being done through the apostles. And all who believed were together and had all things in common. ... And the Lord added to their number day by day those who were being saved. Acts 2:38–47 ✍

On the Michigan Frontier

I know it's Christmas Day, but I don't feel well," said Julia as she sat on the edge of her bed, her long skirts rustling.

"Oh, dear," said Adolf. He fidgeted with his bow tie and fussed over his wife. "We've been so excited about our new church, Julia. I know you've been looking forward to our first service in it!"

"Yes, I have," Julia said, trying to smile. "Not everyone can celebrate Christmas in a log-cabin church!"

Adolf couldn't understand why his wife smiled if she felt sick.

Julia had a surprise. "I don't feel well because I'm expecting a baby. The baby is your present. Merry Christmas!"

Adolf and Julia hoped that someday they would sit beside their children in the log-cabin church in America. One of the first priorities of these Lutheran immigrants was to build places for worship and study. In each place they settled, they established homes and churches. They took seriously God's admonition: "[Let us] not [neglect] ... to meet together, as is the habit of some, but [encourage] ... one another" (Hebrews 10:25).

In worship, God brought these Christians the Good News of forgiveness and new life in Jesus. Through Word and Sacraments God strengthened their faith in Him and their relationships with one another.

_____Let's talk: What do you like best about worship at your church?

_____Let's pray: Heavenly Father, thank You for my church and for the opportunities I have to worship You. In Jesus' name I pray. Amen.

K. M.

United for a Purpose

"(O)uch!" Adolf tugged on the rope that led to a small stump. As he strained to loosen the stump from the ground, the rope broke and Adolf fell backward. He landed—splat—in the mud.

"Hello, Adolf!" called Frederick, who approached on horseback. "Let me help." Together they pulled the stump from the ground with ease.

"Thanks, Frederick. Working together made that a lot easier," said Adolf. "Which reminds me—have you heard any news about the convention in Chicago?"

"Not yet," said Frederick. "I'm praying for a successful meeting. As we've just seen, there is strength in numbers."

In 1847 Franconian leaders from Michigan, Saxon leaders from Missouri, and Lutherans from other nearby states joined in a meeting in Chicago. At this convention, The German Evangelical Lutheran Synod of Missouri, Ohio, and Other States was officially organized. This synod trained and shared pastors and teachers who were taught the truth of God's Word—that Jesus died and rose again for the sins of all. Those saved by the Gospel spread it to people in the vast frontiers of North America and beyond. Religious freedom in the New World was a reality.

Read from God's Word

Grace was given to each one of us according to the measure of Christ's gift. ... And He gave the apostles, the prophets, the evangelists, the pastors and teachers, to equip the saints for the work of ministry, for building up the body of Christ, until we all attain to the unity of the faith and of the knowledge of the Son of God, to mature manhood, to the measure of the stature of the fullness of Christ, so that we may no longer be children, tossed to and fro by the waves and carried about by every wind of doctrine, by human cunning, by craftiness in deceitful schemes. Rather, speaking the truth in love, we are to grow up in every way into Him who is the head, into Christ, from whom the whole body, joined and held together by every joint with which it is equipped, when each part is working properly, makes the body grow so that it builds itself up in love. Ephesians 4:7, 11–16

_____Let's talk: Which of the gifts from God mentioned in Ephesians 4 does a national church organization help give us?

_____Let's pray: Heavenly Father, thank You for the blessing of other believers around me and around the world. Help me to encourage and support my fellow worshipers. In Jesus' name. Amen.

K. M.

The Nebraska Territory

Read from God's Word

And let the peace of Christ rule in your hearts, to which indeed you were called in one body. And be thankful. Let the word of Christ dwell in you richly, teaching and admonishing one another in all wisdom, singing psalms and hymns and spiritual songs, with thankfulness in your hearts to God. Colossians 3:15–16 ✍

Emil stepped onto the depot platform and turned to help his little sister, Mary. Two younger brothers and his mother, Justina, followed.

"Your father is over there, Emil," Mother said over the sound of hissing steam. "Here, please take this satchel to him."

Emil's father, Wilhelm, was a pastor. Wilhelm and Justina had been married for many years. They had lived in Missouri, but now they were heading west to serve a Nebraska community in need of a pastor.

That evening Emil, Mary, and their twin brothers found themselves in the back of a wagon, heading for a new home. Emil tucked his mother's favorite patchwork quilt around the sleepy twins. Just then he heard Mary humming the hymn "I Am Jesus' Little Lamb."

Emil rode along, humming to himself. This land was strange and a little scary. But his father was a pastor who served Jesus, the Good Shepherd. His father cared for God's flock of believers. Emil was proud of him. Emil knew Jesus was his shepherd. Jesus had paid for the sins of Emil, his family, and all people, and He promised to be with them always.

Knowing that Jesus was near, Emil felt safe. He sang along with Mary. Soon they were all fast asleep.

_____Let's talk: What is your favorite Christian song or hymn? What does it tell you about Jesus?

_____Let's pray: Lord God, thank You for giving songs to Your church and for putting them in my heart to remind me of Your great love through Jesus. In His name. Amen.

K. M.

The Prairie

Wilhelm drew his long coat more tightly about himself as his horse followed the wagon ruts into the wind.

Wilhelm thought about his family and home. Emil was growing up so quickly. Justina eagerly watched progress on the wooden parsonage that the men of their small congregation were building for them. Every time the wind blew against the sod house in which they now lived, dust from the ceiling rained down on them.

Wilhelm regularly left home to ride a circuit of preaching stations. The people in those congregations needed to receive God's grace in Word and Sacrament. They needed to receive Jesus' forgiveness and strength.

Wilhelm was generally content. Although he was challenged by work, weather, and few conveniences, his family was healthy. The people he served were very generous, and he was able to bring them God's Word. He didn't even mind the long horse rides. Come winter, though, he wondered how he would deal with the snow.

He patted his horse's neck and sang into the wind, "O Lord, I sing with lips and heart, joy of my soul, to Thee...."

Read from God's Word

Not that I am speaking of being in need, for I have learned in whatever situation I am to be content. I know how to be brought low, and I know how to abound. In any and every circumstance, I have learned the secret of facing plenty and hunger, abundance and need. I can do all things through Him who strengthens me. Philippians 4:11–13

_____Let's talk: Despite many struggles, why was Wilhelm content? What blessings can you count on, even when you don't get everything you want?

_____Let's pray: Heavenly Father, thank You for filling my heart with joy because of Your love in Jesus. Help me be content with what I have. I pray this in Jesus' name. Amen.

K. M.

Read from God's Word

"You are the light of the world. A city set on a hill cannot be hidden. Nor do people light a lamp and put it under a basket, but on a stand, and it gives light to all in the house. In the same way, let your light shine before others, so that they may see your good works and give glory to your Father who is in heaven." Matthew 5:14–16

A Teacher from Michigan

The year was 1865. Adolf and Julia now had a growing family. Their oldest son, Hans, was one of the first students at the Lutheran teachers college in Illinois.

"Do you have to go, Hans?" Lina playfully yanked her older brother's jacket.

"Yes, I have to go!" said Hans, laughing. He hugged Lina and then tickled her. "When I'm a real teacher, you can come for a visit!"

Adolf and Julia watched. They were proud of Hans. He would be a Lutheran schoolteacher. The college was so far away! Yet they knew God would watch over her children.

The family couldn't know it yet, but by the time Hans would graduate, a new church and school building would be waiting for him on the Nebraska prairie. Church schools were common in the growing Lutheran church body. They provided opportunities for the entire curriculum to be taught in light of the Gospel.

Through the years, God has called thousands of young men and women into a teaching ministry to support this system of Lutheran schools. They teach "in words ... taught by the Spirit" (1 Corinthians 2:13), letting their light shine and nurturing the faith of thousands of students each year. It is an exciting future to consider. Perhaps God has such an adventure in store for you!

_____Let's talk: What are some ways you can let the light of Jesus shine in your life—now and in the future?

_____Let's pray: Heavenly Father, thank You for the opportunities to let my light shine. Thank You for being with me! I ask this for Jesus' sake. Amen.

K. M.

Lina and Emil

"Lina, meet Emil, a student of mine!" Lina had come all the way from Michigan to visit Hans in Nebraska.

"I'll show you around," said Emil. Emil showed Lina the remains of the old sod house where they once had lived. He showed her the cottonwood trees his family had planted near the church and school building. Where once there hadn't been a church at all, a cross-crowned steeple stretched to the clouds.

Emil thought of his parents coming from Germany so long ago. He thought of changes since then. America had changed. The church had grown. God's Word had spread.

The church reminded Lina of her home and the beautiful brick church there. Lina thought of her parents. She thought of how their heavenly Father made it possible for them to work hard and change lives around them, even when they were tired or lonely.

Read from God's Word

But the steadfast love of the LORD is from everlasting to everlasting on those who fear Him, and His righteousness to children's children, to those who keep His covenant and remember to do His commandments. Psalm 103:17–18 ✍

Life had changed greatly for these young Christians, and it would change even more in the years to come. But some things do not change. The reality of sin doesn't change. There will always be a need for Jesus' mercy and forgiveness. And God's love won't change. He promises in His Word and Sacraments to continue His love for His people. His protecting presence is always there for us.

——Let's talk: How has life changed since the time of the story? What are some big changes you've seen in your life?

——Let's pray: Thank You, Lord, for being the eternal source of strength in my life. Be with me through the changing conditions of life. In Jesus' name I pray. Amen.

K. M.

The Patchwork Quilt

Allison pushed hair from her face and stretched. "Thanks for telling me these stories about the Saxons and Franconians, Grandpa. It's amazing how God can use a small group of people to make a difference in the world!"

"Amazing," agreed Grandpa, "but they're not just stories. They are real examples of the Holy Spirit working through God's Word." He walked to a linen closet and returned with a big plastic bag.

Allison pulled out a brown patchwork quilt. "Grandpa, where did it come from?"

"It's something your great-great-great-great-grandmother once had," said Grandpa, smiling. "This quilt came from Germany all those years ago."

"Hey, wait! You mean I'm related to those early Lutherans?

"That's right," said Grandpa. "This quilt has been passed down in our family from generation to generation, just as God's Word has been taught by parents to their children throughout the church's history. The Good News of salvation through Christ saved our ancestors, and God's grace in Christ saves us now."

"So just like this church history really is *my* history, the Good News is *my* good news?"

"Yes. But it's also important to everyone else. All Christians are part of the family of God. From St. Paul to Martin Luther to the early Lutherans to us—we're all part of the 'patchwork quilt' of God's people—saved by His Word and grace."

_____Let's talk: Who taught the Good News to you? With whom can you share it?

_____Let's pray: Dear Jesus, thank You for Your love to me. Help me pass on Your love to others. In Your name I pray. Amen.

K. M.

Evangelists

For many Christians, October 18 is the day to recognize the work of St. Luke. God used Luke to write two books of the Bible. One of the books tells us about Jesus' life here on earth. The book has his name—the Gospel of Luke. Since Luke was a doctor, he tells many stories of Jesus making sick people well.

Luke also wrote the Book of Acts to tell about the growth of the Christian church. In Acts, God used evangelists such as Luke and Paul to spread the Good News about Jesus. They believed that Jesus died to save all. The Holy Spirit used them to tell the message of Jesus' death and resurrection on our behalf.

The ending of the Book of Acts is very unusual. It doesn't have a summary or conclusion. Maybe that's because there are still evangelists all over the world who continue to tell the story of Jesus.

Read from God's Word

Inasmuch as many have undertaken to compile a narrative of the things that have been accomplished among us, just as those who from the beginning were eyewitnesses and ministers of the word have delivered them to us, it seemed good to me also, having followed all things closely for some time past, to write an orderly account for you, most excellent Theophilus, that you may have certainty concerning the things you have been taught. Luke 1:1–4

In Baptism God called you to be an evangelist in His Kingdom. Although you are not a pastor or a missionary in a foreign land, the Holy Spirit helps you daily share Christ's love in what you say and do with your friends, neighbors, and relatives. His grace is for all.

_____Let's talk: God uses many people to share the Good News of Jesus. What are some ways that you can be an evangelist?

_____Let's pray: Thank You, God, for sending Your Son, Jesus, to save me from my sins. Thank You for sending people who share the Gospel with me. Help me share the Good News with my family and friends. In Jesus' name. Amen.

J. W.

Generations

Posterity shall serve Him; it shall be told of the Lord to the coming generation; they shall come and proclaim His righteousness to a people yet unborn, that He has done it. Psalm 22:30–31

I watched the Baptisms of my triplet grandsons. Relatives gathered to witness this wonderful step in the babies' 12-day-old lives. Four generations were represented—the boys, their parents, grandparents, aunts and uncles, and one great-grandmother.

Many generations of our family and others had come to this baptismal font. Even the pastor performing the ceremony was baptized at this font many years ago. He was part of the parade of generations. Together, we presented little ones to be forgiven of their sin and filled with faith in Jesus as their Savior.

When is your Baptism birthday? How do you celebrate another year of life in Christ? Read again the words God's Spirit helped you and your sponsors confess in the Rite of Baptism. There, in Baptism, you were given the gift of faith in the one God, who is Father, Son, and Holy Spirit. By the grace God gives you in Word and Sacrament, He will keep you faithful unto death and will enable you to wear the crown of life.

_____Let's talk: What are some ways a sponsor can guide a godchild?

_____Let's pray: Dear Father, Son, and Holy Spirit, keep our faith in You strong. Amen.

J. L.

Twins

G ary and Jacob are brothers—in fact, they are twins. It is amazing to watch them.

Gary is the mover. His arms and legs stop only when he's asleep. Jacob is the thinker. He examines everything carefully. He is also the talker. He loves to hear himself speak.

Watching Gary and Jacob might remind you of another set of twins— Esau and Jacob. They were also different. Jacob grew to be a man who loved to be close to home and family. But he was also good at deceiving people, especially Esau. Esau gave up his birthright as the eldest when he smelled Jacob's stew cooking one day and wanted to eat. Esau also lost the family blessing because of Jacob's trickery. Bad feelings between them lasted for many years, but later God led them to peace.

Jesus is not a twin, but He is our Brother. He became like us when He,

Read from God's Word

When her days to give birth were completed, behold, there were twins in her womb. The first came out red, all his body like a hairy cloak, so they called his name Esau. Afterward his brother came out with his hand holding Esau's heel, so his name was called Jacob. Isaac was sixty years old when she bore them. When the boys grew up, Esau was a skillful hunter, a man of the field, while Jacob was a quiet man, dwelling in tents. Genesis 25:24–27

who was God, became a man. Jesus lived among us, enduring hardships and happy times as all people do. His sinless life made Him the perfect sacrifice for our sin. His sinless life and sacrifice brought us peace with God. As we received this peace in faith, we were brought into the family of God—a blessing that begins at Baptism and lasts forever.

_____Let's talk: Do your siblings believe in Jesus? How can you talk to them about Him and His love?

_____Let's pray: Dear Jesus, thank You for being our perfect Savior and Brother. We can't live eternally without You. Amen.

J. L.

So Much!

Read from God's Word

You shall keep the Feast of Booths seven days, when you have gathered in the produce from your threshing floor and your winepress. You shall rejoice in your feast, you and your son and your daughter, your male servant and your female servant, the Levite, the sojourner, the fatherless, and the widow who are within your towns. For seven days you shall keep the feast to the LORD your God at the place that the LORD will choose, because the LORD your God will bless you in all your produce and in all the work of your hands, so that you will be altogether joyful.
Deuteronomy 16:13–15 ✐

The garden soil is frosted. The harvest is complete. Corn has been frozen. Cucumbers are now pickles. Zucchini has been baked into bread. Tomatoes are spaghetti sauce, chili sauce, and juice. Strawberries, blueberries, and cherries are packed away.

Celebrate these and all the blessings that God rains down. He showers us with more than we deserve—including our Savior, Jesus.

Give God thanks for all these gifts and so much more!

"Now thank we all our God
With hearts and hands and voices,"
Who wondrous things has done,
In whom his world rejoices;
Who from our mothers arms
Has blest us on our way
Wit countless gifts of love
And still ours today." (LW 443:1)

_____Let's do: Make your own raining-down list of blessings.

_____Let's pray: Dear Provider of all, thanks for everything—especially Your love in sending Jesus. Amen.

J. L.

Falling and Rising

F alling leaves. Falling football players. Falling acorns. Falling temperatures.

The word *falling* can bring many pictures to mind. A baby who is learning to walk might fall. An older child may fall trying to ride a bike. A soccer player might fall, angling in his body for a great steal. Friends might suddenly tip then fall while skateboarding. Falling can be painful. Falling can be bad.

The fall into sin was painful and bad. God's earth was a wonderful place before Adam and Eve did what the devil tempted them to do. Once the forbidden fruit was eaten, sin brought fear and punishment.

God did not leave Adam and Eve without hope. He gave them a marvelous promise. He would send a Savior, who would die and rise from death to give us the gifts of His grace—forgiveness and eternal life.

Read from God's Word

But now the righteousness of God has been manifested apart from the law, although the Law and the Prophets bear witness to it—the righteousness of God through faith in Jesus Christ for all who believe. For there is no distinction: for all have sinned and fall short of the glory of God, and are justified by His grace as a gift, through the redemption that is in Christ Jesus. Romans 3:21–24 ∽

God's Old Testament people saw the coming Messiah with eyes of faith. And we also see Christ the Messiah with eyes of faith. Through the Word of God, we are witnesses to His life, death, and resurrection.

God's Word of Law shows us our sin. God's Spirit uses it to drive us to fall on our knees in repentance. God's Gospel raises us up to celebrate.

_____Let's talk: Reread today's text. How is the "righteousness of God" given to us?

_____Let's pray: Dear Jesus, when I am tempted to fall into sin, pull me back into Your safe, loving arms. Amen.

J. L.

Read from God's Word

Live as people who are free, not using your freedom as a cover-up for evil, but living as servants of God. Honor everyone. Love the brotherhood. Fear God. Honor the emperor. 1 Peter 2:16–17 ᔐ

Checkups

O ctober is checkup time at school. The first quarter ends. Grades are averaged. Report cards go out. Parents meet with teachers.

From the first day of school students in Mrs. Luis's class hear her talk about *P* and *R* as valuable habits. P stands for prepared, and R stands for responsible. Being prepared means that homework is done and handed in. Being responsible means students are working cooperatively in a group, showing respect for others and themselves.

God's laws provide another way to check up on classroom attitudes and actions. Teachers and students in Christian schools learn God's laws in religion class, Sunday school, the Divine Service, and family devotions. They learn that if we want to get to heaven by doing things right, then we have to keep God's laws perfectly. But no matter how hard the teachers and students try, each one is failing. That's why teachers and students rejoice as they learn the Gospel—the news that Jesus kept all those laws and then died for the sins of all. Jesus was a perfect student.

Jesus' grace, received in faith, makes us perfect students in God's eyes. God now gives us the special freedom to live as His prepared and responsible servants, loving one another.

_____Let's do: Write about ways to be a servant of God.

_____Let's pray: Dear Jesus, thank You for making my spiritual checkup perfect by taking away my sins. Send Your Spirit to help me live as Your free servant. Amen.

J. L.

Names

"M r. October comes through again!" Mr. October was the nickname of Reggie Jackson, a talented baseball player for the Oakland A's and the New York Yankees. He earned his nickname by hitting key home runs in play-off and World Series games.

Reggie Jackson did something to get his nickname. Others get a nickname—such as Red or Freckles—from the way they look. Some people's given names are shortened to nicknames. Susan becomes Sue; Benjamin becomes Ben. Spelling changes can create another kind of nickname—John to Jack or Dorothy to Dottie.

Jesus had many names, but they aren't nicknames. Many of these names come from His characteristics—Prince of Peace or Mighty God. Some of them tell who He is—King of kings and Son of God. Others come from what He did—Lamb of God, Rabbi (teacher), and, of course, Savior.

How can the Mighty God also be named the Lamb? Because Jesus is God. This multinamed Jesus, the Mighty God, is also the Lamb who took away the sin of the world. That makes Jesus the key player for sinners. He is our Savior for October and for all time. He is the sacrifice who brings us through this life and into eternity.

Read from God's Word

Let each of you look not only to his own interests, but also to the interests of others. Have this mind among yourselves, which is yours in Christ Jesus, who, though He was in the form of God, did not count equality with God a thing to be grasped, but made Himself nothing, taking the form of a servant, being born in the likeness of men. And being found in human form, He humbled himself by becoming obedient to the point of death, even death on a cross. Therefore God has highly exalted Him and bestowed on Him the name that is above every name, so that at the name of Jesus every knee should bow, in heaven and on earth and under the earth, and every tongue confess that Jesus Christ is Lord, to the glory of God the Father. Philippians 2:4–11 ✍

_____Let's talk: List other names for Jesus. What can you learn about Him through these names?

_____Let's pray: Thank You, Lord Jesus, for all You've done for me. Keep Your name on my lips, so others can hear of Your love. In Your holy name. Amen.

J. L.

Poppa's Stuff

Read from God's Word

So we do not lose heart. Though our outer nature is wasting away, our inner nature is being renewed day by day. For this slight momentary affliction is preparing for us an eternal weight of glory beyond all comparison, as we look not to the things that are seen but to the things that are unseen. For the things that are seen are transient, but the things that are unseen are eternal. 2 Corinthians 4:16–18 ✐

Poppa's tiny house was full of stuff. Every year he got more things because his friends and family kept giving him gifts.

Poppa announced his plan to solve his problem—a garage sale. He cleaned out rooms, closets, halls, boxes, and cupboards. He attached price tags to everything. He prepared the garage with a box full of change and some chairs for tired customers. He even had a cooler full of water in case someone was thirsty.

What do you think happened on the day of the sale? It wasn't what Poppa expected. Only five people showed up. And only three people bought anything. But Poppa didn't mind. He was so glad he had sorted through his things and found what was really valuable.

Later that week, Keiko helped him take all the unsold items to the thrift store. "I hope someone can use them," he said with a smile.

"Aren't you sad to lose all those things?" Keiko asked.

But Poppa said, "No, it's not important stuff."

Poppa knows a lot about stuff—important and not so important. Poppa told her the important stuff is God-given and lasts forever. Poppa knows that Jesus loves him and died on the cross for his sins. Someday Poppa will be in heaven with Jesus. "That's the important stuff," says Poppa. "That's forever."

_____Let's talk: What do you think it means to fix your eyes on things unseen? What are some of those eternal things?

_____Let's pray: Thank You, Jesus, for being with us in all we do. Help us to fix our eyes on You. Amen.

K. B.

Eli

Eli was just Eli. He repeatedly ran off with the football and ignored his teammates. He laughed in a basketball game when someone missed an easy lay-up. He sneered at struggling readers and exasperated anyone who had to be his science partner. And Kayla and her brother, Kyle, had Eli on their bus—all the way to school and back.

They didn't know why Eli acted that way. My mom tried to help Kayla and Kyle be patient with him. She told them, "God made Eli, and God made you. He sent Jesus for Eli. He sent Jesus for you. God will help you to be Eli's strong friends."

Then one day while walking by Eli's house, they heard a terrible noise. Someone was screaming and yelling at Eli.

Sin accuses us before God. But instead of yelling and screaming at us for our sins, God acted on our behalf. He gave us His Son, Jesus, who freed us from the hopelessness and condemnation of sin through His death on the cross and His Easter resurrection. He made us friends with God again, and He gives us strength and hope through His Word and Sacraments. He also gives us one another—friends with whom we can share God's love and so glorify God.

Read from God's Word

We who are strong have an obligation to bear with the failings of the weak, and not to please ourselves. Let each of us please his neighbor for his good, to build him up. For Christ did not please Himself, but as it is written, "The reproaches of those who reproached You fell on me." For whatever was written in former days was written for our instruction, that through endurance and through the encouragement of the Scriptures we might have hope. May the God of endurance and encouragement grant you to live in such harmony with one another, in accord with Christ Jesus, that together you may with one voice glorify the God and Father of our Lord Jesus Christ. Romans 15:1–6 ✎

_____Let's do: Do you know someone like Eli? Write three ways you could show Jesus' love and kindness to this person.

_____Let's pray: Dear Jesus, thank You for dying on the cross for all people. Help me to show Your love and kindness to all, even when it is hard for me to do so. Thank You for being my Savior. Amen.

K. B.

Notice the Signs

Read from God's Word

Love does no wrong to a neigh-bor; therefore love is the fulfilling of the Law. Romans 13:10

"Why are there so many different kinds of signs along this high-way?" wondered Michael.

"Because drivers need a lot of information to drive carefully and reach their destinations," answered his dad.

"Why don't we look for all the different kinds of road signs?" Dad suggested. "Let's find out how they help us to reach our destinations and to show love to other drivers."

"Show love to other drivers?" Michael giggled at the thought.

Dad explained that the kind of love God wants us to have for one another is a helpful love; it doesn't harm. And a way to show that kind of love to other drivers is to follow road signs. So Michael and his dad noticed the signs—speed limits, merges, no passing zones, and exits.

God's road signs of love are His commandments. They tell us how to love Him and one another. God requires people to keep all His laws, but our sinful nature and sinful acts make that impossible for us. Jesus came to fulfill the Law. In doing so He gave us a new sign—the cross—to remind us of His perfect victory over sin, death, and the devil. And Jesus' resurrection is God's sign that one day we will be with Him in heaven.

_____Let's do: Think of three more signs that God gave His people in the Bible. Write what they mean to you.

_____Let's pray: Dear Jesus, thank You for being God's sign of love, my Savior. Help me to follow You. Amen.

K. B.

Nana's Quilt

Nana made a quilt using photos. When people come to visit Nana, they reminisce about special days gone by as they look at the quilt. They say that all the baby pictures look alike. They laugh at snapshots of shaving-cream battles and muddy go-cart drivers. They smile at Carmi's baby brother wrapped in Christmas garland. And they ask about all the special people they don't recognize, people who lived long ago.

Once Carmi asked Nana if she missed all those special people who had gone to be with Jesus. She does miss them, Nana said, but she told Carmi that each of them was a Christian—a child of God. She had a twinkle in her eye when she said that she knew she would see them again.

Nana's answer showed that her heart and mind were set on things above—on godly things. God gave Nana that new heart in her Baptism. Her faith in Jesus grew as she was strengthened through church, Bible study, and the Lord's Supper. He helped Nana at very sad times when she lost her friends and family. And He will help you to set your minds on things above while you live out each day of homework and practices, of book reports and family chores, of ups and downs.

Read from God's Word

If then you have been raised with Christ, seek the things that are above, where Christ is, seated at the right hand of God. Set your minds on things that are above, not on things that are on earth. For you have died, and your life is hidden with Christ in God. When Christ who is your life appears, then you also will appear with Him in glory. Colossians 3:1–4

_____Let's do: Draw a picture of a quilt to represent your life. Put at least four pictures in it. Put a cross at the center.

_____Let's pray: Dear Jesus, thank You for dying on the cross to save all people. Give me a mind that is set on things above through all the days of my life. Amen.

K. B.

Read from God's Word

"I, I am the LORD, and besides Me there is no savior. I declared and saved and proclaimed, when there was no strange god among you; and you are My witnesses," declares the LORD, *"and I am God." Isaiah 43:11–12* ✍

Corn Quiz and More

Corn on the cob tastes great, but hidden in those kernels are interesting possibilities and uses. Can you guess?

1. For breakfast you might eat corn in the form of _____.

2. If you eat pancakes or waffles, your topping may contain _____.

3. If you need to fry something, you might put _____ in the pan.

4. Women sometimes put _____ on their lips.

5. If our car runs low on gas, you might find this at the gas station.

   _____

6. If your doctor says you are low on energy and need a boost, your _____ might contain corn.

7. If you get an infection, and you need a prescription filled, your _____ might contain corn.

8. If you wanted to change the color of your wall, you might find corn in

   _____.

ANSWERS:

6. Vitamins 7. Antibiotics 8. Paint

1. Cereal 2. Corn syrup 3. Corn oil 4. Lipstick 5. Gasohol

God created corn. From His loving hand, He has given us so many gifts with hidden and interesting truths. Although God's divine nature was hidden in His earthly body, His saving work was revealed by His death and resurrection. And Scripture reveals these truths to save us from our sin.

_____Let's talk: What qualities about Jesus have been revealed through His Word to you?

_____Let's pray: Dear heavenly Father, work through Your world and Word to reveal Your great love to me. Thank You for Jesus, Your Son, our Savior. In His name I pray. Amen.

K. B.

Family Matters

Read from God's Word

The saying is trustworthy and deserving of full acceptance. For to this end we toil and strive, because we have our hope set on the living God, who is the Savior of all people, especially of those who believe. 1 Timothy 4:9–10

Nick's dad was 59—much older than his classmates' dads. He helped Nick build an award-winning pinewood derby car. He jogged two miles every morning. And Nick's mom and dad taught his Sunday School class.

Rukiya's mom was a single parent who worked evenings. Rukiya called her mom on the phone to say good night every night except Thursday. That was the day they always went out to eat. And Sundays were special too. Rukiya and her mom went to early church and then helped in the nursery during the late service.

José was part of a stepfamily. His mom remarried after she divorced his dad. Now José had three stepsisters. He wasn't used to having that many girls around, but he did like to play computer games with them. They also liked to sing, so all four of them sang in the church choir.

God puts His children in many kinds of families. But we have one thing in common—Jesus. He is the Savior of all. He comes to us in Baptism and Holy Communion. He comes to us in the preaching and teaching of His Word. And He comes for all—children, adults, stepfamilies, single-parent families, two-parent families. With the gift of faith we are made members of God's family for all eternity.

_____Let's do: Draw a cross. At the end of each line of the cross, draw a picture of a family that is different from your own.

_____Let's pray: Dear Jesus, thank You for blessing me with a family. Help me to know that You came to be the Savior of all. I pray in Your holy name. Amen.

K. B.

For by grace you have been saved through faith. And this is not your own doing; it is the gift of God, not a result of works, so that no one may boast. Ephesians 2:8–9

It's Free!

During the 1300s and 1400s, serious abuses occurred in the church in Europe. To obtain money to run the church, many leaders used methods that went against Bible teachings. One of those methods was the sale of indulgences. Indulgences were papers saying that heaven was earned by giving money to charity.

On October 31, 1517, Martin Luther posted his Ninety-five Theses on the door of the Castle Church in Wittenberg, Germany. These theses were a series of statements that attacked the sale of indulgences. Luther believed that people are saved only through faith in Jesus Christ. He believed that God's forgiving grace makes us righteous (put right with God).

Luther was eventually excommunicated (kicked out) of the Roman Catholic Church by Pope Leo X. But Luther was not kicked out of God's holy Christian church. He continued to believe that Jesus had saved him from his sins. Until his death in 1546, he continued to proclaim Jesus as the only way to salvation.

We are blessed to know that God saves us through Jesus. Because of Jesus' death and resurrection, God has given us the most precious gift. And it is free. We can't earn it. We can't work for it. We can't buy it. Salvation is God's free gift in Jesus Christ, our Lord.

_____Let's do: Write a short letter to God, saying thanks for His free gift of Jesus. Tell Him what it means to you to know that you will be in heaven with Him.

_____Let's pray: Dear Jesus, there is nothing in this world I can do to gain heaven on my own. Thank You for being the free gift that saves me. Amen.

K. B.

november

Contributors for this month:

Jan Brunette

Elizabeth Friedrich

Pat List

Ruth Maschke

Dawn Napier

Read from God's Word

What shall I render to the LORD for all His benefits to me? I will lift up the cup of salvation and call on the name of the LORD. I will pay my vows to the LORD in the presence of all His people. Precious in the sight of the LORD is the death of His saints. Psalm 116:12–15 ✍

Is Death Spooky?

Letitia and her friends were in the lunchroom, looking serious.

"Bernie's been absent a long time," said one. "Do you think he's going to die and all that spooky stuff?"

"Are you superstitious or something?" another person asked. "Why worry? When you're gone, you're gone."

Letitia interrupted. "Death's not spooky; it's not like we become Halloween ghosts, you know."

"Ohhhh, let's talk about something else," said her friend.

Letitia was troubled. "Mom," she asked that night, "is Bernie going to die? The kids sounded real spooked today. They seem to be superstitious about death. They didn't want to talk about it."

"Letitia, let's pray for Bernie's recovery." And they did. Then Mom asked, "Remember Grandma's funeral?"

"Yes. I miss her, but I'm glad her pain is over and that she's with Jesus."

"For a Christian, death is a passageway to the next life. Maybe your friends are fearful because ..."

" ... because they don't know that Jesus died for them," Letitia continued. "God wants all people to be with Him forever."

"Exactly. In the church, this day is set aside to remember the faithful departed, like Grandma. God's precious children are remembered as being saved by Jesus' precious blood and living forever with Him in heaven."

_____Let's do: Write about some of the super-precious pictures of everlasting life—a flower bulb or an egg.

_____Let's pray: Dear Jesus, thank You that we are precious to You. Keep us faithful to You until we are with You in heaven. Amen.

R. M.

God's Ladder

Read from God's Word

Behold, I long for Your precepts; in Your righteousness give me life! Let Your steadfast love come to me, O LORD, Your salvation according to Your promise; then shall I have an answer for him who taunts me, for I trust in Your word. Psalm 119:40–42

Tom and Jay like to play Chutes and Ladders. When Tom's marker landed on a square that shows a good deed, he climbed the ladder toward the goal. But on his next move he landed on a picture of a bad deed and plunged down a chute.

"I'm glad it's only a game," said Tom. "If it wasn't, I'd be a loser. I did so many bad things."

"No, you wouldn't," Jay argued. "God promises to be with you always—on good days and bad."

"How can God keep on loving me?" Tom wondered.

"He promised in the Old Testament to send a Savior, and He kept that promise through Jesus, who died on the cross for our sins. When Jesus ascended into heaven, He promised a helper would come to His people. The Holy Spirit came and is with us now—this very minute. So you see," said Jay, "God's love never stops."

"But what about all the *do's* and *don'ts* in God's commandments?"

"God's laws are like a curb along a road to keep us on the right path, Tom. God's Spirit makes us sad over our sins and brings us His love and forgiveness. His forgiveness moves us to follow Christ's teachings. His perfect righteousness received in faith is our 'ladder of success' and makes us winners."

———Let's talk: How can God's constant love help us in our good days and bad days?

———Let's pray: Dear heavenly Father, remind me of Your unfailing love every day. Give me understanding to know Your Law, Your Good News, and Your will in my life. In Jesus' name. Amen.

R. M.

Opening Doors

Read from God's Word

O LORD God of hosts, hear my prayer; give ear. O God of Jacob! Behold our shield, O God; look on the face of Your anointed! For a day in Your courts is better than a thousand elsewhere. I would rather be a doorkeeper in the house of my God than dwell in the tents of wickedness. For the LORD God is a sun and shield; the LORD bestows favor and honor. No good thing does He withhold from those who walk uprightly. O LORD of hosts, blessed is the one who trusts in You! Psalm 84:8–12

Have you ever considered becoming a doorkeeper? You'd be responsible for opening and closing doors at the proper time.

The psalm writer said, "I would rather be a doorkeeper in the house of my God than dwell in the tents of wickedness." Young Samuel, serving the priest Eli, "opened the doors of the house of the LORD" (1 Samuel 3:15). Friends of Peter opened the door to him after an angel released him from prison.

Sam is the doorkeeper at my church. His "doorkeeping" began early in life at a church in Canada, where his father was pastor. Today Sam teaches children reading, writing, math, religion, and other subjects. These skills will open doors for young minds and hearts. But, most important, Sam leads children to Jesus, who said, "I am the door" (John 10:9).

Teachers in Christian schools, pastors, missionaries, and Bible translators are doorkeepers. When they teach the Law and the Gospel, the Holy Spirit works faith in people who are without hope. And when people know and love their Savior, the door to eternal life is open for them.

Try this. Open a door for someone else, just to be kind. Imagine how it might feel to open doors for others through a career in church work so they may know Jesus as their Savior.

_____Let's talk: What special joys might come from a church-work career?

_____Let's pray: Holy Spirit, open the heart doors of young people so many will find joy working in Your kingdom. In Jesus' name. Amen.

R. M.

God's Recycling Center

Can we recycle people? A woman in Canada, Mrs. Y, did just that. Mrs. Y's daughter, Lorna, was almost helpless in the hospital. She needed everything done for her.

Lorna could not speak, but she could respond to people. So Mrs. Y found over 200 volunteers to visit Lorna and other patients. They were all recycled—used again for a good purpose.

One day a very angry teenage girl became a patient at the same hospital. No one could do anything with her. Mrs. Y introduced her to Lorna.

The tense girl noticed Lorna's soft brown hair. She began to comb it gently. The teenage girl relaxed, and she came back every morning to comb Lorna's hair. Mrs. Y knew that God was using Lorna's helplessness to work a miracle in a troubled youth.

"And *we know* that in *all things* God works for the *good* of those who *love* Him" (Romans 8:28 NIV, emphasis added). Speak the passage seven times, emphasizing each italicized word in turn. Did each repetition have a new meaning? You recycled it!

The cross of Christ is God's recycling center. Here a loving Father offered His Son. Here a loving Savior shed His blood for our sins. Here God's Spirit recycles our fears into forgiveness, our failures into faith.

_____Let's talk: What kinds of things do you recycle in your home? your school? How can you be recycled for service to God?

_____Let's pray: Holy Spirit, recycle me for special service. For Jesus' sake. Amen.

R. M.

Read from God's Word

For I know the plans I have for you, declares the LORD, plans for wholeness and not for evil, to give you a future and a hope. Then you will call upon Me and come and pray to Me, and I will hear you. You will seek Me and find Me. When you seek Me with all your heart. Jeremiah 29:11–13

The New Owner

Read from God's Word

At my first defense no one came to stand by me, but all deserted me. May it not be charged against them! But the Lord stood by me and strengthened me, so that through me the message might be fully proclaimed and all the Gentiles might hear it. So I was rescued from the lion's mouth. The Lord will rescue me from every evil deed and bring me safely into His heavenly kingdom. To Him be the glory forever and ever. Amen. 2 Timothy 4:16–18

While walking through town some time ago, Jason noticed an old, rambling house hidden behind overgrown trees. He saw a For Sale sign on the lawn as he peered through branches. The house had broken windows, crooked shutters, and peeling paint. The yard was filled with trash.

A few months later Jason passed by the same house but it looked very different. New owners had trimmed the trees, watered the grass, and planted flowers. A coat of paint and new shutters brightened the old house and made it look new and beautiful again.

Do you ever feel like that dilapidated house looked? Uncared for? Broken down? Neglected? Lonely? Does it seem like Mom and Dad are too busy to notice you? Do you feel like your friends "dump their trash" on you, then leave? Do school assignments confuse and overwhelm you?

Sometimes the apostle Paul felt deserted by his friends. But he wrote to Timothy: "The Lord stood by me and strengthened me." No matter how dark Paul's life looked, he said, "I can do all things through [Christ] who strengthens me" (Philippians 4:13).

You can too! Jesus is your "new owner." He fills your heart with new strength. He repairs the sin of your life forever through His death and resurrection. Jesus makes you shine again!

_____Let's talk: What parts of your life need repairing? What hope do you have in the Lord?

_____Let's pray: Jesus, fill my life with Your love. Refresh me; restore me; renew me. I know I can do all things through You, my strength and my helper. Amen.

E. F.

Fantastic Feet

Read from God's Word

D o you appreciate your feet? Do you think of them as being "swift and beautiful"? Or do you cover them up, neglect them, or take them for granted?

Feet take a lot of criticism. People call them ugly, smelly, and dirty. But feet are a remarkable part of the body. These comparatively small things support your weight for an entire lifetime. Without your feet you couldn't walk, run, or jump. You couldn't even stand up.

Each of your feet has 26 bones. These bones form three arches that put the spring into your walk. These arches act as shock absorbers to protect your spinal column. Many ligaments and muscles support the arches of your foot. In fact, your feet have as many muscles as your hands.

These fantastic "feats" of God's engineering are able to perform many jobs—jobs that help others to hear

How beautiful upon the mountains are the feet of him who brings good news, who publishes peace, who brings good news of happiness, who publishes salvation, who says to Zion, "Your God reigns." The voice of Your watchmen—they lift up their voice; together they sing for joy; for eye to eye they see the return of the LORD to Zion. Break forth together into singing, you waste places of Jerusalem, for the LORD has comforted His people; He has redeemed Jerusalem. The LORD has bared His holy arm before the eyes of all the nations, and all the ends of the earth shall see the salvation of our God. Isaiah 52:7–10

about His love in sending Jesus to be the Savior of all. Those opportunities come as we deliver some cookies and a smile to someone who is sick. They transport us to the store on an errand for Mom. They support us while we sing in church.

Jesus' feet had nails driven through them to save us from sin. Praise God that Jesus' beautiful, sinless feet guide us back to His righteous path!

_____Let's talk: What beautiful news do the feet bring in today's Bible reading?

_____Let's pray: Take my hands and let them do Works that show my love for You; Take my feet and lead their way, Never let them go astray. (*LW* 404:2)

E. F.

Read from God's Word

You will say in that day: "I will give thanks to You, O LORD, for though You were angry with me, Your anger turned away, that You might comfort me. Behold, God is my salvation; I will trust, and will not be afraid; for the LORD God is my strength and my song, and He has become my salvation." With joy you will draw water from the wells of salvation. And you will say in that day: "Give thanks to the LORD, call upon His name, make known His deeds among the peoples, proclaim that His name is exalted. Sing praises to the LORD, for He has done gloriously; let this be made known in all the earth. Shout, and sing for joy, O inhabitant of Zion, for great in your midst is the Holy One of Israel." Isaiah 12:1–6 ✑

A Bear's Advice

Two travelers strolled through the thick forest and observed the natural beauty all around them.

Suddenly a huge bear rushed out at them. The first ran quickly, grabbed a branch, and hid behind its leaves. The second traveler just fell to the ground and buried his face in the dirt.

The bear quickly spotted the traveler lying on the ground. He circled the man, eyeing him carefully. Finally the bear leaned over and sniffed right next to the man's ear. The bear, assuming the man was dead, turned and ambled off back through the trees.

The first traveler came out smiling from his hiding place. "What did the bear whisper in your ear?" he laughed.

The other traveler replied, "He told me never to trust a friend who runs off when I'm in trouble."

We have a Friend who never runs away. Long ago this Friend had the chance to desert us when crowds of people wanted to kill Him. He didn't run away. He knew we were doomed by our sin. Our eternal lives were at stake. Our Friend loved us so much that He gave His life to save us so we could be His forever. He's the best Friend of all. Do you know His name?

_____Let's do: Read the Bible passage again. Write down all the actions of the writer. What do they show you?

_____Let's pray: Dear Jesus, thank You for giving Your life so I may have life eternal. Thank You for always being my best Friend. I love You, Jesus. Amen.

E. F.

Hiding Places

Read from God's Word

Where shall I go from Your Spirit? Or where shall I flee from Your presence? If I ascend to heaven, You are there! If I make my bed in Sheol, You are there! If I take the wings of the morning and dwell in the uttermost parts of the sea, even there Your hand shall lead me, and Your right hand shall hold me. Psalm 139:7–10

Some people search all around the house for the perfect place to hide their valuables. They want to make sure their expensive possessions are hidden from burglars. They bury money in a dirty clothes hamper or tape credit cards to the backs of dresser drawers. They wrap their jewelry in aluminum foil and place it in the freezer like a package of meat.

Sometimes people try just as hard to hide from God. They avoid going to church, forget about praying, or choose friends who aren't Christian. Some do this because they are ashamed of something they did. Others are too busy for God. These people assume that if they don't look to God, He can't see them.

We might be successful in hiding our valuables from burglars. But we can't hide anything from God. The psalm writer said to Him, "You search out my path and my lying down and are acquainted with all my ways" (Psalm 139:3). God knows our actions, our words, and even our thoughts.

His arms are open to *forgive* and to *give* us His love. God gave us His own Son to set us free from slavery to sin. He gives us blessing after blessing every day. Who would ever try to hide from a God like that?

_____Let's talk: Why do we no longer need to hide from God?
Whom does God see when He looks at our sin?

_____Let's pray: Loving God, I know You are always here to forgive, help, and lead me. Thank You for loving me so much. In Jesus' name. Amen.

E. F.

Read from God's Word

Let all bitterness and wrath and anger and clamor and slander be put away from you, along with all malice. Be kind to one another, tenderhearted, forgiving one another, as God in Christ forgave you. Therefore be imitators of God, as beloved children. And walk in love, as Christ loved us and gave Himself up for us, a fragrant offering and sacrifice to God. Ephesians 4:31–5:2 ✐

An Old Pastime

Scene: A playground at recess
Characters: Abby and Kim
        (10-year-old girls)
Abby: Did you see the grade on Yolanda's math test? I wonder what she got this time.
Kim: She usually gets an A. She probably did this time too.
Abby: You know why she always gets A's, don't you?
Kim: She's just smart, I guess.
Abby: She's not *that* smart. She cheats!
Kim: How do you know?
Abby: It just makes sense. Her brother was in Mr. Casey's class last year. He probably gives her all his old tests.

Sometimes people gossip to make themselves look better. Sometimes they gossip to hurt other people. Sometimes they gossip simply because they don't have anything else to talk about.

In the Bible, James tells us about the harm we can do by misusing our words. He also warns us that it isn't easy to stop gossiping. "No human being can tame the tongue. It is a restless evil, full of deadly poison" (James 3:8).

How can we say helpful things? Look to Jesus. He bought you with His own blood. Through His Spirit, Jesus' love fills you and overflows from you. His love forgives our gossip and moves our tongue to speak His words of truth, forgiveness, and love.

_____Let's talk: According to Philippians 4:8, what can we think about instead of gossiping?

_____Let's pray: Dear Jesus, fill our hearts with Your love. Help us control our tongues. For Your sake. Amen.

E. F.

A Story of Faithfulness

It was 3 P.M. according to the big clock on the wall at the railroad station in Tokyo, Japan. A dog called Hachi sat in the middle of the station. Hachi sat firm and kept his eyes on the open door leading to the tracks.

Finally Hachi saw his master. He jumped up and ran forward. The two friends walked home together.

For years and years Hachi faithfully appeared to meet his master's train. But one day Hachi's master didn't arrive on the train because he had died while at work. Yet Hachi waited and waited at the train station for the next 10 years.

Stories of faithfulness like this are rare. Few of us have a friend like Hachi. Or do we?

Our Bible reading tells us that God will keep His covenant of love to a thousand generations of those who love Him and keep His commands. A thousand generations is about 25,000 years. That's real faithfulness!

Read from God's Word

It was not because you were more in number than any other people that the LORD set His love on you and chose you, for you were the fewest of all peoples, but it is because the LORD loves you and is keeping the oath that He swore to your fathers, that the LORD has brought you out with a mighty hand and redeemed you from the house of slavery, from the hand of Pharaoh king of Egypt. Know therefore that the LORD your God is God, the faithful God who keeps covenant and steadfast love with those who love Him and keep His commandments, to a thousand generations. Deuteronomy 7:7–9

His perfect faithfulness received in faith takes away our faithlessness. His constant love for us will never change, nor will it fail. His faithfulness enables us to be faithful unto death and gives us life everlasting.

———Let's talk: What promises did God keep by giving His only Son for us?

———Let's pray: Dear God, it comforts me to know You will always be by my side. Thanks. Keep me always close to You. In Jesus' name I pray. Amen.

E. F.

Read from God's Word

So Jesus said to the Jews who had believed in Him, "If you abide in My word, you are truly My disciples, and you will know the truth, and the truth will set you free." John 8:31–32 ✍

Knowing the Facts

Write True or False by each statement.

1. _____ The world is flat.

2. _____ The sun orbits the earth.

3. _____ Tomatoes are poisonous.

Did you answer *False* for all the statements? They are all false, but at one time or another, people believed that they were true. What people believed didn't change the facts.

Eventually sailors discovered that the world wasn't flat, but round. Scientists proved that the earth orbits the sun. And tomatoes are now enjoyed as a nutritious food.

It's important to get our facts straight about God's love and plans for us. Satan and our own sin are always ready to confuse the facts. Many people believe that we must somehow earn forgiveness and eternal life. It's simply not true! Many years ago, Martin Luther helped straighten out this fact. Our forgiveness was earned by Jesus, who won eternal life for us when He died on the cross.

The Bible gives us the facts about our sin and about God's saving work. The Bible is God's own holy Word, which He inspired people to write. The Bible's truths never change, even if people believe something different. When we are confused, the facts in the Bible set us straight again. Thank God for His Word!

_____Let's talk: What are some ideas you have heard others say about Jesus that are not true? How do you know they are false?

_____Let's pray: O God, Your holy Word is my treasure. Keep me close to You forever. Amen.

D. N.

A Cage of Love

After Patrick played with his hamster, Squeaky, or cleaned the cage, he carefully latched the little door. That's because Whiskers, the cat, was never far away. Whiskers often sat by the cage, twitching her long silky tail, silently watching the little hamster. Sometimes Whiskers would even bat at the cage with her paws.

Still, Squeaky wasn't afraid of the cat. He tried to get out of the cage every chance he got. The little hamster didn't realize the great danger just outside that door. Squeaky was safe only because Patrick carefully latched the cage door.

The people in today's Bible reading didn't want to be caged by God's plans for them. They wanted a king like all the nations around them. So God agreed to give them a king. King Saul was a good ruler at first, but in the end he turned away from God. The people suffered because of it.

Many years later God sent His Son to be our perfect King. Jesus came to keep the laws we could not keep. He died on the cross in our place, winning forgiveness and new life for us. As Patrick lovingly protected his hamster, God protects us from sin and evil in the world. He will always do what's best for us.

All the elders of Israel gathered together and came to Samuel at Ramah and said to him, "Behold, you are old and your sons do not walk in your ways. Now appoint for us a king to judge us like all the nations." But the thing displeased Samuel when they said, "Give us a king to judge us." And Samuel prayed to the LORD. And the LORD said to Samuel, "Obey the voice of the people in all that they say to you, for they have not rejected you, but they have rejected Me from being king over them." ... But the people refused to obey the voice of Samuel. And they said, "No! But there shall be a king over us, that we also may be like all the nations, and that our king may judge us and go out before us and fight our battles." And when Samuel had heard all the words of the people, he repeated them in the ears of the LORD. And the LORD said to Samuel, "Obey their voice and make them a king." 1 Samuel 8:4–9, 19–22

_____Let's talk: How can God's rules keep you from the danger of sin? How can God's grace keep us from sin too?

_____Let's pray: Dear Jesus, thank You for rescuing me from sin and protecting me from harm. In Your name I pray. Amen.

D. N.

Read from God's Word

He committed no sin, neither was deceit found in His mouth. When He was reviled, He did not revile in return; when He suffered, He did not threaten, but continued entrusting Himself to Him who judges justly. He Himself bore our sins in His body on the tree, that we might die to sin and live to righteousness. By His wounds you have been healed.
1 Peter 2:22–24

Two in One

"Did you spill orange juice on the floor?" Mom asked Antoine. Antoine looked down and nodded his head yes.

"I'm sorry," Antoine mumbled. "My imaginary friend made me do it!" Mom smiled. They laughed at the silly excuse. Then Antoine helped clean the floor.

You may smile too. But Antoine is not alone in making silly excuses. Perhaps you have made or heard similar excuses.

"See what you made me do?" "The devil made me do it." "It was her fault." "I couldn't help myself." People are very good at excusing and explaining away their sins.

Each of us is a sinner. We are sinful from birth and separated from God. Sin will affect us all our lives. Because of sin, each one of us will die someday.

But God loved us so much that He would not let us die in sin. In His great mercy, God sent His only Son to take away our sin by dying on the cross.

Because of what Jesus did, God declares us righteous—forgiven and holy. We are at the same time both a saint (made holy through Jesus) and a sinner (still having a sinful nature). Until we die, the sinner and saint will fight within us, but Jesus has given the saint the final victory.

_____Let's do: Draw the shape of a person. Write the words *sinner* and *saint* inside the shape. Now write about how you became both.

_____Let's pray: Lord Jesus, thank You for Your victory over sin. Help me resist sin in my life. In Your name I pray. Amen.

D. N.

It's Worth It!

Read from God's Word

I planted, Apollos watered, but God gave the growth. So neither he who plants nor he who waters is anything, but only God who gives the growth. He who plants and he who waters are one, and each will receive his wages according to his labor.
1 Corinthians 3:6–8 ✍

A missionary named Eric went to a small village in the jungles of South America. For 30 years he worked among the people there. He prayed many prayers for the villagers.

Still, in all the years Eric worked, not one person ever came to faith in Jesus. No one was ever baptized.

Years later another missionary came to the village. Soon, many people came to faith in Jesus and were baptized. A Bible was translated into the language of the people. Two villagers studied to become pastors.

Was the new worker a better missionary than Eric? Perhaps. But more likely, God was answering Eric's countless prayers.

God alone has the power to change lives. He asks only that we remain faithful to His Word and promises as we do His work.

We should not seek to measure our worth or the effectiveness of our efforts by visible results. God's Word tells us to keep living for the Lord. It tells us to keep telling others of Jesus and His gift of salvation. It tells us to wait patiently. God's Word will have an effect. God is at work saving sinners although we might not see the results. Rejoice! God brings about His results in His own time.

_____Let's talk: Where can you plant the seed of God's Word? How can you "water" a growing faith—yours or someone else's?

_____Let's pray: Dear Father, give me joy and patience in serving You. In Jesus' name I pray. Amen.

D. N.

Read from God's Word

And let us consider how to stir up one another to love and good works, not neglecting to meet together, as is the habit of some, but encouraging one another, and all the more as you see the Day drawing near. Hebrews 10:24–25

Keep Your Faith Warm

The November night held a chill. Robert and Dad stacked logs in the fireplace.

"Why can't I go to the game tomorrow?" Robert asked. "What's important about church anyway?"

When the first flames appeared, Robert fanned them with the bellows. Soon the cozy warmth of a blazing fire filled the den.

"Christians are like these logs," Dad began. "When we are gathered together around God's Word and Sacraments, the Holy Spirit fans our faith. We share the warmth of God's love for us as He feeds us with the gifts of His goodness. We grow stronger as we learn and work together. Most important, we shine God's light into a world dark with sin when we tell others how Jesus came to be our Savior."

One log rolled off the stack. Away from the flame the log's orange glow soon faded, and the log cooled.

"When we are away from God's Word, our faith may cool," continued Dad. "We no longer see our own sin. We no longer see our need for God's forgiveness in Christ. But in church, God surrounds us with other believers who help and encourage us. There, God helps us see and confess our sins and He gives us His gifts of grace and salvation to keep our faith burning brightly."

_____Let's talk: What would you do if you were Robert? Why? Name ways your faith can be fueled in church.

_____Let's pray: Heavenly Father, thanks for warming my faith as I gather with others around Your Word and Sacraments. In Jesus' name. Amen.

D. N.

Power for Possibilities

Read from God's Word

Praise the LORD! For it is good to sing praises to our God; for it is pleasant, and a song of praise is fitting. The LORD builds up Jerusalem; He gathers the outcasts of Israel. He heals the brokenhearted and binds up their wounds. He determines the number of the stars; He gives to all of them their names. Great is our LORD, and abundant in power; His understanding is beyond measure. Psalm 147:1–5

You probably remember the Bible's account of Jesus feeding five thousand people. A crowd had followed Jesus out into the country to hear Him speak of God's love and His kingdom. When it was time to eat, they were far away from any food.

"We have only five loaves of bread and two fish. How can we possibly feed this crowd?" The disciples must have asked. Although they'd seen Jesus do many miracles, perhaps they forgot about His godly power.

Jesus asked for the food they had and then prayed. Amazingly, there was enough for everybody. There were even 12 baskets of leftovers!

It's easy for people to be discouraged in times of trouble. We throw up our hands. "It's too hard. I can't do this. There's no solution," we may say.

Jesus solved our most impossible problem—sin—when He died in our place. Our mighty God raised His Son from the grave. Through Him, our sins are forgiven and we have new and eternal life.

God's love and power haven't changed. He is a God who fed thousands. He is a God who can solve impossible problems. He is a God who can bless His people to do mighty things! He is a God of countless possibilities. What can He do for you?

———Let's talk: Do you have a task that seems impossible? Do you have a problem you just can't solve? Read Psalm 147. How can God provide a rescue?

———Let's pray: Most holy God, continue to send Your Spirit into my life. Help me always trust in Your power and possibilities for my life. In Your Son's name. Amen.

D. N.

Read from God's Word

For by grace you have been saved through faith. And this is not your own doing: it is the gift of God, not a result of works, so that no one may boast. Ephesians 2:8–9

How to Get to Heaven

Years ago a television show featured a comedian named Art Linkletter. He asked children questions and waited for them to give answers that were often very silly.

One day Art asked the children how to get to heaven. The first child said, "Well, you gotta do a lot of good stuff." Many in the audience clapped over what they thought was a good answer.

The second child said, "You have to believe in Jesus." The audience clapped loudly because they knew this child was right.

The third child said, "First you gotta die." Everyone laughed!

Who was right? Certainly not the first one. We don't get to heaven because we do a lot of good things. When we have the love of Jesus in our heart, we will do good things, but that's not what gets us into heaven.

Both the second and third children were right, weren't they? Of course you have to die before you go to heaven! But the most important answer was about believing in Jesus as your Savior. This child knew that was the only way to heaven. He knew that Jesus died on the cross and rose again. Jesus took the punishment for every single one of our sins. Having faith in Jesus, we know we will be with Him when we die!

———Let's do: Interview three people and ask them how to get to heaven. If you find someone who doesn't know the true way, tell him or her.

———Let's pray: Dear Jesus, You made it so easy for us to get to heaven. You did all the work. Help everyone to understand this and believe in You as their Savior. Amen.

P. L.

A Clear Message

For Mitchell's birthday, his mom planned a great party. All afternoon the boys and girls played games and won prizes.

"Now," said Mitchell's mom, "You're going on a treasure hunt!"

Some of the clues were easy. Others were tricky, and the boys and girls cheered when they found the next clue. But for the final clue there was a problem. Some of the words in the clue had become smeared. The message wasn't clear, and the children didn't know what to do. How could they ever reach the treasure?

God's messages to us are always clear. The Ten Commandments are clear. God tells us to put Him first, not to steal, not to use His name in cursing, and other commands. But it is also clear that we sinners could not keep God's Law perfectly.

God is very clear as He tells us how He takes away our sin. He says in John 3:16, "For God so loved the world, that He gave His only Son, that whoever believes in Him should not perish but have eternal life." In that one short verse, He told us why He wanted us saved and how we are saved. God's Word brings us a clear message. It is a message that gives us the greatest treasure—eternal life with God in heaven.

Read from God's Word

"For God so loved the world, that He gave His only Son, that whoever believes in Him should not perish but have eternal life. For God did not send His Son into the world to condemn the world, but in order that the world might be saved through Him." John 3:16–17

_____Let's do: Copy several verses from the Bible that tell how people can be saved.

_____Let's pray: Dear heavenly Father, thank You for being very clear about how people are saved. Thank You for sending Jesus. In His name. Amen.

P. L.

Read from God's Word

Blessed are those whose lawless deeds are forgiven, and whose sins are covered; blessed is the man against whom the LORD will not count his sin. Romans 4:7–8 ✐

Outside or Inside

Sophie and Chloe were trying to earn money for a class trip. They could have a lemonade stand, but the weather was too cold for that. They could do chores for people in the neighborhood. But most people in their neighborhood did their own chores.

"Why don't you have a rummage sale?" Mom suggested. "We could go through the toys in the basement that you don't play with anymore. Your brothers could clean out the garage. I'm sure there are lots of things out there for your sale."

"That would be a good idea," Sophie said, "except who would want to buy our junk?"

"Some things you could sell because you've outgrown them," Mom said. "Other things you just don't use anymore. That doesn't mean they're junk."

Days later the girls had to agree with Mom. The sale was a huge success, and they made enough money for their class trip.

When people look at others, they often judge them based on their clothes, grades, or other things. If they don't measure up, they're considered junk.

But when God looks at us, He doesn't see junk. He sees children whose transgressions are forgiven and whose sins are covered by the blood of Jesus. He sees children who are His treasures.

_____Let's do: Make a list of ways God tells you that you are valuable.

_____Let's pray: Dear Jesus, thank You for making me Your treasure. Amen.

P. L.

Grandpa's Gift

Last Saturday Amanda's grandpa died. He was very old and had been sick for a long time. Even so, it was hard for Amanda to believe that he was gone.

"How will I be able to stand it without Grandpa?" Amanda sobbed. "He always told stories about when he was a little boy. He listened when I was upset, and he always knew what to say to make me feel better. I know Grandpa went to heaven because he was a good man."

"Whoa! Wait a minute, Amanda," said Mom. "I'm sure Grandpa is in heaven too, but not because he was a good man. That's not how people get to heaven."

"Then how do people get to heaven?" Amanda wanted to know.

"Salvation is God's gift," Mom explained. "We don't receive it because of what we do; it comes to us through God's mercy. Grandpa received God's gift of forgiveness and life eternal through Baptism, and He continued to receive God's gift through His Word and Holy Communion. Grandpa believed Jesus was his Savior."

"That does make me feel better, Mom," replied Amanda. "I still miss him, but knowing Grandpa is with Jesus makes it easier."

Read from God's Word

But when the goodness and loving kindness of God our Savior appeared, He saved us, not because of works done by us in righteousness, but according to His own mercy, by the washing of regeneration and renewal of the Holy Spirit, whom He poured out on us richly through Jesus Christ our Savior, so that being justified by His grace we might become heirs according to the hope of eternal life. Titus 3:4–7 ᔓ

_____Let's talk: How can children proclaim the Gospel of God's grace?

_____Let's pray: Dear Jesus, I'm so glad that You died for my sins. Help me to proclaim God's love to others. In Your name I pray. Amen.

P. L.

Read from God's Word

"Therefore you also must be ready, for the Son of Man is coming at an hour you do not expect." Matthew 24:44 ᢒ

The End Is Coming

Jake and his dad were watching cartoons one Saturday morning. One cartoon showed an old man carrying a sign saying, "The end is coming."

"What does that mean?" asked Jake.

"I think that man is telling the people the end of the world is coming and they should prepare for it," replied Dad.

"How would he know when the end of the world is coming?" asked Jake.

"There's no way he could know," Dad replied. "God tells us to be ready all the time because He is the only One who knows. Sometimes people pick a date and say that's when the world is going to end. There even have been stories of people sitting on a high hill looking up into the sky, just waiting. But of course they were wrong."

"What are we supposed to do to be ready?" wondered Jake.

"Our doing something doesn't make us ready," responded Dad. "We are made ready because of what Jesus did. He made all the preparations by living perfectly and dying for our sins. We receive His readiness.

"The world is a big place, and many people haven't heard about Jesus. As God gives you time and opportunities, you can tell people about Jesus' love and forgiveness. Let's see. Where should we start?"

_____Let's do: Make a prayer list of people who may not know about Jesus and His love. Say a prayer for each one, and then mark on top of each name with a cross. Look for opportunities to share God's love and forgiveness with them.

_____Let's pray: Dear Jesus, thank You for making me ready for the time when You will come again. Help me tell people about You. In Your name I pray. Amen.

P. L.

Wanting? Asking?

In Mrs. Krueger's backyard was a huge apple tree with many apples. Every time Chiwana and his friends tried sneaking over to climb the tree and pick some apples, Mrs. Krueger chased them away.

"I don't understand why she's so selfish," complained Jordan. "She's just a crabby old lady," added Jathan.

Just then Chiwana's mother walked by. "Boys, have you ever *asked* Mrs. Krueger if you could have some apples? Let's go see what she says."

The boys were nervous as they walked up to her house. "Mrs. Krueger, the boys were wondering if they could have some apples," said Chiwana's mother.

"Of course," said Mrs. Krueger, "but I get nervous when I see children climbing up my tree. I'm afraid they will fall. You can have all the apples you want, as long as you use a sturdy ladder."

Read from God's Word

"Ask, and it will be given to you; seek, and you will find; knock, and it will be opened to you. For everyone who asks receives, and the one who seeks finds, and to the one who knocks it will be opened." Matthew 7:7–8

The boys were surprised. All they had to do was ask, and she was more than willing to give them what they wanted.

God has sent His Son to save us, taking care of our greatest need for a Savior, but He also cares about all our other needs. God wants us to ask Him for these earthly needs in prayer. He is loving and kind. Because of the work of Christ, the Father's ears are always open to hear and answer our prayers.

_____Let's do: Keep a prayer journal. Make notes of what you pray for and how God responds.

_____Let's pray: Heavenly Father, You have told us to come to You with every need. Thank You for hearing and answering all of our prayers for Jesus' sake. Amen.

P. L.

But No One Saw Me!

Read from God's Word

And just as it is appointed for man to die once, and after that comes judgment, so Christ, having been offered once to bear the sins of many, will appear a second time, not to deal with sin but to save those who are eagerly waiting for Him. Hebrews 9:27–28 ∽

Kenny rode his bike all over the neighborhood. At first Kenny followed all the safety rules. He wore his helmet and stopped at the stop signs. He rode only on the street and the bike paths.

But as Kenny became more and more sure of himself, he started doing things differently. If the street was busy, he rode on the sidewalk. If it was a hot day, Kenny left his helmet at home.

One day Kenny's mom got a phone call. Mrs. Hamling was concerned about Kenny's safety. "I know you want him to wear his helmet, but lately I've seen him without it."

Although the rules were for Kenny's own good, he thought if no one saw him disobeying them, it didn't matter. Kenny was wrong. The rules were for his safety.

God's rules are called the Ten Commandments. God gave them to us out of His love for us. God wants us to follow them, even when we think no one is watching. But He also knows that we can't keep His commandments perfectly. That's why He sent Jesus to do away with sin. Jesus kept God's Law perfectly, and then He died on the cross. There He took the punishment for the sin of all people, even the sins no one saw!

_____Let's do: Look at today's Bible reading again. What will Christ bring when He comes again? Write the answer in capital letters.

_____Let's pray: Jesus, thank You for taking the punishment for all my sins, even the ones no one knows about. You are a wonderful and forgiving God! Amen.

P. L.

Did You Know?

id you know these things? Catsup was originally a medicine.

Other than from cows, people also drink milk from yaks, buffalos, goats, zebras, camels, sheep, horses, and reindeer.

Sir Isaac Newton was put in jail for insisting that the law of gravity was true.

Some people said Abraham Lincoln's Gettysburg address was a failure.

There was such a thing as a talking donkey (Numbers 22:26–33).

A man once ran faster than a horse (1 Kings 18:44–46).

Christ became a curse for us so we might inherit eternal life (Galatians 3:13).

Because of Christ's sacrifice, we are forgiven (Ephesians 1:7–8).

We are loved unconditionally and forever (1 John 4:10).

Read from God's Word

For our sake He made Him to be sin who knew no sin, so that in Him we might become the righteousness of God. 2 Corinthians 5:21 ✑

Some questions are very difficult to answer. Others are so simple we take the answer for granted.

Don't take the answer of Jesus and His love for granted. He is the only answer to this question: "Who has made you right with God?" Jesus is the perfect answer.

_____Let's do: List some "Did you know?" questions from the Bible. Share them with others.

_____Let's pray: Father, there is so much to learn in the Bible. Open my eyes to Your truth as I seek You daily in Your Word. In Jesus' name I pray. Amen.

J. B.

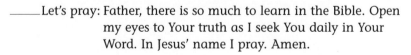

Always Fighting

Boris sat on the side of His bed. His heart ached as he listened to his parents arguing. "Why don't they stop fighting?" he asked himself. "Ever since Dad lost his job last month, all they do is yell at each other."

Boris knew it was not an easy time for his parents. They had trouble paying their bills. Sometimes there wasn't much food on the table.

Families have problems. Anger can explode and be difficult to understand. Children may wonder when and how things can be fixed. Or worse yet, some children feel guilty, thinking they are the cause of the arguments.

We have a Savior who understands those confusing times. He witnessed it in the Garden of Gethsemane, where a friend betrayed Him. He heard the screams and yells of angry people as they refused to believe the truth. He wanted calmness, but found sadness and grief. In the midst of it, Jesus revealed the solution—eternal salvation for us.

Our lives may not always make sense, but we have a Savior who does. God has promised us a Savior to take care of our greatest problem—sin. He died to take away that sin. He strengthens us with His Word and Sacraments and comforts us with His Spirit. He even helps us to trust Him to solve all our problems.

_____Let's talk: Has your family ever experienced difficult times? How did you handle them? How can Jesus help when they happen again?

_____Let's pray: Dear Jesus, be our strength and courage during difficult times. May we never forget to turn to You first. Amen.

J. B.

Smile, Jesus Loves Me

Lightning flashed across the sky and the thunder cracked. Concerned for Jamal's safety, his mother decided to follow his route home from school, hoping to snatch him out of harm's way.

However, as she approached him, she witnessed a strange happening. As the lightning flashed, he stopped, looked up to the heavens, and smiled. With each flash of lightning that followed, Jamal continued to look up and smile. Finally, his mom's curiosity could take it no longer. She pulled up beside him, stopped, and asked, "What are you doing?"

Jamal excitedly responded, "I am trying to look nice because God's taking my picture."

We can look at the picture of Christ's love on the cross with the same kind of happiness and say, "Smile, Jesus loves me." There is no sin He will not forgive and no worry He will not soothe, for as lightning brightens the sky, so His love brightens our lives with guidance and strength. His goodness is generously given, and His power is always available.

The next time you see lightning, just imagine that God is taking your picture, and say, "Smile, Jesus loves me."

_____Let's do: Draw a lightning bolt. Write "Jesus loves me" on the jagged edge.

_____Let's pray: Dear Jesus, thank You for loving me. May I always remember how precious I am in Your sight. I pray in Your name. Amen.

J. B.

Read from God's Word

Whoever confesses that Jesus is the Son of God, God abides in him, and he in God. So we have come to know and to believe the love that God has for us. God is love, and whoever abides in love abides in God, and God abides in him. 1 John 4:15–16

I Wonder

Read from God's Word

Where were you when I laid the foundation of the earth? Tell me, if you have understanding. Who determined its measurements—surely you know! Or who stretched the line upon it? On what were its bases sunk, or who laid its cornerstone, when the morning stars sang together and all the sons of God shouted for joy? Or who shut in the sea with doors when it burst out from the womb, when I made clouds its garment and thick darkness its swaddling band, and prescribed limits for it and set bars and doors, and said, "Thus far shall you come, and no farther, and here shall your proud waves be stayed"? Job 38:4–11

Sometimes I wonder how deep the ocean would be without sponges. Sometimes I wonder why no one is listening until I make a mistake. Sometimes I wonder why my puppy licks my face even after I've left him alone all day. But I wonder most of all why the same God who made the universe also has time for my needs.

God has time to listen to me, even as He maintains the planet's orbits, limits the ocean's waves, or sends lightning bolts on their way. When I cry, He understands my hurt and pain and sends hugs of love through His Word and Sacraments. When I feel unloved, He reminds me of Jesus, who gave His life for me on the cross. When I remember that, I get the biggest hug of comfort, the sweetest feeling of peace, and the greatest assurance of friendship. No one else loves me that much.

Oh, I wonder—how I wonder about Jesus! Why did You go to the mountains to pray? How did You feed all those hungry people? Did it hurt when Judas betrayed You? Why were You willing to die a horrible death?

Oh, yes, I wonder—but this thing I know: His love kept Him on the cross, and His love will guide me safely to Him forever.

_____Let's do: List some things you wonder about. What is the most important question you would like to have answered?

_____Let's pray: Dear Father in heaven, thank You for loving me all the time and for sending Jesus to be my Savior. In His name I pray. Amen.

J. B.

Erasers and Parables

Read from God's Word

He also told this parable to some who trusted in themselves that they were righteous, and treated others with contempt: "Two men went up into the temple to pray, one a Pharisee and the other a tax collector. The Pharisee, standing by himself, prayed thus: 'God, I thank You that I am not like other men, extortioners, unjust, adulterers, or even like this tax collector. I fast twice a week; I give tithes of all that I get.' But the tax collector, standing far off, would not even lift up his eyes to heaven, but beat his breast, saying, 'God, be merciful to me, a sinner!' I tell you, this man went down to his house justified, rather than the other. For everyone who exalts himself will be humbled, but the one who humbles himself will be exalted." Luke 18:9–14 ∽

Ian was drawing cartoons on the chalkboard when the teacher was out of the room. So the teacher said Ian would need to clean the chalkboards for a week. Finally he was done. And with that his teacher said the slate of his offense was also wiped clean.

Jesus used parables to teach about heaven and about forgiveness of sin. Some of the most well-known are the prodigal son (Luke 15:11–32), the seed and the sower (Matthew 13:3–8, 18–23), and the Good Samaritan (Luke 10:30–37).

Another favorite is the Pharisee and the tax collector in today's reading. The proud preacher (Pharisee) stood before God in prayer. He believed he deserved God's favor because of his own righteousness. The tax collector, recognizing his sin, could not look up to heaven, and he pleaded for God's mercy. He realized any goodness received from God was an act of love and forgiveness, totally undeserved. The tax collector, not the Pharisee, found favor with God and received an eternal reward.

Just as with the tax collector, our sin is eliminated because of Jesus' sacrifice on the cross. It is as if a giant eraser followed us around, wiping out every flaw and error in our life. Turning around, we would see a clean slate. All is forgiven.

_____Let's talk: To what (besides a giant eraser) could you compare Christ's forgiveness through His sacrifice on the cross?

_____Let's pray: Dear Jesus, thank You for forgiving all my sin. Give me a humble heart. Amen.

J. B.

Open It, Please!

Read from God's Word

Consequently, He is able to save to the uttermost those who draw near to God through Him, since He always lives to make intercession for them. For it was indeed fitting that we should have such a high priest, holy, innocent, unstained, separated from sinners, and exalted above the heavens. He has no need, like those high priests, to offer sacrifices daily, first for His own sins and then for those of the people, since He did this once for all when He offered up Himself.
Hebrews 7:25–27 ✑

Gina tried hard to twist open the lid on the jar. She wanted the candy inside. When she couldn't get it open, she began to fuss.

Her father stood by watching. "Gina, are you using all the strength you can find?" he asked.

"Yes, Daddy," replied Gina, "but it just won't open."

Her dad picked up the jar, smiled, and said, "But you haven't used all the strength you can find because you haven't asked me." He easily opened the jar and gave her some candy.

We often try to do things on our own. We try to resist temptation alone. We can never succeed because we are sinful. Right beside us is our loving, heavenly Father. He waits to "open the jar." He is there when the subjects in school seem hard, when others make fun of us, or when our cruel words have shown disrespect. He waits for us to call on His strength.

Jesus is the strength God sent to pay for our greatest struggle—our battle with the devil, the world, and our sin. Jesus reached out His hands and died on the cross to take away the sin of all. His sacrifice is the strength for His children. His sacrifice opened the way of salvation for all people. What sweet news that is in the believer's ear.

_____Let's talk: When was the last time you wanted to "do it yourself" and found you couldn't? How could things have been different if you had asked Jesus for help?

_____Let's pray: Father, forgive me for Jesus' sake when I do things my own way or rely on my own power. Lead me in Your ways and with Your power. Amen.

J. B.

Hidden Places

Andrea crawled behind the couch with scissors in her hand. With a few snips, her bangs were gone. Instantly, she realized it would be difficult to cover up her new hairdo. And the longer she sat behind the couch, the more fearful she became. Suddenly she heard Mom calling, "Andrea, where are you?"

She crept from behind the couch, headed for her bedroom, and hid the scissors. She then walked up to Mom, pretending that nothing had changed.

Mother was shocked. "Andrea, what have you done to your hair? Have you seen yourself in the mirror?"

Andrea realized her terrible mistake. Instead of the lovely bangs that once covered her forehead, she now had prickly, pointy hair. She cried, "I'm sorry, Mom."

Temptations face us every day. Some appear harmless and we believe that no one will notice—whether it's taking coins from Mom's purse or watching an inappropriate movie. But when brought to the light through the mirror of others or through God's Word, we realize the prickly, pointy stubble of sin that remains.

Christ's sacrifice covers our sins. Hiding behind couches is no longer necessary. Even when we fail, He promises to forgive. Jesus' love and forgiveness flow to us from the cross. Now our lives, which once looked prickly and pointy, are perfect.

Read from God's Word

Therefore let anyone who thinks that he stands take heed lest he fall. No temptation has overtaken you that is not common to man. God is faithful, and He will not let you be tempted beyond your ability, but with the temptation He will also provide the way of escape, that you may be able to endure it. 1 Corinthians 10:12–13

———Let's talk: Who has forgiven you? What happened? How did they demonstrate God's love in Christ?

———Let's pray: Dear Jesus, may the light of Your love keep me from giving in to the temptations I face every day. Amen.

J. B.

december

Contributors for this month:

Lisa Ellwein

Cheryl Honoree

John Juedes

Arleen Keyne

Mary Krallmann

Valerie Schultz

The Best Gift

M ary's parents were missionaries. They didn't have much money to spend on things like toys. Mary, her parents, and her two brothers lived in three rooms in the back of their small church. Mary didn't feel poor, but all her friends lived in larger houses and had more things. Every now and then, Mary wished she had things like her friends did. Now, it was nearly Christmas and Mary was wishing for a doll.

Today, as soon as Mary's father returned from a meeting, the whole family would take a walk into the woods. Her father would cut down their Christmas tree.

The time finally came. Her father was home. Mary was so happy to see him that she forgot about wanting a doll. She gave him a big hug. Then he put down his suitcase. When he did, a strange thing happened. The suitcase said, "Ma-ma."

Read from God's Word

"For God so loved the world, that He gave His only Son, that whoever believes in Him should not perish but have eternal life. For God did not send His Son into the world to condemn the world, but in order that the world might be saved through Him." John 3:16–17

Her father opened the case and pulled out a beautiful doll dressed in a frilly pink dress and bonnet. "Merry Christmas! I love you very much," he said. Mary squealed with delight.

God, our heavenly Father, loves us so much that He sent His only Son, Jesus, to live for us and die in payment for our sin. This, our best gift, lasts forever. We can be the happiest people on earth.

_____Let's talk: What are some good gifts you have received? Why is Jesus better than any earthly gifts?

_____Let's pray: Heavenly Father, thank You for Your love and for Your Son, Jesus. In His name I pray. Amen.

A. K.

Read from God's Word

A glad heart makes a cheerful face, but by sorrow of heart the spirit is crushed. Proverbs 15:13 ✍

Trying to Get Happy

Moses was a small boy with a big smile. But now he was sick, in a hospital, and his smile wasn't so big.

Moses' daddy came to see him every day before work. His father read stories and rocked him in the chair near his bed. Moses wished the time would never end, but he knew it couldn't last forever.

Finally, Moses' father had to leave. He hugged Moses and said, "Now, Moses, I want you to get happy."

Moses listened, but the tears trickled down his cheeks. He turned his face up to his father's and said, "I'm trying to get happy but I just can't."

There is a special time of year when everyone seems happy—Christmas! We get presents and see family and friends. Above all, we remember that God's Son, Jesus, was born.

God loves us so much that He sent Jesus to live and die as our substitute. He took our sins, grief, and sorrows on Himself. Jesus' birthday at Christmas is a happy time. Prepare and celebrate.

When Jesus was born, an angel said to some shepherds: "I bring you good news of great joy that will be for all the people. For unto you is born this day in the city of David a Savior, who is Christ the Lord. (Luke 2:10–11).

_____ Let's talk: Why can't we get happy just by trying? What's the secret of real happiness?

_____ Let's pray: Dear Jesus, thank You for saving me from my sins and for bringing me great joy. Amen.

A. K.

A Journey of Trust

Alex couldn't see! The snow surrounded him with its raging swirls. Alex could see only one dark object—the back of his father's coat directly in front of him.

"Hold tight," his father shouted. Alex did, leaning as close to his dad as possible. Alex's father plowed a path through the drifts of snow. It seemed an endless journey. At last the brick building loomed in front of them. Dad took Alex by the hand and led him safely inside.

It was another school day. Alex and his dad walked only one block in the Canadian blizzard, but he would always remember how safe he felt clutching his father's coat. It was a journey of trust.

In the same way our heavenly Father goes before us every day. He says, "I'll help you hold tightly to My promises and I will never leave you. I promised you a Savior, and I kept that promise. I sent My Son, Jesus, to live and die for you in payment for your sins."

The blizzards of life howl around us and may even blind us for a time. But the Lord leads the way for us and will overcome every obstacle. Nothing is too hard for God. Remember Psalm 118:6: "The LORD is with me; I will not be afraid."

_____Let's talk: Read Psalm 118:1–9. When have you felt lost or unsure of your way? How did God help you overcome the trouble?

_____Let's pray: I am trusting You, Lord Jesus; trusting only You. Lead me all my journeys through. Amen.

A. K.

Read from God's Word

"Therefore do not be anxious, saying, 'What shall we eat?' or 'What shall we drink?' or 'What shall we wear?' For the Gentiles seek after all these things, and your heavenly Father knows that you need them all. But seek first the kingdom of God and His righteousness, and all these things will be added to you." Matthew 6:31–33 ✍

Full Price

The stores were closing for Christmas Eve. Susan raced toward the store, hoping she wasn't too late.

Susan's husband was in the hospital. His treatment cost a lot of money, so there was little to spend on Christmas. But she wanted their four children to have a tree and a little treat. Their young family was ready for the celebration of Jesus' birthday. They knew the heart and center of Christmas. They knew that God sent His Son to save us from our sins.

"Please, sir," Susan said to the store clerk. "Do you have any trees left?" The store had just one tree left. It had branches missing so the clerk sold it to Susan for half price.

Then Susan rushed to the bakery. There was one coffee cake left, and since it was the end of the day Susan was able to purchase it for half price. It looked wonderful—full of cinnamon and decorated with red and green sprinkles.

On the way home, Susan said a prayer: "Thank You, dear Jesus, for coming to earth and for our wonderful gifts." *How good God is to us!* Susan thought. *I've paid half price today, but God loves us so much that He paid the full price for our redemption.*

_____Let's talk: How has God met your needs today? What special blessings do you look forward to?

_____Let's pray: Lord Jesus, help me always put You first in my life. Thank You for saving me from my sins. Amen.

M. K.

Looking Inside

Read from God's Word

O LORD, You have searched me and known me! You know when I sit down and when I rise up; You discern my thoughts from afar. You search out my path and my lying down and are acquainted with all my ways. Even before a word is on my tongue, behold, O LORD, You know it altogether. Psalm 139:1–4 ✍

"Mommy, what big eyes you have!" exclaimed Corey after the table prayer

Mom nodded. "Corey," she explained, "The doctor put special drops in my eyes. The drops make the black parts of my eyes larger. That way he could look inside better."

"Oh," said Corey, "I can't see in there very well."

"Dr. Vaughn had a special light that doctors are trained to use. He checked all around in my eyes while his light was shining. I had to look up and down, right and left, as far as I could. He said my eyes look healthy."

"Wow! That light must have been bright!" said Corey.

"It was. While the doctor did that, I remembered this Bible verse: 'O LORD, You have searched me and known me' (Psalm 139:1)."

"That can be a little uncomfortable sometimes," Dad remarked.

"Yeah," said Corey, "like when you've done something bad."

"But remember that God looks at us as His forgiven children," Dad said. "He can see what's wrong with us. He also sees that Jesus lived and died to take away the punishment for our sins."

"God looks at us in love," Mom added. "Like the doctor, God cares about us and wants to help us, not hurt us."

———Let's talk: What are some things God knows about you that most people don't know? Why can you be happy that God knows everything about you?

———Let's pray: Dear God, thank You for looking at me as Your forgiven child. Help me to see others the same way. In Jesus' name. Amen.

M. K.

Good Gifts

Read from God's Word

"You have heard that it was said, 'You shall love your neighbor and hate your enemy.' But I say to you, Love your enemies and pray for those who persecute you, so that you may be sons of your Father who is in heaven. For He makes His sun rise on the evil and on the good, and sends rain on the just and on the unjust." Matthew 5:43–45

This is the day of St. Nicholas. In the United States, the traditional time for holiday presents isn't here yet. But in places like Holland, today is the big day for gifts.

The original St. Nicholas died on December 6. He was a church leader, a bishop, who lived hundreds of years ago. He had a reputation for being kind and generous. According to legend, he gave gifts at night to some people who needed help. That's how the idea of presents on St. Nicholas's Day got started. As the custom developed, people dressed like the bishop brought gifts for children. We hear a similar idea about Santa Claus.

God uses a different plan for giving gifts. People don't ever deserve rewards from God. We aren't perfect, even when we try to do good.

Still, God blesses us. God loves us although we haven't earned His love. He sent His greatest gift, Jesus, to be our Savior. We have this gift every day in December and every day all year long. How blessed we are to be loved by the Lord of heaven and earth!

_____Let's talk: What are some good gifts you have received from God? What can you give some people you know who have special needs?

_____Let's pray: Dear God, thank You for blessing me with so many good things I don't deserve. Thank You especially for forgiveness through Your gift of a Savior. Help me share Your gifts with others. In Jesus' name. Amen.

M. K.

December Surprises

On December 7, 1941, Pearl Harbor was bombed. The next day the United States officially entered World War II.

The attack on the Hawaiian naval base was a shock. When radar picked up the signals from the oncoming planes, the readings first looked like a mistake. Radar was still new. People who saw it didn't fully realize what it meant.

The first Christmas startled people too. Even when scholars confirmed the prophecy, Herod didn't understand its meaning. The shepherds were frightened when the angels appeared. Other people were surprised when the shepherds told what had happened.

God's plan wasn't to destroy, but to save. He put signs in the Scriptures. Spokesmen such as Isaiah told about the coming Savior.

While sinful people were God's enemies, He decided to make them His friends. Jesus was born to make peace between us and God. He came to bring us life eternal with God in heaven. It was a most surprising plan, and a very wonderful one.

We still struggle against sin. But as God's forgiven people, we know He is on our side. Jesus has already won the most important battle for us.

The Pearl Harbor surprise meant that for the United States war was starting. God's Christmas surprise meant that for God's children there is heavenly peace.

_____Let's talk: What are some advance messages God gave about His plan to save us?

_____Let's pray: Father, thank You for carrying out Your peace plan through the birth of Jesus, my Savior. In His name. Amen.

M. K.

Read from God's Word

Of this gospel I was made a minister according to the gift of God's grace, which was given me by the working of His power. To me, though I am the very least of all the saints, this grace was given, to preach to the Gentiles the unsearchable riches of Christ, and to bring to light for everyone what is the plan of the mystery hidden for ages in God who created all things, so that through the church the manifold wisdom of God might now be made known to the rulers and authorities in the heavenly places. This was according to the eternal purpose that He has realized in Christ Jesus our Lord.
Ephesians 3:7–11

Read from God's Word

As a deer pants for flowing streams, so pants my soul for You, O God. My soul thirsts for God, for the living God. When shall I come and appear before God? My tears have been my food day and night, while they say to me continually, "Where is your God?" These things I remember, as I pour out my soul: how I would go with the throng and lead them in procession to the house of God with glad shouts and songs of praise, multitude keeping festival. Why are you cast down, O my soul, and why are you in turmoil within me? Hope in God; for I shall again praise Him, my salvation.
Psalm 42:1–5

Ouch!

One night after dinner, Mrs. Thompson asked her daughter if she was well. "You didn't eat much," she said.

"I'm okay, Mom," Sherree said. "It's just that my mouth is kind of sore. One of the brackets on my braces is sharp. I put dental wax over it but the wax came off. The wire pokes me when I eat."

"We will call Dr. Merwil. Maybe he can see you after school tomorrow."

The next evening Mom said, "You look a lot happier, Sherree. You even ate oatmeal cookies for dessert."

"Thanks, they're good. Thanks for taking me to the orthodontist too. He fixed things up in just a few seconds. It feels so much better."

"It's wise to ask for help when we need it," Mom said. "The important thing is to get help from the right person."

Psalm 42 says to look to God for help and praise Him as our Savior and God. God is always the right person to ask for help when we are troubled. Sometimes we think we can handle problems without Him. But God has the only real solution for our basic problems of sin. He offers us forgiveness through the blood of Christ, shed for us. His solution gives us eternal life with Him forever.

_____Let's talk: How do we get relief from our sins or help for our problems?

_____Let's pray: Lord Jesus, when I'm hurting in body and soul, please heal me. Help me remember Your love. Amen.

M. K.

Hide-and-Seek

R eady or not—here I come!" Kevin's heart pounded as he searched for his friends. The pressure was on. Kevin knew he had to find them before they all arrived "home free."

Hide-and-seek is a favorite game to play. As sinful human beings, we, too, play hide-and-seek. We try to cover up our sins. We blame others for our mistakes. We say we've done nothing wrong because we didn't actually do what we were thinking. The Bible says we were sinful from the time we were formed.

How fortunate we are that Jesus is "it" and finds us every time! He knows everything there is to know about every one of us. He knows our deepest secrets. He knows our thoughts even before we think them. Because of His love for us, He forgives our hidden sins. Because of His love for us, He hears our unspoken prayers and fills our needs. God has given us faith in His Son, Jesus, who died for our sins and rose from the dead to guarantee us eternal life.

Don't try to hide from God. Ask Him to help you. He will help you confess your sins. He forgives you. With Jesus on your side, you can be assured that you will always be "home free."

Read from God's Word

The LORD looks down from heaven; He sees all the children of man; from where He sits enthroned He looks out on all the inhabitants of the earth. He who fashions the hearts of them all and observes all their deeds. The king is not saved by his great army; a warrior is not delivered by his great strength. The war horse is a false hope for salvation, and by its great might it cannot rescue. Behold, the eye of the LORD is on those who fear Him, on those who hope in His steadfast love, that He may deliver their soul from death and keep them alive in famine.
Psalm 33:13–19

_____Let's talk: Have you ever hidden because you did something wrong? Why don't we have to try to hide from God?

_____Let's pray: Dear Jesus, what a powerful and caring God You are to know our every thought and concern! Forgive me for the times when I try to hide from You. Thank You for always finding me and being there for me. Amen.

L. E.

Read from God's Word

And do not fear those who kill the body but cannot kill the soul. Rather fear Him who can destroy both soul and body in hell. Are not two sparrows sold for a penny? And not one of them will fall to the ground apart from your Father. But even the hairs of your head are all numbered. Matthew 10:28–30 ✐

No Worries

Marie's favorite movie is *The Lion King*. Her favorite characters are Pumbaa and Timon. She likes the song they sing, "Hakuna Matata," and she likes that the words mean "no worries".

Marie sometimes worries about her problems—the D she got in history, the fight she had with her little brother this morning, and the fact that she didn't get invited to Jennifer's slumber party. She feels like she has so much to worry about. Marie wonders if she'll ever have "hakuna matata."

Worrying can get us down. When that happens, God wants us to remember that His arms are always open to us. He loved us so much that He gave up His Son to pay for our sins. He knows how many hairs we have on our heads, so He certainly knows what is best for us in our lives. God is in control. He promises to be with us always.

When your worries seem too much to handle, seek the comfort of God's Word. Pray to your Father. Place your trust in Him, for He knows what is best for you. He promises to be with you on your earthly journey to the place of perfect "hakuna matata"— heaven!

_____Let's talk: What are some of your worries or fears? What can you remember the next time you're feeling like things are out of control?

_____Let's pray: Dear Lord Jesus, thank You for being my Savior, Protector, and Comforter. Forgive me when I forget to put my trust in You. For Your sake. Amen.

L. E.

What a Creation!

Read from God's Word

I praise You, for I am fearfully and wonderfully made. Wonderful are Your works; my soul knows it very well. Psalm 139:14 ✍

ave you ever wished you had a perfect body? Maybe you want to be taller or shorter, skinnier or more muscular. Maybe you want a different hairstyle, or a smaller nose, or you just want your skin to be clear.

Some people can become so concerned with making their bodies "perfect" that they forget their bodies are already an incredible creation. Adam was the high point of God's six days of work. Every part of the body was designed with a purpose in mind, right down to the fingernails and eyelashes. No scientist has ever been able to duplicate the human body.

What a powerful and loving God we have! He created us in His image. He loves us so much that, through the suffering and death of His Son, He creates us anew—forgiving our sins and changing our hearts to love Him.

As forgiven and loved creatures, we take the best care we can of our bodies, God's wonderful gift to us. But we worship the God who created us, not the bodies He created. As you look in the mirror today, admire the wonderful creation you are—and give praise and thanks to the almighty Creator!

_____Let's talk: What parts of your body amaze you the most? Why? What do you mean when we say God gives us "new hearts"?

_____Let's pray: Heavenly Father, thank You for Your wonderful and awesome creation, the human body. Send Your Spirit to enable me to respect and care for my body. In Jesus' name. Amen.

L. E.

Read from God's Word

But when the fullness of time had come, God sent forth His Son, born of woman, born under the law, to redeem those who were under the law, so that we might receive adoption as sons. Galatians 4:4–5

More Than Candy

The candy cane has been a popular treat during the Christmas season for many years. You may be surprised to learn that the candy cane was originally created for another purpose.

A number of years ago, a candy maker in Indiana wanted to make a candy that would show his faith in Jesus Christ as his Savior. He started with a stick of white hard candy. He used white to symbolize that Jesus was without sin. Its hardness reminded him that God's promises are firm.

The candy maker formed the candy in the shape of a J to represent Jesus' name. The cane is also a reminder of the shepherd's staff and of Jesus, our Good Shepherd.

Finally, the candy maker added three red stripes to the candy to represent the blood shed by Christ on the cross so we may have eternal life. The three strips remind us that Jesus is one Person in the Trinity.

The next time you eat a candy cane, remember why the candy maker made them. Share a candy cane and its story with someone you know. It will be a wonderful Christmas witness.

_____Let's do: Draw some other symbols of the Christian faith.
Think of some ways to share the story of Jesus during this Advent season.

_____Let's pray: Dear Jesus, thank You for being my Good Shepherd.
And thank You for shedding Your blood for me. Help me be a witness of Your love in all that I do. Amen.

L. E.

What's in a Name?

D o you know what your name means? Why did your parents choose it for you?

Lisa's name means "consecrated to God." Lisa's brother's name is Michael, which means "who is like God." Your parents chose your name for a special reason too. Your name is unique to you.

God planned Jesus' name. He knew we needed a Savior. God chose the name Jesus, which means "the Lord saves."

Jesus' name is sacred and holy. Martin Luther's explanation of the Second Commandment helps us to know how to use God's name rightly. "We should fear and love God so that we do not curse, swear, use satanic arts, lie, or deceive by His name, but call upon it in every trouble, pray, praise, and give thanks" (*Luther's Small Catechism*).

When someone says your name today, remember that you are lovingly chosen as a child of God. When you hear the name of Jesus, remember that "At the name of Jesus every knee should bow, in heaven and on earth and under the earth, and every tongue confess that Jesus Christ is Lord, to the glory of God the Father" (Philippians 2:10–11).

Read from God's Word

In the sixth month the angel Gabriel was sent from God to a city of Galilee named Nazareth, to a virgin betrothed to a man whose name was Joseph, of the house of David. And the virgin's name was Mary. And he came to her and said, "Greetings, O favored one, the Lord is with you!" But she was greatly troubled at the saying, and tried to discern what sort of greeting this might be. And the angel said to her, "Do not be afraid, Mary, for you have found favor with God. And behold, you will conceive in your womb and bear a son, and you shall call His name Jesus. He will be great and will be called the Son of the Most High. And the Lord God will give to Him the throne of His father David, and He will reign over the house of Jacob forever, and of His kingdom there will be no end." Luke 1:26–33

_____Let's talk: Why is your name special? How can you remind others what Jesus' name means?

_____Let's pray: Dear Jesus, help me use Your name to Your glory and honor. Thank You for being my Savior. Amen.

L. E.

A Constant Reminder

Read from God's Word

Therefore, since we are surrounded by so great a cloud of witnesses, let us also lay aside every weight, and sin which clings so closely, and let us run with endurance the race that is set before us, looking to Jesus, the founder and perfecter of our faith, who for the joy that was set before Him endured the cross, despising the shame, and is seated at the right hand of the throne of God. Hebrews 12:1–3

Ryan threw socks, an extra sweatshirt, and long underwear into his duffle bag. His first week-long campout—a winter experience—would begin tomorrow.

As Ryan packed, his older sister, Carin, walked into his room and sat on his bed. "Hey, are you excited?" she asked.

"Well," Ryan admitted, "I think so. But I have a funny feeling in my stomach. I've never been away from home that long and I'm kind of nervous."

Carin nodded. "I remember my first trip away from home; I was terrified! But mom gave me a picture of our family to keep in my suitcase. Whenever I felt homesick, I peeked at the picture and felt better."

"That's a good idea," Ryan replied.

"I thought so too," said Carin. "So here's a family picture to take with you."

Ryan smiled his thanks.

We all feel like Ryan sometimes. We face new and scary situations. But we Christians have something even greater than a picture to give us comfort. We have Jesus!

Jesus loved us so much that He died so we might live forever with Him. The cross reminds us of His great love and care. He promises to be with us through every problem we face. The next time you are worried or afraid, remember that Jesus endured the cross for you.

_____Let's talk: Where have you seen a cross? What can you
remember when you look at a cross?

_____Let's pray: Dear Jesus, help me not be afraid when I face scary
situations. In Your name I pray. Amen.

L. E.

Worthless Dust?

D o I have to?" whined Kyle. "You know we always clean the house on Saturday, and your job is to sweep and vacuum," his mother reminded.

Does this sound familiar? In homes all over the world, parents and their children argue about chores. The next time your mom or dad ask you to help, here's something to think about:

We usually see dirt as worthless and bothersome. We are always scrubbing and cleaning, trying to get rid of dust and dirt that never seem to stay away. The Bible says that we were created out of dirt (Genesis 2:7). God formed humans from the worthless dust on the ground and turned us into living, breathing beings. We are different from all other living creatures on earth. We are unique and special. We are created in God's image!

But the story doesn't end there. That image was soiled with the filth of sin. We deserved eternal punishment. But through God's endless love we were saved. By the blood of Jesus we have been washed clean. No longer are we filthy with sin. We are new creations!

Next time you're asked to help clean the house, remember your Creator and Redeemer. Praise and thank God for the gift of life and salvation. You are clean.

Read from God's Word

We have all become like one who is unclean, and all our righteous deeds are like a polluted garment. We all fade like a leaf, and our iniquities, like the wind, take us away. There is no one who calls upon Your name, who rouses himself to take hold of You; for You have hidden Your face from us, and have made us melt in the hand of our iniquities. But now, O LORD, You are our Father; we are the clay, and You are our potter; we are all the work of Your hand. Isaiah 64:6–8

_____Let's talk: What makes us different from all of God's other creations? How do you feel, knowing you are clean from sin?

_____Let's pray: Dear Savior, thank You for shedding Your blood for me. Forgive me for my many sins. In Your name I pray. Amen.

L. E.

Are You Mixed Up?

"I can hardly wait for Santa Claus to hide the colored eggs," Nikoleta said.

"You're mixed up!" shouted Almir. "Claus discovered America on the Fourth of July. And he had three dogs—Nina, Pinta, and the Santa Cupid."

"I think you're both mixed up!" Derek piped in. "Let's look it up in the encyclopedia."

"There's a better book to use to discover what is important about Christmas," said William.

What book do you think William was talking about?

When the Wise Men saw the star in the sky and went to worship Jesus, they had trouble finding Him.

King Herod's helpers knew what book to look in to help them. They found the place in the Bible that said: "But you, O Bethlehem Ephrathah ... from you shall come forth for Me one who is to be ruler in Israel, whose origin from of old." (Micah 5:2). King Jesus would be born in the town of Bethlehem.

Lots of people are mixed up about what Christmas means and who Christ Jesus is. They don't know that He is the world's Savior from sin. They don't know that He is the way to eternal life. You can find out the truth, and help other people to find the truth, by reading the best book about Christmas—the Bible.

_____Let's talk: What confusing messages about Jesus have you heard? Why are these messages wrong?

_____Let's pray: Dear Lord God, thank You for Your Word, which guides me in Your truth and Your way. In Jesus' name. Amen.

J. J.

What's Missing

Read from God's Word

What good is it, my brothers, if someone says he has faith but does not have works? Can that faith save him? If a brother or sister is poorly clothed and lacking in daily food, and one of you says to them, "Go in peace, be warmed and filled," without giving them the things needed for the body, what good is that? So also faith by itself, if it does not have works, is dead. James 2:14–17

Peanut butter and jelly. Shoes and socks. Chips and salsa. Computer and mouse. Some things just naturally go together.

So it is with our Christian faith. Words and actions should go together. In the Bible, James tells us that faith without works is dead. But that truth is not always reflected in our lives.

Sometimes we confess our faith in Jesus and tell others how we love Jesus, but our actions don't show it. We follow the crowd. We say one thing but do another. Or we act as Jesus wants us to, but we forget to share why we act the way we do. We're too embarrassed or afraid to share our faith in Jesus and what He has done for us.

This happens because of sin. The apostle Paul wrote in Romans 7:19: "For I do not do the good I want, but the evil I do not want is what I keep on doing." Thanks be to God! He has forgiven our sin through Jesus Christ. Through the help of God's Spirit we confess our shortcomings and receive courage to speak our faith in Jesus as our Savior. We can have strength to live this faith through our actions.

_____Let's do: Think of some words about Jesus you can share with others. Make a list of the ways your actions can reflect your faith.

_____Let's pray: Dear God, forgive me when I don't act or speak as I should. Help me share Your love with all those I meet. In Jesus' name and for His sake I pray. Amen.

L.E.

Read from God's Word

Whoever trusts in his riches will fall, but the righteous will flourish like a green leaf. Proverbs 11:28

True Riches

Susan and her family were headed for their favorite Christmas tree lot. "I hope we find the biggest tree in the world. I want to show it off to all my friends."

"Christmas is about the rich gift God gave us, not about showing off riches to others," said Mom.

Susan spotted the trees but was confused by the sign that read, "Xmas Trees for Sale." Her mother explained that Xmas is sometimes used to save space on a sign. The X in Xmas could refer to Greek letter *chi* (X), the first letter of Christ's name in Greek. But many people remove Christ from Christmas, so they X out His name.

Susan thought about that as she and her family searched for their Christmas tree. "Mom," Susan confessed on the way home, "I'm removing Christ from Christmas when I want to brag about our tree. I'm sorry. I love God, and I don't want to X Him out of my celebration."

Susan and her mom planned to put Christ in Christmas. Susan's friends came over to help decorate the tree. As they worked they sang carols about Christ, the Savior of the world. Christ who came to suffer and die for us. Christ who gives us the riches of forgiveness and life with Him forever.

_____Let's do: Instead of a list of gifts you want this year, make a list of some things about your Christmas tree that can remind you of Jesus and the gifts He brings.

_____Let's pray: Dear Jesus, help me to trust You—my richest blessing. Amen.

C. H.

Follow That Star!

Read from God's Word

Keep your life free from love of money, and be content with what you have, for He has said, "I will never leave you nor forsake you." Hebrews 13:5

I t's really Deborah!" squealed Bailee. Bailee grabbed Maddie's arm and ran toward the crowd surrounding her favorite singing star. "Isn't she the greatest?!"

"She has a nice voice," Maddie said, "but I don't like her new song."

"Oh, I guess it's kind of crude," Bailee said. "But look at her picture on the CD. Isn't she pretty?"

"Yes," Maddie agreed. "She is. But she wears such tight tops and short skirts."

"Deborah is awesome," Bailee snapped. "Why are you criticizing her?"

Maddie apologized. "I'm sorry. I know she's a star and you really like her. But she's not the kind of star I want to follow."

"Just what kind of star do you want to follow?" Bailee wanted to know.

"Someone who cares about me and wants to know me."

Just then a man stepped in front of the crowd and told them Deborah was finished signing autographs.

Bailee was disappointed. "She left before I could get her autograph. I wish there were stars like the one you're talking about."

"There is," Maddie explained. "He's Jesus. He didn't walk out on us; He walked among us. He came from heaven to earth to suffer and die for us all. He's the only star that never leaves or forsakes us. He's the star for all time."

_____Let's do: List ideas or attitudes that a star you admire promotes. Put a star next to the ones that are God pleasing.

_____Let's pray: Thank You, Lord, for loving me and caring about me so much that You sent Your Son, Jesus, to be my Savior. Help me to trust You above everyone else in my life. Amen.

V. S.

Read from God's Word

For God gave us a spirit not of fear but of power and love and self-control. Therefore do not be ashamed of the testimony about our Lord, nor of me His prisoner, but share in suffering for the gospel by the power of God.
2 Timothy 1:7–8 ✍

Ornaments

The lights are hung, the ornaments dangle from the tree branches, there may even be presents wrapped and under the tree waiting to be opened. How does your family celebrate Christmas? Think of all the things you do to make this time of year so special.

Unfortunately, a week or so after Christmas, the lights will come down, the ornaments will be packed up, and the gifts will be put away. People will go on with their everyday routines and soon forget about Christmas—until next year. The bad thing is that some people put Jesus away until next Christmas too.

What if there was a way to keep Christmas going all year? You could leave lights up all year, but that might annoy your neighbors. You could leave the tree up all year, but the dry needles would fall off. You could "ornament" yourself. Whenever people saw you, it would remind them of Christmas.

Actually, you would look silly wearing Christmas ornaments. They would get in the way and the hooks would hurt. You could, however, wear the "ornaments" of Christ's love.

For God, who in love "ornamented" you with the gift of His Son, keeps Christmas all year. He adorns believers through His Word and Sacraments. With God's help, your ornamented life can show and tell the message of Jesus' victory over sin, death, and the devil.

_____Let's do: Draw a tree. Decorate it with ornaments that remind you of the things that God has done for you.

_____Let's pray: Dear Jesus, live in my heart. Strengthen and encourage me that I might testify of Your love. Amen.

V. S.

Wait

Wait: Don't eat that snack now; it's almost dinnertime.

Wait: Finish your homework; then you can watch TV.

Wait: Don't open your eyes; it's a surprise.

Waiting can be hard, especially if you are waiting for something special. It may seem as if what you are waiting for will never happen.

The children of Israel were experienced "waiters." They waited 430 years to be freed from slavery in Egypt. They wandered around for another 40 years waiting to get into the land God had promised them. They waited thousands of years for God to send His promised Savior.

Sometimes the children of Israel waited patiently. Sometimes they got tired of waiting and grew angry with God. They thought He wasn't listening to their prayers—but He was.

Why did God make them wait so long? We don't know, but we do know that God's timing is perfect. He knew just what the children of Israel needed and when. He didn't ignore their prayers. It wasn't God's time.

God knows just what you need too. He knew you needed a Savior, and at just the right time, He sent Jesus. He knows, and cares, about everything in your life. He never ignores your prayers. And in love He sometimes says to you, "Wait."

Read from God's Word

But when the fullness of time had come, God sent forth His Son, born of woman, born under the Law, to redeem those who were under the Law, so that we might receive adoption as sons. Galatians 4:4–5

———Let's do: Make a prayer list. As you see God answer your prayers, thank Him and check them off your list.

———Let's pray: Heavenly Father, thank You for hearing my prayers. Help me to wait for Your perfect timing. Amen.

V. S.

Read from God's Word

"Therefore do not be anxious, saying, 'What shall we eat?' or 'What shall we drink?' or 'What shall we wear?' For the Gentiles seek after all these things, and your heavenly Father knows that you need them all. But seek first the kingdom of God and His righteousness, and all these things will be added to you. Therefore do not be anxious about tomorrow, for tomorrow will be anxious for itself. Sufficient for the day is its own trouble." Matthew 6:31–34

First Time, First Place

First times can be fun. Your first basketball game. First dance recital. First band concert. First times can also be sad. Your first Christmas without a loved one. First holiday in a new town far away from family and friends. First D on a report card.

First place can be exciting. First in the two-mile race. First chair in the clarinet section. First in line for concert tickets. First place can also be sad. First person to get knocked out of a dodgeball game. First car in an accident. First person in line to get a vaccination.

Jesus came for all the times and all the places in our lives. He gave up His heavenly home at just the right time to be born and live in just the right place so He could be our Savior from sin, death, and the devil. He never sinned—not even once. Yet He died for all sinners—every single one.

For all time and all places, God wants to be first in our hearts. That means He wants us to think about how He can help us in times of trouble and how He blesses us with just what we need. We can't put Him there by ourselves. God's Spirit enlightens our hearts and keeps God first in our lives. With God in first place, we have nothing to worry about!

_____Let's do: Make a list of your memorable firsts. Thank Jesus for the exciting ones. Talk to Him about the tough ones.

_____Let's pray: Thank You, Jesus, for coming to earth to be my Savior. Help me through Your Spirit to put You first in my life. Amen.

V. S.

Out of the Darkness

Ever been spelunking? Spelunking is cave exploration. Some people like it. Others don't.

For one thing, caves are damp and cold. Even if it is very warm outside, inside it's chilly. Some caves have bats hanging from the ceilings. Bats are very necessary and useful animals, but some people find them a little creepy.

The thing most people dislike most about caves is the complete darkness. Since caves form underground or deep in hills or mountains, sunlight doesn't get in. If you go into a cave and turn off your light, you can't see anything at all.

Want to know something good about a cave? It is thought that Jesus was born in one. Bethlehem is in a very hilly area with lots of caves. Instead of building stables, people used caves to keep their animals.

Jesus, the Son of God, the light of the world, lit up that darkened place when He was born. Jesus, the Son of God, the light of the World, lights up hearts through His Word. Without Jesus we are trapped in the dark cave of sin. Jesus, our Savior, rescues us from sin and gives us His love and forgiveness.

Jesus gives us hope of life forever with Him. Through God's grace in Jesus, we are out of the dark, living in light.

Read from God's Word

Again Jesus spoke to them, saying, "I am the Light of the world. Whoever follows Me will not walk in darkness, but will have the light of life." John 8:12 ◇

_____Let's do: Write about a time when you felt as if you were alone in the dark. Compare that time to the darkness of a life without Jesus. Then thank God for Jesus.

_____Let's pray: Jesus, light of the world, thank You for chasing away the darkness of my sinful life and this sin-filled world. Amen.

V. S.

Read from God's Word

For we did not follow cleverly devised myths when we made known to you the power and coming of our Lord Jesus Christ, but we were eyewitnesses of His majesty. For when He received honor and glory from God the Father, and the voice was borne to Him by the Majestic Glory, "This is My beloved Son, with whom I am well pleased," we ourselves heard this very voice borne from heaven, for we were with Him on the holy mountain.
2 Peter 1:16–18

What's Real?

"That movie was awesome!" Patrick exclaimed as the boys came out of the theater. "Let's go see it again!"

"I don't know," Adam hesitated. "Those giant grasshoppers looked real."

"Come on," Patrick urged. "It's only a movie."

It's hard to tell sometimes what's real and what isn't. What I'm going to tell you is not a make-believe story; it is real. It happened more than two thousand years ago in Bethlehem. It happened in a stable, filled with animals. There, a baby was born. No emergency room doctors or nurses were there. No lights flashed on monitors. There was just a baby, Jesus, God's Son, the Savior of the world.

News of this birth spread, but not by newspapers or television. God sent His angel messengers to shepherds. They found the baby and worshiped Him, and then spread the news.

This baby grew up and became a teacher. He taught everyone He saw about God's love and forgiveness. He walked from town to town, speaking to people, forgiving them, healing them.

Some people didn't like His message. They had Him arrested and killed. They thought they had won; but they hadn't.

Jesus rose from the dead. He won the battle over sin and death. He did this for you. He loves you. There is no questioning this reality!

_____Let's do: Write down three things you know are true about Jesus.

_____Let's pray: Thank You, Jesus, for coming to earth to save me from my sin. Help me to believe that what You did for me is real. In Your name I pray. Amen.

V. S.

News of Great Joy

The night was dark and quiet. The peaceful bleating of the sheep lulled the shepherds to sleep. Suddenly an angel of the Lord appeared.

It was just that simple. One minute all was quiet. The next minute there was an angel and the glory of the Lord shone around the shepherds. The shepherds were terrified! God's angels came to deliver a message to them, and they were afraid.

Why would they have been afraid of God? Perhaps it was because they did not understand why God was there. Maybe they were afraid because they knew they hadn't lived according to God's commandments and assumed God was there to punish them.

They could not have been more wrong. God did know the shepherds had not lived according to His plan. And because He knew this, He knew they would rejoice in the good news the angels brought.

Read from God's Word

And in the same region there were shepherds out in the field, keeping watch over their flock by night. And an angel of the Lord appeared to them, and the glory of the Lord shone around them, and they were filled with fear. And the angel said to them, "Fear not, for behold, I bring you good news of a great joy that will be for all the people. For unto you is born this day in the city of David a Savior, who is Christ the Lord. And this will be a sign for you: you will find a baby wrapped in swaddling cloths and lying in a manger." Luke 2:8–12 ↩

The angel said, "I bring you good news of a great joy that will be for all the people" (v. 10). That news is also for us. God did not send Jesus into the world to condemn us for the wrong things we have done. He sent Jesus to save us. That truly is great joy for us all!

_____Let's do: Write out the angel's words to the shepherds in fancy and joyful script.

_____Let's pray: Dear Father, thank You for the good news that Jesus' birth brings to us: that we are saved through Christ the Lord. In His name we pray. Amen.

C. H.

Aliens

The music was eerie and threatening. The giant alien from Xyplon jumped onto the screen. Some people in the audience screamed when they saw his three green heads and long, tentaclelike arms.

Deuteronomy 10 tells us to love aliens, but even aliens from Xyplon? Let's take a closer look.

Latitia felt overwhelmed walking into her new school. She had moved to her new home only a few days ago and hadn't had time to make new friends. She didn't know anyone. Even worse, Latitia was from another country and couldn't speak the language of this new school. Latitia was an alien, someone from another country.

Cooper surprised his teacher with a hug. He laughed as he offered hugs to other students. Most of them pushed him away or walked away. Cooper has a mental handicap. He's different from others. His strange behaviors are alien.

People who are different from us or come from different places sometimes make us feel uncomfortable. Jesus was a kind of alien when He lived on earth. Maybe He made people uncomfortable because He was different from them. He was not born with a sinful nature. His character was different.

Although we are sinfully imperfect, Jesus still loves us. His out-of-this-world love also gives us His Spirit. His in-this-world power helps us to love others.

_____Let's talk: How can you show Jesus' love to someone in your neighborhood or school who is different from others?

_____Let's pray: Lord Jesus, help me to see others as You see them. Help me to love as You love. In Your name I pray. Amen.

C. H.

Disappointments

Read from God's Word

For I know the plans I have for you, declares the LORD, plans for wholeness and not for evil, to give you a future and a hope. Jeremiah 29:11 ✐

Timmy carefully lifted the package. It was the right size. It was the right weight. He listened as he shook it. Timmy was sure it was the game he wanted. What else could it be?

He untied the ribbon and removed the wrapping paper. As the wrappings fell, so did Timmy's face. There in the box was a white shirt. *What?* Timmy thought. *This isn't want I wanted!*

Have you ever been disappointed like Timmy? Disappointments attack us when we get a C instead of an A, when we don't get to go to the mall with our friends, or when the summer camping trip is rained out.

Disappointments came into the world with sin. They come through people, sinful people, and through our sinful world. But there is One who never disappointments us.

It is God. He called us by the Gospel and bestowed saving faith in our Baptism. He keeps all of His promises. He keeps us in the one true faith, in which there are no disappointments. He keeps us as His own dear children—those who know Jesus as the Savior of the world.

_____Let's do: Write about a disappointment you have experienced. Write about God, who fills your every need. How did He help you with your disappointments?

_____Let's pray: Dear God, when I am feeling disappointed, help me to remember that You always keep Your promises. In Jesus' name I pray. Amen.

C. H.

Darkness to Light

Timmy and John were gasping for air. As they hiked higher up the mountain, it became harder to breathe. But they kept going, focused on the goal.

Suddenly swirling clouds surrounded them. The clouds covered the whole mountain. Now they couldn't see anything around them. It was cold and wet and scary.

"Let's keep going uphill to find a way out," John said.

The boys continued their cautious climb. Would they be able to see obstacles in their path? Would they reach the top? Finally they saw sunlight and moved quickly again. Now that they could see, they knew where they were headed.

The Gentiles had lived in uncertainty for hundreds of years. They weren't sure who the Savior would be. It was if they were walking in a dark cloud.

The birth and death of Jesus changed that. Now Gentiles have the light of the world. Jesus' life and death eliminated the darkness of sin and freed all people to live without the burden of sin. Jesus died to dispel the darkness of death with eternal life.

That light, which has dawned for us too, is Jesus. He has taken away the dark curse of our mean thoughts and our angry words, our lazy obedience and our selfish actions. We, too, are saved! Rejoice!

_____Let's do: Write about a time darkness scared you and how God showed He was with you.

_____Let's pray: Dear Jesus, thank You for coming to shine in our lives so we no longer walk in the darkness of sin or death. in Your name we pray. Amen.

C. H.

Water, Water Everywhere

Read from God's Word

And going into the house they saw the child with Mary His mother, and they fell down and worshiped Him. Then, opening their treasures, they offered Him gifts, gold and frankincense and myrrh. Matthew 2:11

Tammy opened her gift from her little sister. Inside the box, Tammy found a paper clip, a rubber band, and a rock.

"The paper clip is for holding your school papers together," her sister explained. "The rubber band is for holding your ponytail. And the rock is for holding your papers down when we open the window."

Tammy saw the joy on her sister's face and smiled. "These are the best gifts I've ever received. Thank you!"

Jesus received some unusual gifts too. When the Wise Men visited Him, the Bible tells about three gifts: gold, frankincense, and myrrh.

Each of these gifts was very valuable, expensive, and rare. Each had a special purpose. The frankincense was incense burned on the altar during worship. Myrrh was an oil used for anointing people when they died. Gold was a symbol of wealth, a treasure of kings.

These gifts are symbols of the roles Jesus played in our salvation. The frankincense reminds us that He is our High Priest, going to God on our behalf. The myrrh reminds us that He died for us and for our sins. The gold reminds us that He is the King of kings and is victorious over the devil. These gifts remind us of the most wondrous gift—Jesus.

_____Let's do: List some unusual gifts you have received and why these gifts turned out to be important.

_____Let's pray: Dear Jesus, thank You for coming to be our wondrous Savior from sin. In Your name we pray. Amen.

C. H.

Whiter Than Snow

Purge me with hyssop, and I shall be clean; wash me, and I shall be whiter than snow. Psalm 51:7 ✍

Ben tugged his mom's hand. "Hurry, Mom, this is my favorite part." Ben's mom walked a little quicker. Around the next corner were the polar bears.

Every trip to the zoo, Ben watched the polar bears play in the moat and hide behind the rocks. The crowd stood on tiptoes to watch the zookeeper feed the bears. Somehow the large bears were able to catch the flying fish.

Ben loved learning about polar bears. When he went home after a zoo trip, he would search on the Internet for information. He'd read for hours about his favorite animal, often sharing what he learned with his mother. "Mom, did you know that polar bears' skin is black?"

"No," mom said, "I thought it was white."

"That's what I thought too," informed the scholar. "Their fur is really hollow, clear hairs. And their skin is black."

God made it so the black appears white on polar bears. And only God can change the darkness of sin in the lives of humans. Only God can wash away our sin. Only God, in Christ, can give us a new look—His whiter than snow robe of righteousness won for us on Calvary.

The Bible makes it clear! When Jesus washes away our sins, we are whiter than polar bears, whiter than snow.

_____Let's do: Draw the outline of a cross. Inside the shape, list things that are white as snow.

_____Let's pray: Dear Lord, thank You for coming to me in Baptism and washing me clean. In Jesus' name I pray. Amen.

C. H.

Fading Christmas

Read from God's Word

Blessed be the God and Father of our Lord Jesus Christ! According to His great mercy, He has caused us to be born again to a living hope through the resurrection of Jesus Christ from the dead, to an inheritance that is imperishable, undefiled, and unfading, kept in heaven for you, who by God's power are being guarded through faith for a salvation ready to be revealed in the last time. 1 Peter 1:3–5 ✑

Walking past the Christmas tree, Tina heard the tinkling sound of needles falling off the tree. Then she noticed that some of the bulbs had burned out. Was Christmas fading?

Later she saw her dog chewing on the leftover bone from the Christmas ham. "It seems that everywhere I look, Christmas is over. Even the candles don't seem to burn as brightly. Everything seems sad now."

"It does seem sad when the needles fall, the lights burn out, and the festive meals are gone. But Christmas isn't over," said her mom. "The shiny decorations, parties, cards, even the gifts—the things we do to help us celebrate Christmas—fade away. But the real meaning of Christmas never fades.

"In Baptism, we receive the living hope that God provided through the sacrifice of His Son. Hope in Him won't die like those needles. Hope in Him won't burn out like those lights. Hope in Him won't get used up like our Christmas ham."

For Tina, for her mom, and for us, Jesus won His fight against sin, death, and Satan. God's Christmas gift came to us at Easter. On the Good Friday cross, He won a crown of glory for each of us, and that crown will never "perish, spoil or fade" (1 Peter 1:4, NIV.)

———Let's talk: What are some Christmas things that are fading away? What do you know about Jesus that never fades away?

———Let's pray: Dear Jesus, thank You for the living hope we have been given through Your death and resurrection. Amen.

C. H.